AUDUBON GUIDE
to the National Wildlife Refuges

California
& Hawaii

AUDUBON GUIDE
to the National Wildlife Refuges

California
& Hawaii

California · Hawaii

By Loren Mac Arthur

Foreword by Theodore Roosevelt IV

Series Editor, David Emblidge
Editor, Donald Young

A Balliett & Fitzgerald Book
St. Martin's Griffin, New York

Cartography: © Balliett & Fitzgerald, Inc. produced by Mapping Specialists Ltd.
Illustrations: Mary Sundstrom
Cover design: Michael Storrings and Sue Canavan
Interior design: Bill Cooke and Sue Canavan

Balliett & Fitzgerald Inc. Staff
Sue Canavan, Design Director
Maria Fernandez, Production Editor
Alexis Lipsitz, Executive Series Editor
Rachel Deutsch, Associate Photo Editor
Kristen Couse, Associate Editor
Paul Paddock, Carol Petino Assistant Editors
Howard Klein, Editorial Intern
Scott Prentzas, Copy Editor

Balliett & Fitzgerald Inc. would like to thank the following people for their assistance in creating this series:
At National Audubon Society:
    Katherine Santone, former Director of Publishing, for sponsoring this project
    Claire Tully, Senior Vice President, Marketing
    Evan Hirsche, Director, National Wildlife Refuges Campaign
At U.S. Fish & Wildlife Service:
    Richard Coleman, former Chief, Division of Refuges, U.S. Fish & Wildlife Service
    Janet Tennyson, Outreach Coordinator
    Craig Rieben, Chief of Broadcasting & Audio Visual, U.S. Fish & Wildlife
        Service, for photo research assistance
    Pat Carrol, Chief Surveyor, U.S. Fish & Wildlife Service, for map information
    Regional External Affairs officers, at the seven U.S. Fish & Wildlife Service
        Regional Headquarters
    Elizabeth Jackson, Photographic Information Specialist, National
        Conservation Training Center, for photo research
At St. Martin's Griffin:
    Greg Cohn, who pulled it all together on his end, as well as Michael
        Storrings and Kristen Macnamara
At David Emblidge—Book Producer:
    Marcy Ross, Assistant Editor
Thanks also to Theodore Roosevelt IV and John Flicker.

ISBN 0-312-20689-5
First St. Martin's Griffin Edition: March 2000

10 9 8 7 6 5 4 3 2 1

CONTENTS

Foreword   **viii**
Theodore Roosevelt IV

Preface   **x**
John Flicker, President, National Audubon Society

Introduction   **1**
Introduction to the National Wildlife Refuge System
Migratory flyways map
How to use this book

California and Hawaii   **15**
A Regional Overview
Regional Refuge map

CALIFORNIA

Cibola NWR   **28**
Cibola, Arizona

Coachella Valley NWR   **33**
Thousand Palms

**Don Edwards
    San Francisco Bay NWR**   **36**
Fremont

Farallon NWR   **43**
San Francisco

Havasu NWR   **45**
Lake Havasu City, Arizona, and Needles, California

**Hopper Mountain NWR Complex
    and Blue Ridge NWR**   **52**
Hopper Mountain NWR and Bitter Creek NWR
Ventura and Porterville

Humboldt Bay NWR   **58**
Loleta

Imperial NWR   **61**
Yuma, Arizona

Kern NWR 68
Delano

Klamath Basin NWR Complex 71
Bear Valley NWR, Clear Lake NWR, Klamath Marsh
NWR, Lower Klamath NWR, Tule Lake NWR, Upper
Klamath NWR
Tulelake

Modoc NWR 89
Alturas

Sacramento NWR Complex 95
Sacramento NWR, Sacramento River NWR,
Colusa NWR
Willows

Salinas River NWR 109
Castroville

San Diego NWR Complex 112
Sweetwater Marsh NWR, Tijuana Slough NWR,
San Diego NWR
Imperial Beach

San Luis NWR Complex 126
San Luis NWR, Merced NWR
Los Banos

San Pablo Bay NWR 138
Vallejo

Seal Beach NWR 142
Seal Beach

Sonny Bono Salton Sea NWR 144
Calipatria

Stone Lakes NWR 152
Elk Grove

HAWAII & PACIFIC ISLANDS

**Hawaiian and Pacific Islands
  NWR Complex** 154
Hakalau Forest NWR, James Campbell NWR, Kealia
Pond NWR, Kilauea Point NWR, Hanalei NWR, Midway
Atoll NWR, Pacific/Remote Islands NWR Complex

Appendix

Nonvisitable National Wildlife Refuges 186

Federal recreation fees 187

Volunteer activities 188

U.S. Fish & Wildlife Service general information 189

National Audubon Society Wildlife Sanctuaries 190

Bibliography and Resouces 192

Glossary 194

Index 200

Acknowledgements 210

About the author 210

Photography credits 210

National Audubon Society mission statement 211

National Audubon Society application form 212

Foreword

America is singularly blessed in the amount and quality of land that the federal government holds in trust for its citizens. No other country can begin to match the variety of lands in our national wildlife refuges, parks and forests. From the Arctic Refuge on the North Slope of Alaska to the National Key Deer Refuge in Florida, the diversity of land in the National Wildlife Refuge (NWR) System is staggering.

Yet of all our public lands, the National Wildlife Refuge System is the least well known and does not have an established voting constituency like that of the Parks System. In part this is because of its "wildlife first" mission, which addresses the needs of wildlife species before those of people. That notwithstanding, wildlife refuges also offer remarkable opportunities for people to experience and learn about wildlife—and to have fun doing so!

The Refuge System was launched in 1903 when President Theodore Roosevelt discovered that snowy egrets and other birds were being hunted to the brink of extinction for plumes to decorate ladies' hats. He asked a colleague if there were any laws preventing the president from making a federal bird reservation out of an island in Florida's Indian River. Learning there was not, Roosevelt responded, "Very well, then I so declare it." Thus Pelican Island became the nation's first plot of land to be set aside for the protection of wildlife. Roosevelt went on to create another 50 refuges, and today there are more than 500 refuges encompassing almost 93 million acres, managed by the U.S. Fish & Wildlife Service.

The Refuge System provides critical habitat for literally thousands of mammals, birds, amphibians and reptiles, and countless varieties of plants and flowers. More than 55 refuges have been created specifically to save endangered species. Approximately 20 percent of all threatened and endangered species in the United States rely on these vital places for their survival. As a protector of our country's natural diversity, the System is unparalleled.

Setting NWR boundaries is determined, as often as possible, by the needs of species that depend on the protected lands. Conservation biology, the science that studies ecosystems as a whole, teaches us that wildlife areas must be linked by habitat "corridors" or run the risk of becoming biological islands. The resulting inability of species to transfer their genes over a wide area leaves them vulnerable to disease and natural disasters. For example, the Florida panther that lives in Big Cypress Swamp suffers from a skin fungus, a consequence, scientists believe, of inbreeding. Today's refuge managers are acutely aware of this precarious situation afflicting many species and have made protection of the System's biodiversity an important goal.

Clearly, the job of the refuge manager is not an easy one. Chronic underfunding of the System by the federal government has resulted in refuges operating with less money per employee and per acre than any other federal land-management agency. Recent efforts by some in Congress to address this shortfall have begun to show results, but the System's continued vulnerability to special interests has resulted in attempts to open refuges to oil drilling, road building in refuge wilderness areas, and military exercises.

The managers of the System have played a crucial role in responding to the limited resources available. They have created a network of volunteers who contribute tens of thousands of hours to help offset the lack of direct financing for the Refuge System. Groups like refuge "friends" and Audubon Refuge Keepers have answered the call for local citizen involvement on many refuges across the country.

I hope Americans like yourself who visit our national wildlife refuges will come away convinced of their importance, not only to wildlife but also to people. I further hope you will make your views known to Congress, becoming the voice and voting constituency the Refuge System so desperately needs.

—*Theodore Roosevelt IV*

Preface

Thank you for adding the *Audubon Guide to the National Wildlife Refuge System* to your travel library. I hope you will find this nine-volume series an indispensable guide to finding your way around the refuge system, as well as a valuable educational tool for learning more about the vital role wildlife refuges play in protecting our country's natural heritage.

It was nearly 100 years ago that Frank Chapman, an influential ornithologist, naturalist, publisher and noted Audubon member, approached President Theodore Roosevelt (as recounted by Theodore Roosevelt IV in his foreword), eventually helping to persuade him to set aside more than 50 valuable parcels of land for the protection of wildlife.

Because of limited funding available to support these new wildlife sanctuaries, Audubon stepped up and paid for wardens who diligently looked after them. And so began a century of collaboration between Audubon and the National Wildlife Refuge System. Today, Audubon chapter members can be found across the country assisting refuges with a range of projects, from viewing tower construction to bird banding.

Most recently, National Audubon renewed its commitment to the Refuge System by launching a nationwide campaign to build support for refuges locally and nationally. Audubon's Wildlife Refuge Campaign is promoting the Refuge System through on-the-ground programs such as Audubon Refuge Keepers (ARK), which builds local support groups for refuges, and Earth Stewards, a collaboration with the U.S. Fish and Wildlife Service and the National Fish and Wildlife Foundation, which uses refuges and other important bird habitats as outdoor classrooms. In addition, we are countering legislative threats to refuges in Washington, D.C., while supporting increased federal funding for this, the least funded of all federal land systems.

By teaching more people about the important role refuges play in conserving our nation's diversity of species—be they birds, mammals, amphibians, reptiles, or plants—we have an opportunity to protect for future generations our only federal lands system set aside first and foremost for wildlife conservation.

As a nation, we are at a critical juncture—do we continue to sacrifice wetlands, forests, deserts, and coastal habitat for short-term profit, or do we accept that the survival of our species is closely linked to the survival of others? The National Wildlife Refuge System is a cornerstone of America's conservation efforts. If we are to leave a lasting legacy and, indeed, ensure our future, then we must build on President Theodore Roosevelt's greatest legacy. I invite you to join us!

—John Flicker, President, National Audubon Society

Introduction
to the National Wildlife Refuge System

He spent entire days on horseback, traversing the landscape of domed and crumbling hills, steep forested coulees, with undulating tables of prairie above. The soft wraparound light of sunset displayed every strange contour of the Badlands and lit the colors in each desiccated layer of rock—yellow, ochre, beige, gold.

Theodore Roosevelt was an easterner. As some well-heeled easterners were wont to do, he traveled west in 1883 to play cowboy, and for the next eight years he returned as often as possible. He bought a cattle ranch, carried a rifle and a six-gun, rode a horse. North Dakota was still Dakota Territory then, but the Plains bison were about gone, down to a scattering of wild herds.

The nation faced a new and uneasy awareness of limits during Roosevelt's North Dakota years. Between 1776 and 1850, the American population had increased from 1.5 million to more than 23 million. National borders were fixed and rail and telegraph lines linked the coasts, but Manifest Destiny had a price. The ongoing plunder of wildlife threatened species such as the brown pelican and the great egret; the near-total extermination of 60 million bison loomed as a lesson many wished to avoid repeating.

Despite the damage done, the powerful landscapes of the New World had shaped the outlooks of many new Americans. From Colonial-era botanist John Bartram to 19th-century artists George Catlin and John James Audubon, naturalists and individuals of conscience explored the question of what constituted a proper human response to nature. Two figures especially, Henry David Thoreau and John Muir, created the language and ideas that would confront enduring Old World notions of nature as an oppositional, malevolent force to be harnessed and exploited. The creation in 1872 of Yellowstone as the world's first national park indicated that some Americans, including a few political leaders, were listening to what Thoreau, Muir, and these others had to say.

Roosevelt, along with his friend George Bird Grinnell, drew upon these and other writings, as well as their own richly varied experiences with nature, to take the unprecedented step of making protection of nature a social and political cause. Of his time in the Badlands, Roosevelt remarked "the romance of my life began here," and "I never would have been president if it had not been for my experiences in North Dakota." As a hunter, angler, and naturalist, Roosevelt grasped the importance of nature for human life. Though he had studied natural history as an undergraduate at Harvard, believing it would be his life's work, Roosevelt owned a passion for reform and had the will—perhaps a need—to be effective. Rather than pursuing a career as a naturalist, he went into politics. His friend George

Barren-ground caribou

New England Region
Middle Atlantic Region
Southeast Region
Northern Midwest Region
South Central Region
Southwest Region
Rocky Mountains Region
Alaska and Pacific Northwest Region
California and Hawaii Region

Migratory Flyway

Great Lakes

Minnesota

Michigan

Wisconsin

New Hampshire
Vermont
Massachusetts

Maine

New York

Iowa

Pennsylvania

Rhode
Island
Connecticut

New Jersey
Delaware
Maryland

Illinois

Indiana

Ohio

West
Virginia

Virginia

Missouri

Kentucky

North
Carolina

Tennessee

South
Carolina

Arkansas

Mississippi

Alabama

Georgia

Atlantic
Ocean

Louisiana

Florida

Puerto
Rico

Gulf of Mexico

Bird Grinnell, publisher of the widely read magazine *Forest and Stream,* championed all manner of environmental protection and in 1886 founded the Audubon Society to combat the slaughter of birds for the millinery trade. Fifteen years later, TR would find himself with an even greater opportunity. In 1901, when he inherited the presidency following the assassination of William McKinley, Roosevelt declared conservation a matter of federal policy.

Roosevelt backed up his words with an almost dizzying series of conservation victories. He established in 1903 a federal bird reservation on Pelican Island, Florida, as a haven for egrets, herons, and other birds sought by plume hunters. In eight years, Roosevelt authorized 150 million acres in the lower 48 states and another 85 million in Alaska to be set aside from logging under the Forest Reserve Act of 1891, compared to a total of 45 million under the three prior presidents. To these protected lands he added five national parks and 17 national monuments. The NWR system, though, is arguably TR's greatest legacy. Often using executive order to circumvent Congress, Roosevelt established 51 wildlife refuges.

The earliest federal wildlife refuges functioned as sanctuaries and little else. Visitors were rare and recreation was prohibited. Between 1905 and 1912 the first refuges for big-game species were established—Wichita Mountains in Oklahoma, the National Bison Range in Montana, and National Elk Refuge in Jackson, Wyoming. In 1924, the first refuge to include native fish was created; a corridor some 200 miles long, the Upper Mississippi National Wildlife and Fish Refuge spanned the states of Minnesota, Wisconsin, Illinois, and Iowa.

Atlantic puffins, Petit Manan NWR, Maine

Still, the 1920s were dark years for America's wildlife. The effects of unregulated hunting, along with poor enforcement of existing laws, had decimated once-abundant species. Extinction was feared for the wood duck. Wild turkey had become scarce outside a few southern states. Pronghorn antelope, which today number perhaps a million across the West, were estimated at 25,000 or fewer. The trumpeter swan, canvasback duck, even the prolific and adaptable white-tailed deer, were scarce or extirpated across much of their historic ranges.

The Depression and Dust-bowl years, combined with the leadership of President Franklin Delano Roosevelt, gave American conservation—and the refuge system in particular—a hefty forward push. As wetlands vanished and fertile prairie soils blew away, FDR's Civilian Conservation Corps (CCC) dispatched thousands of unemployed young men to camps that stretched from Georgia to California. On the sites of many present-day refuges, they built dikes and other

Saguaro cactus and ocotillo along Charlie Bell 4WD trail, Cabeza Prieta NWR, Arizona

water-control structures, planted shelterbelts and grasses. Comprised largely of men from urban areas, the experience of nature was no doubt a powerful rediscovery of place and history for the CCC generation. The value of public lands as a haven for people, along with wildlife, was on the rise.

In 1934, Jay Norwood "Ding" Darling was instrumental in developing the federal "Duck Stamp," a kind of war bond for wetlands; hunters were required to purchase it, and anyone else who wished to support the cause of habitat acquisition could, too. Coupled with the Resettlement Act of 1935, in which the federal government bought out or condemned private land deemed unsuitable for agriculture, several million acres of homesteaded or settled lands reverted to federal ownership to become parks, national grasslands, and wildlife refuges. The Chief of the U.S. Biological Survey's Wildlife Refuge Program, J. Clark Salyer, set out on a cross-country mission to identify prime wetlands. Salyer's work added 600,000 acres to the refuge system, including Red Rock Lakes in Montana, home to a small surviving flock of trumpeter swans.

The environmental ruin of the Dust bowl also set in motion an era of government initiatives to engineer solutions to such natural events as floods, drought, and the watering of crops. Under FDR, huge regional entities such as the Tennessee Valley Authority grew, and the nation's mightiest rivers—the Columbia, Colorado, and later, the Missouri—were harnessed by dams. In the wake of these and other federal works projects, a new concept called "mitigation" appeared: If a proposed dam or highway caused the destruction of a certain number of acres of wetlands or other habitat, some amount of land nearby would be ceded to conservation in return. A good many of today's refuges were the progeny of mitigation. The federal government, like the society it represents, was on its way to becoming complex enough that the objectives of one arm could be at odds with those of another.

Citizen activism, so integral to the rise of the Audubon Society and other groups, was a driving force in the refuge system as well. Residents of rural Georgia applied relentless pressure on legislators to protect the Okefenokee Swamp. Many other refuges—San Francisco Bay, Sanibel Island, Minnesota Valley, New Jersey's Great Swamp—came about through the efforts of people with a vision of conservation close to home.

More than any other federal conservation program, refuge lands became places where a wide variety of management techniques could be tested and refined. Generally, the National Park system followed the "hands off" approach of Muir and Thoreau while the U.S. Forest Service and Bureau of Land Management, in theory, emphasized a utilitarian, "sustainable yield" value; in practice, powerful economic interests backed by often ruthless politics left watersheds, forests, and grasslands badly degraded, with far-reaching consequences for fish and wildlife. The refuge system was not immune to private enterprise—between 1939 and 1945, refuge lands were declared fair game for oil drilling, natural-gas exploration, and even for bombing practice by the U.S. Air Force—but the negative impacts have seldom reached the levels of other federal areas.

Visitor use at refuges tripled in the 1950s, rose steadily through the 1960s, and by the 1970s nearly tripled again. The 1962 Refuge Recreation Act established guidelines for recreational use where activities such as hiking, photography, boating, and camping did not interfere with conservation. With visitors came opportunities to educate, and now nature trails and auto tours, in addition to beauty, offered messages about habitats and management techniques. Public awareness of wilderness, "a place where man is only a visitor," in the words of long-time advocate Robert Marshall of the U.S. Forest Service, gained increasing social and political attention. In 1964, Congress passed the Wilderness Act, establishing guidelines for designating a host of federally owned lands as off-limits to motorized vehicles, road building, and resource exploitation. A large number of refuge lands qualified—the sun-blasted desert of Arizona's Havasu refuge, the glorious tannin-stained waters and cypress forests of Georgia's Okefenokee Swamp, and the almost incomprehensible large 8-million-acre Arctic NWR in Alaska, home to vast herds of caribou, wolf packs, and bladelike mountain peaks, the largest contiguous piece of wilderness in the refuge system.

Sachuest Point NWR, Rhode Island

Nonetheless, this was also a time of horrendous air and water degradation, with the nation at its industrial zenith and agriculture cranked up to the level of "agribusiness." A wake-up call arrived in the form of vanishing bald eagles, peregrine falcons, and osprey. The insecticide DDT, developed in 1939 and used in World War II to eradicate disease-spreading insects, had been used throughout the nation ever since, with consequences unforeseen until the 1960s. Sprayed over wetlands, streams, and crop fields, DDT had entered watersheds and from there the food chain itself. It accumulated in the bodies of fish and other aquatic life, and birds consuming fish took DDT into their systems, one effect was a calcium deficiency, resulting in eggs so fragile that female birds crushed them during incubation.

Partially submerged alligator, Anahuac NWR, Texas

Powerful government and industry leaders launched a vicious, all-out attack on the work of a marine scientist named Rachel Carson, whose book *Silent Spring,* published in 1962, warned of the global dangers associated with DDT and other biocides. For this she was labeled "not a real scientist" and "a hysterical woman." With eloquence and courage, though, Carson stood her ground. If wild species atop the food chain could be devastated, human life could be threatened, too. Americans were stunned, and demanded an immediate ban on DDT. Almost overnight, the "web of life" went from chalkboard hypothesis to reality.

Protecting imperiled species became a matter of national policy in 1973 when President Nixon signed into law the Endangered Species Act (ESA), setting guidelines by which the U.S. Fish & Wildlife Service would "list" plant and animal species as *threatened* or *endangered* and would develop a program for their recovery. Some 56 refuges, such as Ash Meadows in Nevada and Florida's Crystal River, home of the manatee, were established specifically for the protection of endangered species. Iowa's tiny Driftless Prairie refuge exists to protect the rare, beautifully colored pleistocene land snail and a wildflower, the northern monkshood. Sometimes unwieldy, forever politicized, the ESA stands as a monumental achievement. Its successes include the American alligator, bald eagle, and gray wolf. The whooping crane would almost surely be extinct today without the twin supports of ESA and the refuge system. The black-footed ferret, among the rarest mammals on earth, is today being reintroduced on a few western refuges. In 1998, nearly one-fourth of all threatened and endangered species populations find sanctuary on refuge lands.

More legislation followed. The passage of the Alaska National Interest Lands Conservation Act in 1980 added more than 50 million acres to the refuge system in Alaska.

The 1980s and '90s have brought no end of conservation challenges, faced by an increasingly diverse association of organizations and strategies. Partnerships now link the refuge system with nonprofit groups, from Ducks Unlimited and The Nature Conservancy to international efforts such as Partners in Flight, a program to monitor the decline of, and to secure habitat for, neotropical songbirds. These cooperative efforts have resulted in habitat acquisition and restoration, research, and many new refuges. Partnerships with private landowners who voluntarily offer marginally useful lands for restoration—with a sponsoring conservation group cost-sharing the project—have revived many thousands of acres of grasslands, wetlands, and riparian corridors.

Citizen activism is alive and well as we enter the new millennium. Protecting and promoting the growth of the NWR system is a primary campaign of the National Audubon Society, which, by the year 2000, will have grown to a membership of around 550,000. NAS itself also manages about 100 sanctuaries and nature centers across the country, with a range of opportunities for environmental education. The National Wildlife Refuge Association, a volunteer network,

Coyote on the winter range

keeps members informed of refuge events, environmental issues, and legislative developments and helps to maintain a refuge volunteer workforce. In 1998, a remarkable 20 percent of all labor performed on the nation's refuges was carried out by volunteers, a contribution worth an estimated $14 million.

A national wildlife refuge today has many facets. Nature is ascendant and thriving, often to a shocking degree when compared with adjacent lands. Each site has its own story: a prehistory, a recent past, a present—a story of place, involving people, nature, and stewardship, sometimes displayed in Visitor Center or Headquarters exhibits, always written into the landscape. Invariably a refuge belongs to a community as well, involving area residents who visit, volunteers who log hundreds of hours, and a refuge staff who are knowledgeable and typically friendly, even outgoing, especially if the refuge is far-flung. In this respect most every refuge is a portal to local culture, be it Native American, cows and crops, or big city. There may be no better example of democracy in action than a national wildlife refuge. The worm-dunker fishes while a mountain biker pedals past. In spring, birders scan marshes and grasslands that in the fall will be walked by hunters. Compromise is the guiding principle.

What is the future of the NWR system? In Prairie City, Iowa, the Neal Smith NWR represents a significant departure from the time-honored model. Established in 1991, the site had almost nothing to "preserve." It was old farmland with scattered remnants of tallgrass prairie and degraded oak savanna. What is happening at Neal Smith, in ecological terms, has never been attempted on such a scale: the reconstruction, essentially from scratch, of a self-sustaining 8,000-acre native biome, complete with bison and elk, greater prairie chickens, and a palette of wildflowers and grasses that astonish and delight.

What is happening in human terms is equally profound. Teams of area residents, called "seed seekers," explore cemeteries, roadside ditches, and long-ignored patches of ground. Here and there they find seeds of memory, grasses and wildflowers from the ancient prairie, and harvest them; the seeds are catalogued and planted on the refuge. The expanding prairie at Neal Smith is at once new and very old. It is reshaping thousands of Iowans' sense of place, connecting them to what was, eliciting wonder for what could be. And the lessons here transcend biology. In discovering rare plants, species found only in the immediate area, people discover an identity beyond job titles and net worth. The often grueling labor of cutting brush, pulling nonnative plants, and tilling ground evokes the determined optimism of Theodore and Franklin Roosevelt and of the CCC.

As the nation runs out of wild places worthy of preservation, might large-scale restoration of damaged or abandoned lands become the next era of American conservation? There are ample social and economic justifications. The ecological justifications are endless, for, as the history of conservation and ecology has revealed, nature and humanity cannot go their separate ways. The possibilities, if not endless, remain rich for the years ahead.

—John Grassy

How to use this book

Local conditions and regulations on national wildlife refuges vary considerably. We provide detailed, site-specific information useful for a good refuge visit, and we note the broad consistencies throughout the NWR system (facility set-up and management, what visitors may or may not do, etc.). Contact the refuge before arriving or stop by the Visitor Center when you get there. F&W wildlife refuge managers are ready to provide friendly, savvy advice about species and habitats, plus auto, hiking, biking, or water routes that are open and passable, and public programs (such as guided walks) you may want to join.

AUDUBON GUIDES TO THE NATIONAL WILDLIFE REFUGES

This is one of nine regional volumes in a series covering the entire NWR system. **Visitable refuges**—over 300 of them—constitute about three-fifths of the NWR system. **Nonvisitable refuges** may be small (without visitor facilities), fragile (set up to protect an endangered species or threatened habitat), or new and undeveloped.

Among visitable refuges, some are more important and better developed than others. In creating this series, we have categorized refuges as A, B, or C level, with the A-level refuges getting the most attention. You will easily recognize the difference. C-level refuges, for instance, do not carry a map.

Rankings can be debated; we know that. We considered visitation statistics, accessibility, programming, facilities, and the richness of the refuges' habitats and animal life. Some refuges ranked as C-level now may develop further over time.

Many bigger NWRs have either "satellites" (with their own refuge names) separate "units" within the primary refuge or other, less significant NWRs nearby. All of these, at times, were deemed worthy of a brief mention.

ORGANIZATION OF THE BOOK

■ **REGIONAL OVERVIEW** This regional introduction is intended to give readers the big picture, touching on broad patterns in landscape formation, interconnections among plant communities, and diversity of animals. We situate NWRs in the natural world of the larger bio-region to which they belong, showing why these federally protected properties stand out as wild places worth preserving amid encroaching civilization.

We also note some wildlife management issues that will surely color the debate around campfires and

ABOUT THE U.S. FISH & WILDLIFE SERVICE Under the Department of the Interior, the U.S. Fish & Wildlife Service is the principal federal agency responsible for conserving and protecting wildlife and plants and their habitats for the benefit of the American people. The Service manages the 93-million-acre NWR system, comprised of more than 500 national wildlife refuges, thousands of small wetlands, and other special management areas. It also operates 66 national fish hatcheries, 64 U.S. Fish & Wildlife Management Assistance offices, and 78 ecological services field stations. The agency enforces federal wildlife laws, administers the Endangered Species Act, manages migratory bird populations, restores nationally significant fisheries, conserves and restores wildlife habitats such as wetlands, and helps foreign governments with their conservation efforts. It also oversees the federal-aid program that distributes hundreds of millions of dollars in excise taxes on fishing and hunting equipment to state wildlife agencies.

congressional conference tables in years ahead, while paying recognition to the NWR supporters and managers who helped make the present refuge system a reality.

■ **THE REFUGES** The refuge section of the book is organized alphabetically by state and then, within each state, by refuge name.

There are some clusters, groups, or complexes of neighboring refuges administered by one primary refuge. Some refuge complexes are alphabetized here by the name of their primary refuge, with the other refuges in the group following immediately thereafter.

■ **APPENDIX**

Nonvisitable National Wildlife Refuges: NWR properties that meet the needs of wildlife but are off-limits to all but field biologists.

Federal Recreation Fees: An overview of fees and fee passes.

Volunteer Activities: How you can lend a hand to help your local refuge or get involved in supporting the entire NWR system.

U.S. Fish & Wildlife General Information: The seven regional headquarters of the U.S. Fish & Wildlife Service through which the National Wildlife Refuge System is administered.

National Audubon Society Wildlife Sanctuaries: A listing of the 24 National Audubon Society wildlife sanctuaries, dispersed across the U.S., which are open to the public.

Bibliography & Resources: Natural-history titles both on the region generally and its NWRs, along with a few books of inspiration about exploring the natural world.

Glossary: A listing of specialized terms (not defined in the text) tailored to this region.

Index

National Audubon Society Mission Statement

PRESENTATION OF INFORMATION: A-LEVEL REFUGE

■ **INTRODUCTION** This section attempts to evoke the essence of the place, The writer sketches the sounds or sights you might experience on the refuge, such as sandhill cranes taking off, en masse, from the marsh, filling the air with the roar of thousands of beating wings. That's a defining event for a particular refuge and a great reason to go out and see it.

■ **MAP** Some refuges are just a few acres; several, like the Alaskan behemoths, are bigger than several eastern states. The scale of the maps in this series can vary. We recommend that you also ask refuges for their detailed local maps.

■ **HISTORY** This outlines how the property came into the NWR system and what its uses were in the past.

■ **GETTING THERE** General location; seasons and hours of operation; fees, if any (see federal recreation fees in Appendix); address, telephone. Smaller or remote refuges may have their headquarters off-site. We identify highways as follows: TX14 = Texas state highway # 14; US 23 = a federal highway; I-85 = Interstate 85.

Note: Many NWRs have their own web pages at the F&W web site, http://www.fws.gov/. Some can be contacted by fax or e-mail, and if we do not provide that information here, you may find it at the F&W web site.

■ **TOURING** The **Visitor Center**, if there is one, is the place to start your tour. Some have wildlife exhibits, videos, and bookstores; others may be only a kiosk. Let someone know your itinerary before heading out on a long trail or into the backcountry, and then go explore.

Most refuges have roads open to the public; many offer a wildlife **auto tour,** with wildlife information signs posted en route or a brochure or audiocassette to guide you. Your car serves as a bird blind if you park and remain quiet. Some refuge roads require 4-wheel-drive or a high-chassis vehicle. Some roads are closed seasonally to protect habitats during nesting seasons or after heavy rain or snow.

Touring also covers **walking and hiking** (see more trail details under ACTIVITIES) and **biking.** Many refuge roads are rough; mountain or hybrid bikes are more appropriate than road bikes. When water is navigable, we note what kinds of **boats** may be used and where there are boat launches.

■ **WHAT TO SEE**

Landscape and climate: This section covers geology, topography, and climate: primal forces and raw materials that shaped the habitats that lured species to the refuge. It also includes weather information for visitors.

Plant life: This is a sampling of noteworthy plants on the refuge, usually sorted by habitat, using standard botanical nomenclature. Green plants bordering watery places are in "Riparian Zones"; dwarfed trees, shrubs, and flowers on windswept mountaintops are in the "Alpine Forest"; and so forth.

Wildflowers abound, and you may want to see them in bloom. We give advice about timing your visit, but ask the refuge for more. If botany and habitat relationships are new to you, you can soon learn to read the landscape as a set of interrelated communities. Take a guided nature walk to begin.

(Note: In two volumes, "Plants" is called "Habitats and Plant Communities.")

Animal life: The national map on pages 4 and 5 shows the major North American "flyways." Many NWRs cluster in watery territory underneath the birds' aerial superhighways. There are many birds in this book, worth seeing simply for their beauty. But ponder, too, what birds eat (fish, insects, aquatic plants), or how one species (the mouse) attracts another (the fox), and so on up the food chain, and you'll soon understand the rich interdependence on display in many refuges.

Animals use camouflage and stealth for protection; many are nocturnal. You may want to come out early or late to increase your chances of spotting them. Refuge managers can offer advice on sighting or tracking animals.

Grizzly bears, venomous snakes, alligators, and crocodiles can indeed be dangerous. Newcomers to these animals' habitats should speak with refuge staff about precautions before proceeding.

■ **ACTIVITIES** Some refuges function not only as wildlife preserves but also as recreation parks. Visit a beach, take a bike ride, and camp overnight, or devote your time to serious wildlife observation.

Camping and swimming: If not permissible on the refuge, there may be federal or state campgrounds nearby; we mention some of them. Planning an NWR camping trip should start with a call to refuge headquarters.

Wildlife observation: This subsection touches on strategies for finding species most people want to see. Crowds do not mix well with certain species; you

---

A NOTE ON HUNTING AND FISHING Opinions on hunting and fishing on federally owned wildlife preserves range from "Let's have none of it" to "We need it as part of the refuge management plan." The F&W Service follows the latter approach, with about 290 hunting programs and 260 fishing programs. If you have strong opinions on this topic, talk with refuge managers to gain some insight into F&W's rationale. You can also write to your representative or your senators in Washington.

For most refuges, we summarize the highlights of the hunting and fishing options. You must first have required state and local licenses for hunting or fishing. Then you must check with refuge headquarters about special restrictions that may apply on the refuge; refuge bag limits, for example, or duration of season may be different from regulations elsewhere in the same state.

Hunting and fishing options change from year to year on many refuges, based on the size of the herd or of the flock of migrating birds. These changes may reflect local weather (a hard winter trims the herd) or disease, or factors in distant habitats where animals summer or winter. We suggest what the options usually are on a given refuge (e.g., some birds, some mammals, fish, but not all etc..). It's the responsibility of those who wish to hunt and fish to confirm current information with refuge headquarters and to abide by current rules.

COMMON SENSE, WORTH REPEATING

Leave no trace Every visitor deserves a chance to see the refuge in its pristine state. We all share the responsibility to minimize our impact on the landscape. "Take only pictures and leave only footprints," and even there you'll want to avoid trampling plant life by staying on established trails. Pack out whatever you pack in. Ask refuge managers for guidance on low-impact hiking and camping.

Respect private property Many refuges consist of noncontiguous parcels of land, with private properties abutting refuge lands. Respect all Private Property and No Trespassing signs, especially in areas where native peoples live within refuge territory and hunt or fish on their own land.

Water Protect the water supply. Don't wash dishes or dispose of human waste within 200 ft. of any water. Treat all water for drinking with iodine tablets, backpacker's water filter, or boiling. Clear water you think is OK may be contaminated upstream by wildlife you cannot see.

may need to go away from established observation platforms to have success. Learn a bit about an animal's habits, where it hunts or sleeps, what time of day it moves about. Adjust your expectations to match the creature's behavior, and your chances of success will improve.

Photography: This section outlines good places or times to see certain species. If you have a zoom lens, use it. Sit still, be quiet, and hide yourself. Don't approach the wildlife; let it approach you. Never feed animals or pick growing plants.

Hikes and walks: Here we list specific outings, with mileages and trailhead locations. Smooth trails and boardwalks, suitable for people with disabilities, are noted. On bigger refuges, there may be many trails. Ask for a local map. If you go bushwacking, first make sure this is permissible. Always carry a map and compass.

Seasonal events: National Wildlife Refuge Week, in October, is widely celebrated, with guided walks, lectures, demonstrations, and activities of special interest to children. Call your local refuge for particulars. At other times of the year there are fishing derbies, festivals celebrating the return of migrating birds, and other events linked to the natural world. Increasingly, refuges post event schedules on their web pages.

Publications: Many NWR brochures are free, such as bird and wildflower checklists. Some refuges have pamphlets and books for sale, describing local habitats and species.

Note: The categories of information above appear in A and B refuges in this book; on C-level refuges, options are fewer, and some of these headings may not appear.

—*David Emblidge*

California and Hawaii
A Regional Overview

The idea of California began as a fantasy (and many would say it's remained so ever since) described in 1510 by the Spanish writer Garcia Ordones de Montalvo. There was no metal but gold on the isle of California, he wrote. Ruled by the Amazon Queen Calafia, California was found "on the right hand of the Indies. . .very close to the side of Terrestial Paradise." Myth merged with reality when Spanish explorers sailed to find this land of gold. The gold was there but remained undiscovered for another three centuries—while the true wealth of California, a biological abundance unparalleled in the United States, went unremarked.

Some 735 years before Hernán Cortés, conqueror of the Aztecs, sent his ships north from Mexico in 1535 to search for the fabled California, another group of seafarers had discovered a second earthly Paradise, the Hawaiian Islands. Polynesians, most probably from the Marquesas Islands, sailed in open canoes 2,400 miles across the vast Pacific, perhaps guided to shore by the burning fires of a Hawaiian volcano. They brought with them chickens, dogs, pigs, taro, sugarcane, breadfruit, yams, and bananas, thus instigating the changes that would over the centuries decimate Hawaii's native flora and fauna.

National wildlife refuges play a particularly important role in California and Hawaii because, along with the two states' national parks and local nature preserves, they are the chief bulwarks against the disappearance of natural ecosystems unique in the world.

In this book we cover great refuges from two "Pacific Ocean" states (California and Hawaii) with others located on remote Pacific islands. While many of these refuges have some bird or marine mammal life in common, there are obvious differences between and among such far-flung properties: Their climates, landscapes, and resulting habitats are strikingly distinct. Desert California is drastically different from Hawaiian rain forest, and both of these habitats differ starkly from those of California's High Sierra or Hawaii's snow-capped volcanoes. But it is just these contrasts that make the natural world in the California and Hawaii-Pacific region of the United States so fascinating. Travelers planning a California and Hawaii tour, on one grand trip or on several visits over the years, are in for a rare treat from seeing all this diversity.

This book describes 11 wildlife refuges in Hawaii and 33 in California. Six refuges that spill over state boundaries are also profiled—three in Oregon's half of the Klamath Basin, which straddles the Oregon-California border, and three on both sides of the Colorado River, which defines the Arizona-California border.

GEOLOGY
California and Hawaii owe their spectacular scenery to geological cataclysms that began millions of years ago. At the time, neither California nor Hawaii existed (the West Coast ended somewhere in what is now Nevada); but around 30 million years

California poppies, the state flower

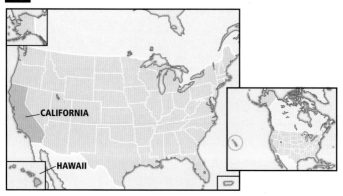

CALIFORNIA

HAWAII

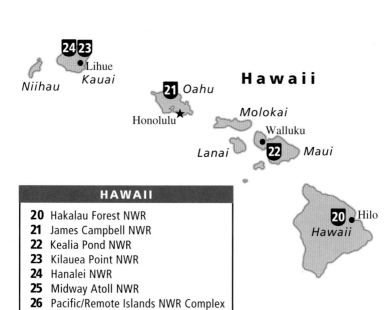

Niihau

24 **23** •Lihue
Kauai

H a w a i i

21 Oahu

Molokai

Honolulu ★

Walluku

22

Lanai

Maui

•Hilo

20
Hawaii

HAWAII

20 Hakalau Forest NWR
21 James Campbell NWR
22 Kealia Pond NWR
23 Kilauea Point NWR
24 Hanalei NWR
25 Midway Atoll NWR
26 Pacific/Remote Islands NWR Complex

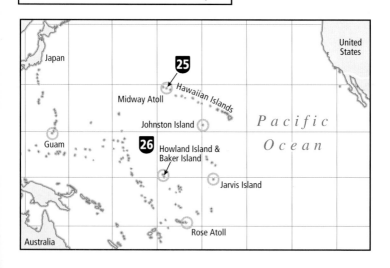

Japan

United
States

25

Midway Atoll

Hawaiian Islands

Johnston Island ⊙

P a c i f i c

Guam

26

Howland Island &
Baker Island

O c e a n

Jarvis Island

Australia

Rose Atoll

11

CALIFORNIA

1 Cibola NWR
2 Coachella Valley NWR
3 Don Edwards
   San Francisco Bay NWR
4 Farallon NWR
5 Havasu NWR
6a Hopper Mountain NWR
   Complex (Bitter Creek NWR
   and Hopper Mountain NWR)

6b Blue Ridge NWR
7 Humboldt Bay NWR
8 Imperial NWR
9 Kern NWR
10 Klamath Basin NWRs
   (Bear Valley NWR, Clear Lake NWR,
   Klamath Marsh NWR, Lower
   Klamath NWR, Tule Lake NWR, and
   Upper Klamath NWR)
11 Modoc NWR
12 Sacramento Valley NWR Complex
   (Sacramento NWR, Sacramento
   River NWR, and Colusa NWR)
13 Salinas River NWR
14 San Diego NWR Complex
   (Sweetwater Marsh NWR, Tijuana
   Slough NWR, and San Diego NWR)
15 San Luis NWR Complex
   (Merced NWR and San Luis NWR)
16 San Pablo Bay NWR
17 Seal Beach NWR
18 Sonny Bono Salton Sea NWR
19 Stone Lakes NWR

ago, in the center of the Pacific Ocean, a hot spot, or rift in the oceanic floor, began to pour lava from the molten outer core of the earth into the ocean. As eons passed, the eruptions continued to build up lava until finally it surfaced; and the first of the Hawaiian islands appeared.

A beautiful Hawaiian legend tells of Pele, the goddess of fire and volcanoes. Fleeing a cruel older sister, Pele dug a crater home on Ni'ihau with her digging stick, but fled again as her sister, Na Maka o Kaha'i, goddess of the sea, forced her way into that shallow home. Pele dug a bigger house on Kaua'i but was chased from there to O'ahu, then to Moloka'i, Lana'i, Kaho'olawe, Molokini, and Maui. Today she lives on the island of Hawaii in a mountain fortress, where Na Maka has not yet forced her out.

The legend parallels the geological explanation for the order of creation of the Hawaiian Island chain—although scientists describe it in different terms. Giant tectonic plates, rafting atop the earth's molten interior, carry islands, continents, and oceans with them. The Pacific hot spot, anchored firmly to the earth's molten interior, has not moved, but under the floor of the Pacific Ocean, the Pacific Plate (6,000 miles long and 50 miles thick) is moving sedately northwest at the rate of around 2 to 4 inches a year, carrying the ocean floor and the Hawaiian Islands with it. Midway Atoll, one of the first islands formed by the hot spot, is some 1,150 miles northwest of Honolulu; and the earliest islands in the chain, now sunk beneath the sea, extend the length of the volcanic formations to 2,500 miles.

Even before the Hawaiian Islands formed, California was taking shape, the result of a series of violent collisions between the Pacific and North American plates. As the North American plate rafted west, it scraped up the ocean floor (because continental rocks are lighter than oceanic rocks, the North American Plate floated over the Pacific Plate, which sank beneath it). The rocks and mud scooped up in this 200-million-year abrasion became California.

Volcanoes and earthquakes remind us that the process of creation is not complete. A new island is being built on the ocean floor southeast of Hawaii; it is already 15,000 feet high. (The ocean floor lies about 18,000 feet below the surface.) When measured from the ocean floor, Hawaii's Mauna Loa volcano, at 13,667 feet above sea level, is one of the greatest mountain masses in the world. It has erupted almost 40 times since 1832. Kilauea volcano, Pele's home and the sister volcano to Mauna Loa, has erupted more than 20 times since 1924.

Earthquakes mark the violent encounters of the earth's great tectonic plates, and California is earthquake country. The San Andreas Fault, notorious for its violent earthquakes, is one of the dividing lines between the Pacific and North American plates. Earthquakes strike when growing stress wrenches apart two plates that have temporarily joined together, or when two plates collide. (Earthquakes along the Pacific Coast from Alaska to California account for around 90 percent of the seismic activity in the United States.)

California holds the dubious statistical record of sustaining eight of the 15 strongest known earthquakes in the Lower 48. A quake in California's Owens Valley in 1872 flattened 52 of 59 houses and killed 27 people. The 1906 San Francisco quake killed an estimated 3,000 persons and tore apart the pipeline carrying water to the city, allowing fires to destroy what the earthquake hadn't. Movement along the San Andreas Fault was observed from San Juan Bautista to Point Arena, a distance of 186 miles. The San Andreas Fault slipped again in 1989, collapsing two freeways and several viaducts in the San Francisco Bay area, killing 63 people. Californians, however, don't get all shook up about quakes. Their black humor points out that "It's not our fault, it's San Andreas' Fault."

CLIMATE AND TOPOGRAPHY

Both California and Hawaii start at sea level and rise to more than 13,000 feet. California's Mount Whitney (14,495 feet) is the highest point in the Lower 48. Less than 60 miles to the east, Death Valley's desolate landscapes contain the country's lowest point, Badwater, 282 feet *below* sea level. Two great deserts, the Mojave and the Colorado, cover much of the state's southeastern corner; desert sand dunes can be seen in Coachella Valley NWR. Although irrigation disguises the San Joaquin Valley with a covering of crops, the southern section of the valley receives less than 10 inches of rain annually, qualifying it, too, as a desert.

The contrast between the irrigated fields around the valley's Kern NWR and the natural landscape within the refuge is startling. Rain (up to 200 inches a year) and fog, enough to sustain the coast redwoods, bathe the northern reaches of California's 1,100-mile coastline. The Humboldt Bay refuge is in this misty environment. The romantic, rocky scenery along California's north coast gives way to the stunning vistas in Big Sur on the central coast and to the broad sand beaches in southern California, where moderate weather allows beachgoing even in February. Tijuana Slough and Sweetwater Marsh NWRs hug the San Diego coastline.

The Sierra Nevada mountain range, around 400 miles long and 50 miles wide, isolates California (only seven roads cross it). Called the "Range of Light" by John Muir, the Sierra is a single uplifted fault block. Its eastern face rises 11,000 feet

Common murres nest along the rocky coastal islands of northern California.

Sunset over wetlands in Lower Klamath NWR

above the Owens Valley (the drive north up US 395 from Olancha to Mono Lake is one of the most spectacular in the country). The Cascade Mountains merge into the Sierra at the northern end of the state. (Mount Lassen and Mount Shasta are the southernmost volcanoes in the Cascades.) The area around Mammoth Mountain in the southern Sierra is also active volcanically.

The state's Great Central Valley, around 500 miles long and 40 miles wide, is drained by two major rivers, the Sacramento in the north and the San Joaquin in the south. Some of the state's most prolific birdlife is found in the valley refuges of Kern NWR and the Sacramento and San Luis complexes.

The vast differences in elevation have created numerous microclimates within California (the highest recorded temperature in Death Valley is 134 degrees, two degrees short of the world record), but overall the state's climate is Mediterranean—mild temperatures with dry summers and rain falling from November through April. Hawaii's seaside climate stays in the balmy 70s and 80s, with an occasional dip into the 60s during winter, but rain can fall at any time of the year. Only the high peaks experience cold weather, with snow falling at the 10,000-foot level on Mauna Loa.

The islands of Kau'ai, Maui, and Hawaii share rugged volcanic landscapes fringed by the beaches for which Hawaii is famous. Hawaii, the largest of the islands, is about the size of Connecticut and is composed of five large volcanoes (Kilauea and Mauna Loa have both been active recently). Maui was formed by two volcanoes, West Maui and Haleakala, joined by an isthmus. Kealia Pond NWR lies at the southern end of the isthmus.

Kaua'i, the oldest of the central Hawaiian Islands, is deeply eroded by water cutting through the lava. In the Hanalei Valley, streams have cut through 2,000 feet of lava, creating an exquisite valley around 4 miles wide and surrounded by walls that in places reach to 3,000 feet. The fluted cliffs of Pali on Oahu show the ability of warm acidic rainwater to erode rock. The rainwater clings to shady surfaces for a longer time than it does to rock exposed to the sun. Over time, the shady side erodes, leaving the sunny side as a ridge. All of the Hawaiian Islands offer fascinating lessons in the actions of volcanoes, and the island of Hawaii is one of the few places in the world where it's easy to see an active volcano.

PLANT COMMUNITIES

California's position on the precarious edge of the North American Plate has not only made it one of the most beautiful and spectacular places in the world, it has also given it 6,300 plant species, nearly one-fourth of all species found in North America north of the Mexican border and more than in any other single state. (All of New England, about the same size, has fewer than 2,000 plant species.) California's variations in climate, elevation, and soil types are responsible for this extraordinary diversity of species. As assorted terranes attached themselves to the West Coast, creating California, they brought with them the diverse soils of their origins, eventually blanketing the state with all 11 of the world's major soil groups. Within the state, these soils have broken down into around 1,200 different types of dirt, each home to plants adapted to that specific soil.

California has the world's tallest, biggest, and oldest trees. Coast redwoods have a life span of around 1,000 years and grow to more than 300 feet in height (one measured 385 feet tall), making them the tallest living things. The Big Trees (giant redwoods) are the world's most massive living things, with diameters to 30 feet and heights of around 325 feet. They weigh around 6,000 tons and live to more than 3,500 years. Bristlecone pines grow in the spare landscape of the White Mountains at elevations ranging from 9,500 to 11,500 feet. They are the world's oldest living trees; one has been dated at more than 4,600 years of age.

Visitors to Coachella Valley and Sonny Bono Salton Sea refuges will see cacti, California fan plans, and smoke trees, some of the many plants adapted to another extreme within California's plant communities—the desert. The wetlands of the Great Central Valley abound in cattails and tules (which gave the notorious ground-clinging tule fog its name); along with marsh plants, there is a glorious display of spring wildflowers in the refuge meadows. As John Muir walked out of Pacheco Pass on his way to Yosemite Valley for the first time in 1868,

Hanalei NWR, Hawaii

he saw the San Joaquin Valley spread before him. "There, extending north and south as far as I could see, lay a vast level flower garden, smooth and level like a lake of gold—the floweriest part of the world I had yet seen," he wrote. "The flowers were so crowded together that in walking through the midst of them and over them more than a hundred were pressed down beneath the foot at every step." The remnants of these vast flower beds can be seen in San Luis and Merced refuges, in the valley below Pacheco Pass. The Sacramento refuges have similar displays.

The flora of the Hawaiian Islands evolved under circumstances quite different from those of California. Beginning life as volcanic rocks barren of vegetation— in the middle of a vast ocean—the islands developed a unique flora, so that today at least 98 percent of their approximately 1,700 species grow only here, on these islands. Some scientists believe that these 1,700 species descended from fewer than 150 seeds surviving among the millions that occasionally drifted ashore or were deposited by a wayward bird in its droppings or off its wings.

The Polynesians, arriving from the Marquesas Islands and Tahiti, beginning around A.D. 400, brought with them plants that began the transformation of Hawaii's flora from endemic species to an overwhelming number of exotics. The arrival of Capt. James Cook in Hawaii in 1778 marked the beginning of the second wave of introduced species. Today most of the gorgeous tropical flowers for which Hawaii is renowned are introduced species.

Several native species survive in the seaside marshes. At James Campbell refuge, look for the water hyssop, a creeping herb with white flowers, and the succulent sea purslane, with dainty pink flowers, growing where it is periodically exposed to salt spray or salt water. Hakalau Forest NWR preserves a segment of Hawaii's rain forest; its dense stands of koa and 'ohi'a trees are the last refuge of Hawaii's native birds and, in the case of the 'ohi'a's red blossoms, a major source of food for them. Twelve of the 29 rare plant species growing in Hakalau Forest and surrounding lands are endangered or proposed for listing as endangered.

ANIMAL LIFE

When Capt. Cook visited Hawaii for the first time about 200 years ago, there were 70 species of birds on the islands, birds found nowhere else in the world. The Hawaiian honeycreepers, believed to have descended from a small flock of finch-like ancestors—probably the first birds to colonize Hawaii—were the dominant group among Hawaiian forest birds. They are famous among bird biologists for their numerous adaptations (unequaled in any continental bird family) that suited them to specific niches within the forest ecosystem. Seven of the species alive in Hakalau Forest at the time of Cook's visit are now extinct, but the survivors can be seen in the Hakalau refuge.

Hawaii's saltwater marsh refuges, including James Campbell, Kealia Pond, and Pearl Harbor, were established to protect four native birds, the Hawaiian duck, coot, moorhen, and stilt, all endangered. Among Hawaii's mammals, only the monk seal and a small brown bat came to the islands under their own power. All other Hawaiian mammals, including the undesirable feral pig and mongoose, are introduced species.

The same diversity of species found in California's plants occurs in the state's populations of mammals, amphibians, and reptiles. They're found from the desert, where the fringe-toed lizard burrows into sand to survive the 111-degree temperatures, to the High Sierra, where the yellow-bellied marmot hibernates to avoid winter temperatures that drop into the teens. North America's fastest mammal, the pronghorn, summers near and in the Modoc refuge; and a herd of tule elk, in a fenced enclosure at the San Luis refuge, is often visible. More difficult to see but present on several of the refuges are black bear, mountain lions, bobcats and foxes.

California lies directly under the path of the Pacific Flyway, and the millions of birds that pass through the state on their annual migrations make for spectac-

Yellow-bellied marmots make their home in the High Sierra.

Canada goose family, Modoc NWR, California

ular birdwatching. The migrating birds stop off—or stay for the winter—in refuges stretching from the Sonny Bono Salton Sea NWR around 100 miles north of the Baja California (Mexican) border to the Modoc NWR in the state's northeast corner. Migrants to Hawaii arrive from Alaska, the golden plover by air and the humpback whale by sea.

OUR ALTERED LANDS

Hawaii has the unfortunate distinction of having more endangered species—both plant and animal—than any other state. California is the only state where its citizens have managed to exterminate the animal that appears on its flag as a symbol of the state—the grizzly (the last California grizzly was shot in the 1920s). Together, the two states serve as an example of what happens when Paradise opens its doors for colonization. Everyone comes in.

The first to suffer with the arrival of the Spaniards in California were the native peoples, who died by the thousands from European diseases inadvertently introduced by the Spanish military. Yankee traders, bringing Aleut hunters with them from Alaska, hunted sea otters and fur seals nearly to extinction. One Yankee ship left the coast with 73,402 fur seal pelts, having killed them at the rate of 200 a day. (Sea otters, now protected as an endangered species, are making a robust comeback but are eating the California abalone, much to the consternation of the state's gourmets.) Gold, discovered in 1848, changed the face of California, bringing the first great wave of immigration. Hydraulic mining, where high-powered jets of water washed out entire hillsides, muddied clear streams and left massive piles of cobbles that can still be seen throughout the foothills. (Hydraulic mining was outlawed after complaints from citizens downstream whose drinking water was muddied.)

California eventually became the market basket for the nation, and it is agriculture that has most directly affected the state's wildlife. California's Great Central Valley was once a maze of wetlands, so extensive they prevented travelers from crossing them. Today 95 percent of the state's wetlands, both inland and

The California condor population, once depleted to less than 30 birds, is on a comeback.

along the coast, are gone, filled in to make farm fields; and 90 percent of the state's riverine habitat along rivers and creeks has disappeared. Agricultural runoff has collected in streams and reservoirs, causing an environmental disaster in Kesterson Reservoir, where excessive selenium in the water caused birth defects in the birds. Selenium concentrations in the Salton Sea have been measured at levels matching those at Kesterson.

The loss of native habitat has caused 215 species of California's plants and animals to be listed as endangered or threatened.

Hawaii has 290 threatened and endangered species. The state's native wildlife evolved without needing defenses against predators such as mosquitoes, reptiles, or carnivorous mammals. Plants lost their chemical defenses and thorns, and birds lost the power of flight. The introduction of mongeese, rats, feral pigs, insects, and hardy alien plant and bird species has devastated the endemic flora and fauna of the islands. Hawaii's rich volcanic soil is now used to grow sugarcane and pineapple, adding to the loss of habitat where formerly native plants grew. Even before the arrival of Capt. Cook, about half of Hawaii's endemic birds had become extinct. At the turn of the 20th century, about 40,000 ducks wintered in the Hawaiian wetlands. Today the number is around 2,000. Currently, in the Hakalau Forest alone, eight of the 14 native bird species are endangered. These beautiful birds, all descended from one species of ancestral Hawaiian honeycreeper, may be seen in the Hakalau Forest NWR.

TAKING CARE OF THE LAND

Protecting Hawaii's rare endemic species is the chief concern of the Hawaiian wildlife refuges. Ridding the refuges of introduced rats, mongeese, barn owls, cattle egrets, bullfrogs, dogs, and cats by trapping them and fencing the refuges prevents the predators from killing the native birds that nest on the refuge lands. Allowing feral pig hunts in Hakalau Forest NWR reduces damage to the vegetation caused when the pigs root through the undergrowth. The refuges also burn out alien plants, spray them with herbicides, disc them, and pull them by hand. Native species are planted in the cleared land. On Midway Island debris is removed from beaches to prevent monk seals from becoming entangled, and all rats on the islands have been eradicated.

Similar methods for controlling alien plants are used in California—prescribed burning and spraying with herbicides—but restoring filled-in wetlands is equally important. The U.S. Fish & Wildlife Service plans more land acquisitions such as adding 5 square miles of cropland at Lower Klamath NWR to be used for water storage—a place for migrating and nesting birds. Depleted riparian habitat is replaced by plantings. Volunteers and wildlife service personnel at San Luis NWR have planted 40,000 cottonwood and willow cuttings, oak seedlings, and native shrubs. Because many wetlands in the refuges are constructed rather than natural, water levels are controlled with a pump system. Water is drawn down in summer to kill alien species and allow the growth of native plants that serve as food for migrating birds when the ponds are refilled in autumn for their arrival.

THE FUTURE

Between 1950 and 1960 California's population surged from 10,586,000 to 15,717,000. This explosive increase continued in the 1980s at a rate of 25 percent, compared with a national average of 9.8 percent. More than 30 million people now live in California, making it the most populous state. The ever spreading suburbs across the state's most desirable empty land bode poorly for the remaining wildlife and cause increasing conflicts between developers and environmentalists. San Diego County, in the southwest corner of the state, stretches from the Pacific Ocean halfway across the state to the Anza Borrego Desert. Its more than 200 threatened, endangered, or rare plants and animals, a number greater than that of any other county in the nation, and its growth rate, one of the highest in the nation during the past 20 years, typify the dilemma facing the state in preserving its remaining wildlife and open spaces. Regional solutions are needed to preserve corridors of open space that prevent wildlife from being trapped in too small an area for survival.

A new approach to conservation is being attempted in San Diego County and may serve as a model for future conservation efforts in the state. In 1991, the State of California Resources Agency established a program, the Natural Community Conservation Planning program, that encourages local governments and landowners to develop their own conservation plans by identifying and agreeing to protect sufficient habitat to allow long-term conservation of sensitive habitats. The Otay-Sweetwater Unit of the San Diego National Wildlife Refuge was established as part of the F&W Service's contribution to a regional reserve set up under the Multiple Species Conservation Plan, which was organized in San Diego County as part of the NCCP. The plan covers a 900-square-mile area (581,600 acres) and provides for both economic development and a preserve of around 268 square miles (171,917 acres) The plan, however, has come under attack by environmentalists, who believe it is not strong enough for the effective conservation of endangered species, and F&W has been sued by 14 environmental groups over the plan. A continuing debate on how to save what is left of California and Hawaii's precious biological communities will occupy the states' environmental agendas in the first decades of the new century.

Our wildlife refuges are microcosms of the wildlife communities that once existed throughout Hawaii and California. A visit to them will show you what's been lost, what's been saved, and what should be preserved.

Cibola NWR
Cibola, Arizona

Refuge landscape, Cibola NWR

Large marshes and farm fields are fed by waters drawn from the Colorado River at Cibola NWR. Abundant flocks of ducks, geese, and sandhill cranes are drawn to the refuge by warm winters and abundant food crops; their vociferous calls, honks, and furious wingbeats fill the air. Out on the valley's desert fringes, you might see other wildlife in action, perhaps a roadrunner chasing down a chuckwalla.

HISTORY

Cibola refuge was created in 1964 to mitigate the effects on wildlife of dam construction and channelization projects on the Colorado River. Today it provides important wintering grounds for migratory waterfowl and other resident wildlife. Encompassing 17,267 acres, Cibola has an annual visitation of around 50,000, almost all in winter.

GETTING THERE

Cibola is located on the Arizona-California border 17 mi. south of Blythe, California. To get there take I-10 west 4 mi. and exit south onto Neighbor's Blvd. (CA 78), which crosses the Colorado River on Cibola Bridge. Follow refuge signs 3.5 mi. to the Visitor Center. The Visitor Center is also accessible via a long dirt road (Cibola Rd.) from the Arizona side off US 95. Lands on the west side of the Colorado River are accessible from CA 78.

■ **SEASON:** Open year-round.

■ **HOURS:** Refuge open dawn to dusk. Visitor Center open weekdays, 8 a.m.– 4:30 p.m.

■ **FEES:** Free entry.

■ **ADDRESS:** Rte. 2, Box 138, Cibola, AZ 85328-9801

■ **TELEPHONE:** 520/857-3253

TOURING CIBOLA

■ **BY AUTOMOBILE:** A 3-mile auto-tour route, Goose Loop, gives exposure to the Arizona side of the refuge, near the Visitor Center. The one-way route runs through farm fields favored by many waterfowl, cranes, and other wildlife in winter. Its final 0.25 mile parallels a water channel that attracts wading birds. On this road, people are required to stay in or close by their vehicles to avoid spooking the wildlife. You may also drive the refuge's extensive system of gravel roads, open to the public.

■ **BY FOOT:** The refuge recently converted 34 acres of agricultural land to native flora. A 1-mile footpath begins in upland mesquite brush, then descends into riparian willow and cottonwood woodlands to an observation tower overlooking a 20-acre pond where thousands of ducks, geese, and sandhill cranes winter. The trailhead is located along Goose Loop Drive, which is an auto-tour route only and not open to foot traffic. Most of the other public roads, however, are open to foot traffic. Several areas are closed to all public entry.

■ **BY BICYCLE:** Biking is allowed on all the public roads except Goose Loop.

■ **BY CANOE, KAYAK, OR BOAT:** Canoes, kayaks, and motorized boats are permitted on the Old River Channel, Pretty Water, Three-Finger Lake, the main Colorado River channel, and Cibola Lake (on the latter, March 15 through Labor Day only). Nonmotorized boats may use Hart Mine Marsh from 10 a.m. to 3 p.m. daily during hunting season. All backwaters (all bodies of water other than the main Colorado River channel) are no-wake zones.

WHAT TO SEE

■ **LANDSCAPE AND CLIMATE** Situated in the historic floodplain of the Colorado River, Cibola refuge is predominately flat river bottomland fringed by low desert ridges cut by washes. The dredged river channel bisects the refuge, flanked on the west by the river channel, and 2,300 acres of wetlands, ponds, and lakes. The largest water body here is 600-acre Cibola Lake.

One-third of the refuge lies in California, the remainder in Arizona. Spanning a 12-mile section of the river, Cibola abuts Imperial NWR on its south border.

This is Sonoran Desert (at its northwesternmost limit), with a hot and dry climate, scant rainfall (only 3 to 5 inches on average), and temperatures exceeding 90 degrees for seven months. Winter days, however, are pleasant.

■ **PLANT LIFE**

Wetlands Growing in the refuge's extensive wetlands along the river, ponds, and lakes are cattail, bulrush, and various sedges.

Forests Also on the river bottomlands but on slightly higher ground are vast areas covered by honey and screwbean mesquite (see sidebar, Brazoria NWR) and tamarisk (see sidebar, Bosque del Apache NWR), an invasive tree that has taken over large swaths of land in the Southwest, crowding out the native cottonwoods and willows. Refuge staff are busy rolling back the tide of tamarisk by planting "reveg" plots with native flora. At ground level here you will find abundant arrowweed.

Arid lands The 785 acres or so of raised desert uplands flanking the valley floor are home to their own flora. Common plants include such desert stalwarts as creosote (see sidebar, Bitter Lake NWR), quailbush, and various cacti.

Farmlands Domestic crops, including corn, milo, millet, wheat, and alfalfa, plus native food stocks, such as grasses and aquatic plants grown on flooded sectors,

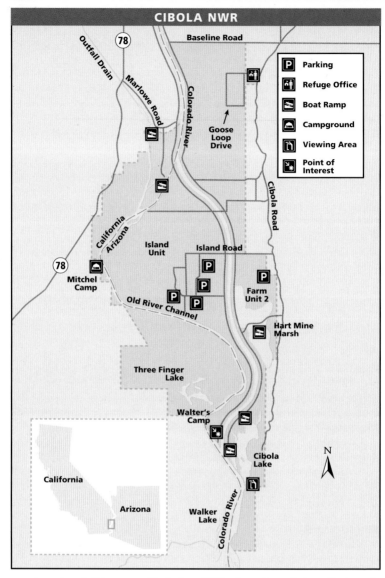

CIBOLA NWR

Parking
Refuge Office
Boat Ramp
Campground
Viewing Area
Point of Interest

Baseline Road

Outfall Drain

Marlowe Road

Colorado River

Goose Loop Drive

Cibola Road

California
Arizona

Island Unit

Island Road

Mitchel Camp

Old River Channel

Farm Unit 2

Hart Mine Marsh

Three Finger Lake

Walter's Camp

Cibola Lake

California

Arizona

Walker Lake

Colorado River

N

are planted on 1,600 acres at Cibola for wildlife. Goose Loop Drive rolls through one of these farm units.

■ ANIMAL LIFE

Birds Cibola is an important wintering area for waterfowl, in particular Canada geese and greater sandhill cranes. The geese spend summers in southern Canada, on the Great Salt Lake of Utah, and in Idaho, Montana, and Wyoming. The Great Basin subspecies frequenting Cibola is among the largest of its kind, standing 2 feet high and weighing up to 10 pounds. These birds have dark gray heads and necks, with a white throat patch. They love alfalfa, eating about a pound of green fodder a day. Peak concentrations of geese—15,000 to 20,000 birds—arrive in December and January, along with about 1,500 sandhill cranes.

The riparian zones are also home to many types of ducks, particularly mallards, northern pintails, northern shovelers, gadwall, bufflehead, common mergansers, and green-winged and cinnamon teal. The duck families reach peak concentrations in fall and winter, although some species are found here year-round.

The wetlands attract wading and shorebirds as well. Sora rails, common moorhens, least bitterns, snowy egrets, and great blue, night-, and green herons all nest here and are present year-round. Avocets, stilts, plovers, and 14 species of sandpipers, phalaropes, and allies also stop over. Most abundant are spotted and least sandpipers and long-billed dowitchers. Take a walk by the marshes and you will hear many chattering red-winged and yellow-headed blackbirds.

In the fields on Goose Loop look for western meadowlarks, brown-headed cowbirds, and northern mockingbirds. Meadowlarks have one of the more distinctive voices of any western bird: 7 to 10 gurgling notes, a *chupp* sound. This is a plump, 9-inch bird, brown with white tail patches in flight; it has a bright yellow breast with a black V across it. The mockingbird is shaped like a robin but is largely gray and displays prominent white wing patches in flight.

The desert fringes are home to white-winged dove, phainopepla, and greater roadrunner, among others. Spring and fall bring such migrant neotropical songbirds as western wood-pewee, Pacific-slope flycatcher, and lark sparrow; nesters include Lucy's warbler and the common yellowthroat.

A handful of endangered or threatened bird species appears at Cibola refuge at various times of the year, including the southwest willow flycatcher, brown pelican, peregrine falcon, bald eagle, and Yuma clapper rail (this one favors cattail marshes and is extremely difficult to see). Birders will be impressed to know that, altogether, 249 species of birds have been recorded here at Cibola NWR.

Mammals Mule deer, coyote, bobcat, and rabbit are the mammals visitors are most likely to see on Cibola refuge.

Reptiles and amphibians Two turtle species, the wetlands-loving spiny softshell and the upland desert tortoise, reside here, along with 13 kinds of lizards, 6 toads and frogs, and 15 types of snakes, including 3 varieties of rattlesnake—the western diamondback, sidewinder, and Mojave. The Mojave is a large rattler that

Snowy egret, Cibola NWR

measures up to 4 feet long; it is distinguished by a diamond pattern and black rings on a white base around its tail (quite similar to the western diamondback). It's handsome to admire—from a respectful distance.

ACTIVITIES

■ **CAMPING:** Camping is not allowed on Cibola refuge.

■ **SWIMMING:** Swimming is permitted, but not encouraged, in the swift waters of the main river channel.

■ **WILDLIFE OBSERVATION:** Goose Loop provides excellent opportunities to watch wildlife at Cibola, because both birds and mammals are drawn to its dry and flooded farm fields in the day to

Northern shoveler

feed; those you're most likely to spot include sandhill cranes, ducks, geese, and wading and shorebirds. The cranes—tall gray birds—prefer the corn and milo fields. Along the way, look to the dense stands of salt cedar, where meadowlarks, sparrows, flycatchers, and shrikes perch and seek cover. Keep an eye out, too, for kestrels hunting insects over the fields or perching on power lines. You might also see burrowing owls standing outside their burrows. An observation tower overlooks a portion of a farm unit located near the Visitor Center.

Serious birders will also want to explore three sites: the island unit (between old and new river channels—continue south past Visitor Center 4.2 miles and turn west/right); Cibola Lake (east bank of the Colorado River on the refuge's southern sector, another 5 miles or so south of Island Unit Road); and Three-Finger Lake (west bank of Colorado River). There is an observation point for views over Cibola Lake on the lake's south end. Drive the levee road until it veers away from the river, then follow it east for about .125 mile. Waterfowl, pelicans, and bald eagles are regularly seen from this high overlook.

HUNTING AND FISHING Large- and **smallmouth bass, striped bass, channel catfish, crappie, sunfish,** and **tilapia** are all taken by anglers here. Boat ramps are found at Cibola Lake and Three Fingers Lake (no access to main river). A river boat ramp is located nearby on Bureau of Land Management (BLM) land. Hunters stalk **mule deer, waterfowl, dove, rabbit,** and **quail**.

You can also drive the upper and lower levee roads paralleling both Colorado River banks. Hart Mine Marsh is another prime place for spotting various birds and other wildlife (south of Island Unit Road, on east bank of Colorado River).

Certain sections of the refuge are closed periodically to provide undisturbed waterfowl roosting areas. Check with staff about birding outside of Goose Loop. With all these options, be sure to pick up a refuge map before you go exploring.

■ **SEASONAL EVENTS:** Slide presentations, and guided tours of the Goose Loop are conducted in winter.

■**PUBLICATIONS:** Brochure, bird list, reptile and amphibian list, auto-tour leaflet.

Coachella Valley NWR
Thousand Palms, California

A March day in the desert at Coachella Valley NWR

Wise folk visit the Colorado Desert in the wintertime, when temperatures do not blast the land, transforming it into a furnace whose thermometer routinely reaches 110 degrees F. The heat is so intense here that light seems to dissolve in front of you. Even the sand dunes appear to move, but it is only the light playing with the shimmering heat. This is the Coachella Valley, one of the driest, hottest places on earth.

HISTORY

The 5.1-square-mile (3,276-acre) Coachella Valley NWR was established in 1985, a year after the establishment of the Coachella Valley Preserve, which includes the refuge. The refuge welcomes around 400 visitors annually.

GETTING THERE

From Los Angeles, take I-10 east past Palm Springs through Thousand Palms. Exit north at Washington St., which bounds the refuge's east side. Washington swings west, becoming Ramon Rd., and cuts through the refuge. To see other areas of the Coachella Valley Preserve, turn north off Ramon Rd. onto Thousand Palms Rd.

   To return to the freeway, either retrace your route or turn east on Dillon Rd. to Indio or west on Dillon Rd., then south on Palm Dr.

■ **SEASON:** Coachella Valley NWR is closed to the public except for a small section of a horse trail, open year-round, that crosses one corner of the refuge.

■ **HOURS:** 7 a.m.–3:30 p.m., weekdays.

■ **ADDRESS:** Coachella Valley NWR, c/o Salton Sea NWR, 906 West Sinclair Rd., Calipatria, CA 92233-0120

■ **TELEPHONE:** 760/348-5278

TOURING COACHELLA VALLEY

■ **BY FOOT AND HORSEBACK:** Both hikers and horseback riders can explore the refuge fan on the horse trail that crosses 1 mile of the refuge (the trail enters the refuge off Ramon Road).

WHAT TO SEE

■ **LANDSCAPE AND CLIMATE** The Coachella Valley's sand dunes are one of its most striking features. Sand dunes are created when prevailing winds pick up a deposit of sand and carry it until the wind meets an obstacle such as a plant or rock, slows, and deposits the sand. Over time, as wind continues to blow in the same pattern, a dune forms—in the Coachella Valley, high winds can lift the dunes to 60 feet in height. The refuge rises from 100 feet in elevation at the south end to 300 feet on the alluvial fan spreading out of Thousand Palms Canyon. (California's highest dunes, between Death Valley and the Owens Valley in the Eureka Valley, reach 680 feet and are the oldest dunes in North America—more than 10,000 years old.)

The Coachella Valley dunes—and a large part of the Colorado Desert—lie in the Salton Trough, a long valley dropping 274 feet below sea level, formed by shifting tectonic plates along the San Andreas Fault, which runs along the east side of the trough. A careful inspection of the trough's east side will reveal offset stream channels and tilted layers of earth.

A striking feature of the desert landscape are the alluvial fans that pour out of the canyons. It looks as if a giant had spilled countless buckets of sand down the canyon until they rolled out into a fan shape as they slid toward the valley floor. The fan shape was created from sand and rocks deposited out of the canyon over the years by flash floods.

Rainfall in the Colorado Desert's Coachella Valley averages around 4 inches a year (but two years can pass with no sign of rain). Temperatures can soar to 120 degrees F. in July (summer lows sometimes hit 34 degrees), and the average July high is 110 degrees. January temperatures are markedly cooler, with the thermometer reading from 15 to 73 degrees.

The rain that does fall on the dunes sinks in rather than drains off; while the dunes appear dry, a layer of slightly damp sand is actually present below the surface. It cools the subsurface sand enough to allow small reptiles to survive beneath a surface that routinely heats up to more than 100 degrees.

■ **PLANT LIFE**
Arid lands Smoke trees and creosote bushes grow on the alluvial fan. From a distance the gray twigs of the nearly leafless smoke tree appear to embrace the twisted trunk in a smoky haze. The tree's gray-blue flowers are so close in tone to the tree's branches that they are virtually invisible from a distance.

A rare but thorough rainstorm can prompt the Coachella Valley milk vetch to burst into pinkish-rose blooms. Look for them from February to May, after a rain. The sand verbena spreads its trailing stems to form a mat over disturbed, sandy areas, flowering, like the milk vetch, after rain.

■ **ANIMAL LIFE**
Reptiles Suddenly aware of human presence, the 4-inch lizard darts across the dune and dives in, disappearing completely into the sand. The endangered Coachella Valley fringe-toed lizard is well adapted for life in one of the hottest

Fringe-toed lizard

places on earth. It lives only in the fine sand of windblown sand dunes. The lizard's toes are fringed with projecting and pointed scales that allow it to run more easily on sand. It has adapted over the years ways to keep its eyes, nose, and ears free of sand—valves shut off its nasal passages and ears, and eyelids overlap.

Another reptile that takes advantage of the sand is the sidewinder, a desert rattlesnake. Active only at night, it shelters during the day beneath a creosote bush with only its head extended from the sand. If a wind is not blowing, morning hikers may see its distinctive track left on the sand's surface.

■ **COACHELLA VALLEY PRESERVE** The Coachella Valley refuge is part of the 20.3-square-mile (13,000-acre) Coachella Valley Preserve, administered jointly by the U.S. Fish & Wildlife Service, the California Department of Fish and Game, the Bureau of Land Management, and the Center for Natural Lands Management. Don't miss the Visitor Center next to the preserve (on Thousand Palms Canyon Road off Ramon Road), with its self-guiding nature trail and stand of California fan palms, the only native palm in the state. The fan palm grows along the Salton Trough, where the San Andreas Fault has allowed water to rise near the surface in the dry desert. For information on the preserve, write Coachella Valley Preserve, P.O. Box 188, Thousand Palms, CA 92276; 760/343-2733.

Don Edwards San Francisco Bay NWR
Fremont, California

Black-necked stilts in San Francisco Bay wetlands

Before Europeans arrived in San Francisco Bay, the wildlife was vast and rich beyond imagining. Geese and ducks were said to rise in dense clouds with a noise like a hurricane. Grizzly bears roamed the shore, and giant condors floated overhead. Whales were commonly seen in the bay, and magnificent wetlands supported millions of birds. What is left of this pristine environment is preserved in a small corner of the east bay in the Don Edwards San Francisco Bay NWR. Surrounded by housing tracts, industrial parks, and a freeway, the refuge is a cherished reminder of what once was.

HISTORY

In 1960 an Army Corps of Engineers study observed that San Francisco Bay—California's largest and most spectacular bay, 12 miles across at its widest point and some 55 miles long—would be a river by the year 2010 if draining, fill, and development continued at its current rate. A slogan developed by local activists—Do you want a bay or a river?—awakened the public. Save the Bay and other grassroots organizations cropped up, including the South San Francisco Baylands Planning, Conservation, and National Wildlife Refuge Committee. Beginning in the early 1960s, they submitted petitions to Congress requesting the establishment of a refuge—although the National Wildlife Service at first expressed no interest in establishing a refuge in an area populated by 4 million people. Ten years later—in 1972—the San Francisco Bay NWR was established, the nation's first refuge in an urban area that is now, with a population of 6 million, the fourth largest urban area in the country. The 33.6-square-mile (21,500-acre) refuge, which has been renamed to honor the U.S. representative who introduced the bill that established the refuge, is California's most visited national wildlife area, tallying some 300,000 visitors annually.

GETTING THERE

From Oakland, drive south on I-880. In Fremont take H-84 west. Exit on Thornton Ave., the last exit before the Dumbarton Bridge. Drive south on Thornton about 1 mi. and take the first right to the refuge on Marshlands Rd.

From San Francisco, drive south on US 101 (Bayshore Freeway). Turn east on CA 84 and cross the Dumbarton Bridge. Swing south on Thornton Ave. and follow directions above. To reach the Environmental Education Center, take US 101 (Bayshore freeway) or I-880 (Nimitz Freeway) and exit at CA 237 toward Alviso. Follow CA 237 to Zanker Rd. (which becomes Los Esteros at 1 mi.). Drive 2.1 mi. past the San Jose/Santa Clara water pollution control plant and continue over railroad tracks, taking a sharp right turn onto the center's entrance road at the corner of Grand Blvd. and Los Esteros.

■ **SEASON:** Refuge open year-round.

■ **HOURS:** Refuge open April–Oct., 7 a.m.–8 p.m.; Nov.–March, 7 a.m.–6 p.m. Visitor Center open Tues.–Sun., 10 a.m.–5 p.m. Closed holidays. Environmental Education Center open to general public Sat.–Sun., 10 a.m.–5 p.m.

■ **ADDRESS:** Don Edwards San Francisco Bay NWR, San Francisco Bay Complex, P.O. Box 524, Newark, CA 94560

■ **TELEPHONE:** 510/792-0222; Environmental Education Center, 408/262-5513

TOURING DON EDWARDS SAN FRANCISCO BAY NWR

■ **BY FOOT:** The refuge has some 16 trails totaling more than 36 miles. Hiking near Mallard Slough at the Environmental Education Center is prohibited from March to August, when the herons are nesting.

■ **BY BICYCLE:** Bicyclists may ride the 5-mile Newark Slough loop trail that passes the salt ponds and eight other trails totaling about 25 miles.

■ **BY CANOE, KAYAK, OR BOAT:** Refuge sloughs, the bay, and its tributaries are open to all boating. Mallard Slough is closed to boaters March to August, and Mowry Slough is closed mid-March to mid-June during harbor-seal pupping. A boat launch is available off Thornton. Warning: Find a tidal chart and expect tidal changes of 8 to 12 feet. If your boat sticks in the mud at low tide, do not try to walk across the mudflats as you probably will become stuck in the mud yourself.

WHAT TO SEE

■ **LANDSCAPE AND CLIMATE** The great waterway that empties through the Golden Gate into the Pacific is formed by two bays—San Francisco Bay to the south and San Pablo Bay, draining the Sacramento and San Joaquin (Wha-KEEN) river delta, to the north. The two bays are usually known jointly as San Francisco Bay, which is separated from the Pacific Ocean by the San Francisco Peninsula south of the Golden Gate Bridge and Marin County to the north. The Don Edwards San Francisco Bay refuge skirts the southeast edge of the bay with a small segment across the bay on the west side near East Palo Alto.

The refuge might very well have served as the site of another expensive condo development except for its long-time use by Leslie Salt, a salt manufacturing company, to extract table salt in a series of evaporation ponds. Some 18 square miles (12,000 acres) on the refuge continue in use as salt ponds, where salt is extracted by moving the salty bay water into increasingly salty ponds as the water evaporates. The depletion of water in deep aquifers has caused land in the south bay to subside. Since 1934, the area around Alviso has dropped about 9 feet. The refuge's elevation rises from sea level to 150 feet.

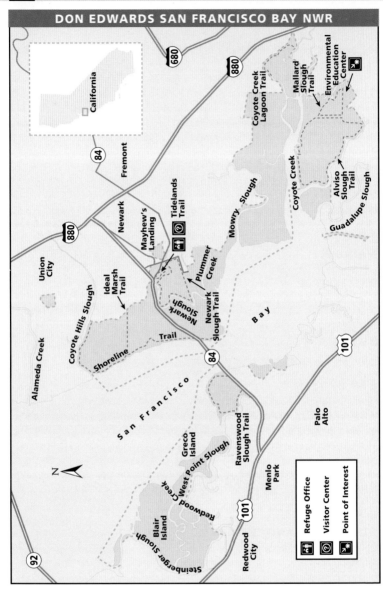

DON EDWARDS SAN FRANCISCO BAY NWR

Like most of California, the Bay Area has a Mediterranean climate—winter rains from November to April (16 inches) and dry but foggy summers. (The fog usually burns off by afternoon.) Influenced by the Pacific, temperatures can range widely—January extremes are 28 to 74 degrees F; in July the range is from 49 to 100 degrees F. Winds blow regularly, usually from the northwest, becoming brisk in the afternoon.

■ PLANT LIFE

Wetlands The mechanisms used by plants to survive in the salty tidal mudflats of San Francisco Bay have a remarkable similarity to the survival strategies of desert plants—the one contends with a lack of water, the other with too much salty water. Pickleweed, the most common plant of the higher tidal flats (its roots are covered with water only at high tide), stores water in its tissues, not, as desert plants, to survive drought but to dilute the salty cell sap that it accumulates. A plant takes in water by a process using osmosis (water moves to a more concentrated solution from a less concentrated one). The sap in a plant is usually more concentrated than water, which causes water to move into the plant until a balance is reached. But the concentration of the salty water of San Francisco Bay is higher than that of a normal plant's sap so the sap would drain out of the plant, which would droop and die just like garden plants you forgot to water. Pickleweed has the ability to store extra water it uses to dilute the salt it accumulates. At season's end, the pickleweed drops its tiny green stems that look like pickles, thus losing the accumulated salt and preparing for new growth the next season.

A paintbrush look-alike, the salt-marsh bird's beak is an endangered plant growing in the same environment as pickleweed, sea blite, and salt grass.

Coastal scrub A drought-tolerant native adopted for xeriscapes by California gardeners is the coyote brush (chaparral broom). This species of baccharis is a many-branched evergreen shrub 6 to 10 feet high with glossy green leaves and cottony white flowers from January to March. Although it does not need summer water, once established it can grow in heavy, wet areas as well as shallow and dry soils.

The coast live oak—one of the most common of California's 16 species of native oaks—has shiny, stiff, green leaves that tend to curve under. The leaves have sharp spines on the edges. Mature trees have great character with extended branches growing in picturesque shapes, forming a tree that is broader than high—from 35 to 80 feet wide and 30 to 60 feet high. The coast live oak grows in the coast ranges from San Diego to Mendocino counties.

Grasslands California poppies with their intense golden orange blossoms bloom from March to September. The state flower is joined by scarlet pimpernels, blooming February to November; blue dicks seen in bloom February to May; and the toyon, a dense evergreen native shrub that grows to 15 feet and is used by many gardeners for its showy red berries maturing December to February and its white flowers, July to September.

Bicyclists on wetlands trail

ANIMAL LIFE

Birds As the largest estuary in California, San Francisco Bay is one of the most important coastal areas for wintering and migrating waterfowl—besides having a bird list that includes 281 species. The bay's 1,600 square miles are home to at least 800,000 waterbirds throughout the year. At peak migration, millions of birds pass through the area—70 percent of the birds using the Pacific Flyway. Nearly 221,000 ducks are found in the bay during winter months—7 percent of all ducks in the state. The canvasback, found in the winter bay in numbers approaching 18,500, has more reason than other ducks to be wary of hunters. This diving duck is con-

Great egret

sidered the best-tasting of North American waterfowl. Gathered in flocks, the canvasbacks sometimes flush all in a group, their wings sounding like thunder. Recognized by their red heads and white bodies, separated by a band of black at the base of their necks, they dive for the succulent roots of marsh plants but will also eat seeds and grain. At night they sleep with heads tucked under their wings while several members of the flock act as sentinels, giving warning if danger is sensed. Canvasbacks are commonly seen on the bay in all seasons except spring.

Both the great and snowy egrets are commonly seen in the bay. To distinguish them, look for size (the great egret reaches 41 inches in height, the snowy egret 27 inches). The great egret has a yellow bill and black legs; the snowy egret has a black bill and legs and yellow feet. The great egret was almost wiped out a century ago by a millinery rage for plumed hats. By the 1890s stylish women wore hats decorated not only with feathers but with entire birds (40 species of native birds or bird parts were observed on the hats of some 700 women in New York City in 1886). The National Audubon Society's first successful campaign halted the feather trade, and the great egret became the society's emblem.

Mammals As treated sewage water is released into San Francisco Bay, the salinity of the water decreases, causing a chain of events that, among other things, has placed the salt-marsh harvest mouse on the endangered species list. As bay water decreases in salinity, the dense beds of pickleweed, intermixed with fat hen and alkali heath in the refuge's salt marshes, thin out, replaced by bulrush and salt grass. The salt-marsh harvest mouse is dependent on pickleweed; as the pickleweed declines, so does this tiny, nocturnal mouse that builds a nest on the ground and has the ability to drink saltwater.

Harbor seals use tidal salt marshes and mudflats for haul-out and breeding sites—the largest haul-out sites in San Francisco Bay are in the south bay. Around 25,000 harbor seals live in California's coastal waters, preferring to remain near convenient haul-out sites. The seals eat crustaceans and a variety of fish, includ-

Harbor seals

ing flounder, sole, herring, and codfish. The seals hump along awkwardly on land; their rear flippers don't bend forward so they must slide along on their bellies. Agile swimmers, they propel themselves like a fish, their rear flippers and torso swaying from side to side. They can dive to 680 feet and stay submerged for 30 minutes, although a typical fishing dive lasts around 3 minutes.

Forty-seven species of mammals live in the bay area, including raccoons, red and gray foxes, and several species of bats.

Fish and invertebrates Bay fish include shiner perch, staghorn sculpin, halibut, striped bass, starry flounder, and king salmon. Crabs, bay shrimp, and mussels can be found around the bay, but read the warning in the hunting and fishing sidebar before considering a clamming, mussel-hunting, or fishing expedition.

ACTIVITIES

■ **WILDLIFE OBSERVATION:** Six species of ducks are present throughout the year—look for northern pintails, blue-winged and cinnamon teals, northern shovelers, canvasbacks, and ruddy ducks. The black-shouldered kite, American kestrel, clapper rail, and killdeer also can be found throughout the year. The Tidelands Trail, a one-mile loop, offers views of shorebirds and a chance to hear the harsh clatter of the clapper rail. Fall may bring white sharks to the bay to attack elephant seal pups.

Tip: When exploring the refuge, keep your distance from a Forster's tern. They are protective of their nests and will dive-bomb you if they think you are too close.

■ **PHOTOGRAPHY:** Weather conditions set up the possibility of very subtle shots of birds silhouetted against the fog. The sun glinting against the bay with shorebirds in the foreground is another possibility. La Riviere Marsh, a part of the refuge hidden behind a business park, offers good photo opportunities. To reach it, drive south on I-880 from the Visitor Center. Exit right at Fremont Boulevard and head south. Take an immediate left onto a dirt road on the levee before reaching West Warren Avenue. A jogging trail on the levee provides great views of the marsh and Coyote Creek Lagoon.

■ **HIKES AND WALKS:** The 9-mile Alviso Slough Trail (muddy in wet wea-

DON EDWARDS SAN FRANCISCO BAY HUNTING AND FISHING SEASONS

Hunting
(Seasons may vary)

	Jan	Feb	Mar	Apr	May	Jun	Jul	Aug	Sep	Oct	Nov	Dec
geese	■									■	■	■
duck	■									■	■	■
coot	■									■	■	■

Fishing

	Jan	Feb	Mar	Apr	May	Jun	Jul	Aug	Sep	Oct	Nov	Dec
striped bass	■	■	■	■	■	■	■	■	■	■	■	■
sturgeon	■	■	■	■	■	■	■	■	■	■	■	■
tiger shark	■	■	■	■	■	■	■	■	■	■	■	■

Warning: Mercury, PCBs, and other chemicals have been found in San Francisco Bay fish, which should be eaten only occasionally and in limited quantities. To reduce your exposure to chemicals, eat smaller fish and only the fillet; avoid guts, liver, or fat, and bake, broil, grill, or steam fish, allowing chemical-containing juices to drain away.

ther) allows views of canoe routes followed by Ohlone Indians. Before the arrival of the Spaniards, more than 10,000 Indians lived near the coast between San Francisco Bay and Point Sur. The Ohlones lived an easy life on the bay's east shore in houses built of tules—plentiful game, birds, shellfish, fish, acorns, and berries were mainstays of their diet. In spring, when muddy trails dried enough for walking, they left the shore for the hills. Exhibits in the Visitor Center illuminate some aspects of the Ohlone culture.

The 5-mile Newark Slough loop trail winds through the salt ponds, and the 3-mile Marshlands Road is part of the Bay Trail, which, when completed, will be a 200-mile trail around San Francisco Bay. In wet weather be prepared for mud on the Mallard Slough Trail (5.5-mile loop).

■ **SEASONAL EVENTS:** The refuge celebrates National Wildlife Refuge Week in October.

■ **PUBLICATIONS:** *Exploring Our Baylands*, by Diane R. Conradson, San Francisco Bay Wildlife Society, Fremont, California, 1996; $9.95. *San Francisco Bay Shoreline Guide*, by Jerry Emory; project director, Rasa Gustaitis; University of California Press, Berkeley, California, 1995; $16.95.

SATELLITE REFUGE

■ **Ellicott Slough NWR** Ellicott Slough, established in 1975, protects the largest known remaining population of the endangered Santa Cruz long-toed salamander, recognized by yellow-orange spots or blotches on a black body. The 0.2-square-mile (144-acre) refuge, covered with willow thickets and an oak woodland, is closed to the public but can be seen from San Andreas Road near Watsonville, 0.5 mile northwest of Ellicott railroad station.

■ **ADDRESS:** Ellicott Slough NWR, Watsonville, California, c/o San Francisco Bay Complex, P.O. Box 524, Newark, CA 94560-0524

■ **TELEPHONE:** 510/792-0222

Farallon NWR
San Francisco, California

Black oystercatcher

The fog melts into the water, a gray landscape without boundaries. It is a cold, gray summer day in San Francisco, and on the offshore Farallons, some 250,000 seabirds have gathered to breed and nest. As our boat slips through the chilly, fog-shrouded landscape off San Francisco, the last visible piece of California's southern coastal mountains emerges from the Pacific Ocean: the Farallons. We have cruised three hours to see these four groups of tiny rocks lying in a northeasterly direction 28 miles west of the Golden Gate Bridge. These rocks are home to the largest continental seabird breeding colony south of Alaska.

HISTORY

Now appreciated for their immense colonies of seabirds, the Farallons were viewed quite differently by Gold Rush entrepreneurs. In the 1850s the islands, like all of California, were there to be looted. Reports indicated that in the 1850s, in just two days, the Farallon Egg Company gathered 120,000 seabird eggs from the islands and sold them for $1 per dozen. By the time President Theodore Roosevelt established a refuge on the islands in 1909 (only two years after Three Arch Rocks became the first national wildlife refuge west of the Mississippi), the Farallons' bird populations were in serious decline; but it was only in the early 1970s, when the Coast Guard automated the Farallon lighthouse, that serious efforts began to focus on actively protecting the wildlife there. Around 2,300 visitors take the boat tour annually to view the 0.3-square-mile (211-acre) refuge.

GETTING THERE

The Oceanic Society leads one-day boat trips to the Farallons from June through November. Call 415/474-3385 for information.

■ **SEASON:** The rocks are closed to public access and must be viewed from a boat.

■ **ADDRESS:** Farallon NWR, c/o San Francisco Bay Complex, P.O. Box 524, Newark, CA 94560-0524
■ **TELEPHONE:** 510/792-0222

WHAT TO SEE

These gaunt rocks, lashed by storms, wind, and waves, support little vegetation. Farallon weed creates a thick mat on the few low-lying areas in the south Farallons, where a thin layer of soil covers the granite. Cormorants and gulls use the weed to build nests. A thick layer of guano coats much of the islands, making it even more difficult for plants to get a foothold.

Among the 12 nesting seabird species, the little-known ashy storm-petrel looks much like the slightly larger black storm-petrel. In flight the black storm-petrel can be distinguished by its more pointed wings. Three species of cormorants—pelagic, double-crested, and Brandt's—pigeon guillemots, black oystercatchers,

Tufted puffin

and rhinoceros and Cassin's auklets all come to the Farallons to breed and nest. Like other seabirds, they spend much of their life at sea, diving for fish or skimming food off the top of the water. The pelagic cormorant has been known to dive to 180 feet. The gaudy tufted puffin, with its parrot's beak, is common in spring and summer.

The rich sea waters around the Farallons have attracted a number of sea mammals, including blue whales and humpback whales, which winter in the waters off Baja. White shark sightings are rare; blue sharks are more common. Elephant seals, harbor seals, and California and Steller sea lions haul out on rocks, and leatherback sea turtles feed on the water's abundant jellyfish.

Northern fur seals have begun breeding on the Farallons for the first time in 150 years. Note: Weather conditions are usually cold and often wet. Dress in layers for possible rain and fog, bringing raingear and binoculars. To avoid seasickness, take a pill before embarking. Summer seas are rough, but this is the season when the most birds are present. Fall seas are calmer, but many birds have left.

Havasu NWR
Lake Havasu City, Arizona, and Needles, California

Lake Havasu, along the border between California and Arizona

Water recreation is the big draw at Havasu NWR. Some 500,000 people come annually to boat, swim, and fish in Lake Havasu, the star and centerpiece of the refuge. But nature lovers will discover another, equally entrancing Havasu NWR. Look for the sunset spectacle of thousands of teal banking in the air or the last rays of light bathing the spires of the Needles in a warm red glow. Spot a kit fox emerging from its den in the rugged desert uplands, its large ears straining to detect the patter of mouse feet across the sands; see a desert bighorn commanding Topock Gorge high above the banks of the Colorado River.

HISTORY

The canyons of the Colorado River south of today's I-40 have a long human history, having seen periodic prehistoric and historic inhabitation, as attested by petroglyphs found at Picture Rock in Topock Gorge and at other sites and by relics of the 1800s' mining era. In 1941, to mitigate environmental damage caused by series of dams and huge reservoirs along the lower Colorado River, a vast wildlife refuge was established encircling Lake Havasu and lands just above the lake. The name of the lake and refuge is believed to derive from an Indian term meaning "blue-green waters." Over the years various pieces were split off from the refuge for state parks, Lake Havasu City, and other uses—including creation of Bill Williams River NWR in 1991. Today Havasu NWR encompasses 37,515 acres. As an extremely popular spot for water recreation—in particular its southern sector near Lake Havasu City—the refuge entertains some 500,000 visitors a year.

GETTING THERE

Havasu refuge is strung along the Colorado River for 28 mi. between Needles, California, and Lake Havasu City, Arizona. Both its northern sector, which includes the popular birding area Topock Marsh, and its southern sector can be accessed by car. Its central section (Topock Gorge/ Needles Wilderness) is accessible only on foot or by boat. To reach Topock Marsh, take Exit 1 off I-40 on the east bank of the Colorado River and proceed north on old Rte. 66. Sideroads branch off to access New South Dike and Catfish Paradise. Just south of the community of Golden Shores at an intersection where Rte. 66 continues north toward Oatman, bear left to reach 5 Mile Landing and Pintail Slough. Another part of the northern marsh sector—a farming unit on the refuge's west side—is reached from Needles (see "Touring Havasu" below).

The southern sector, including popular Mesquite Bay and Castle Rock water recreation areas, is accessed via London Bridge Rd. off AZ 95 just north of Lake Havasu City.

■ **SEASON:** Open year-round.

■ **HOURS:** Refuge open dawn to dusk; office open weekdays, 7 a.m.–3:30 p.m. in winter; 7:30 a.m.–4 p.m. otherwise.

■ **FEES:** Free entry.

■ **ADDRESS:** P.O. Box 3009, 317 Mesquite Ave., Needles, CA 92363

■ **TELEPHONE:** 760/326-3853

White pelican

TOURING HAVASU

■ **BY AUTOMOBILE:** The east side of Topock Marsh is reached via automobile as described above in "Getting There." In addition, a gravel/dirt road winds 7 to 8 miles along the marsh's western edge to a large farm unit, Topock Farm. From Needles, cross over the Colorado River on K St., turn right at the second street (Levy Way), and at the T-intersection turn right onto Barrackman. Follow it until the pavement ends, then proceed 2 miles to the refuge boundary and continue south to the farm unit. You can continue on down this road several more miles until you reach a closure chain.

■ **BY FOOT:** A 4-mile loop begins and ends at the farm unit described above. Visitors can also hike along the dikes and levees throughout the refuge. The Needles/ Havasu Wilderness Areas are open exclusively to hikers, but their extremely rugged terrain and isolation should not be tackled without thorough preparation.

■ **BY BICYCLE:** All the refuge's public roads are open to mountain biking.

■ **BY CANOE, KAYAK, OR BOAT:** One of western Arizona's prime adventures is a float trip through Havasu's Topock Gorge in April, May, or early fall. The daylong, 16-mile outing begins in Topock Bay, just north of the I-40 bridge crossing of the Colorado and ends at Castle Rock. Commercial boat rentals (including dropoff and pickup) are available. Make inquiries through the Visitor Center. Be aware of upriver motorized traffic. Canoes, kayaks, and no-wake boats are also allowed on Topock Marsh. A small area is always closed October 1 to January 31 to decrease disturbance to birds, and other areas are subject to seasonal closure. Inquire at Visitor Center. Boat ramps at Catfish Paradise, 5 Mile Landing, and North Dike.

WHAT TO SEE

■ **LANDSCAPE AND CLIMATE** Havasu National Wildlife Refuge is a three-headed entity. Spanning the Colorado River on the Arizona-California border, its

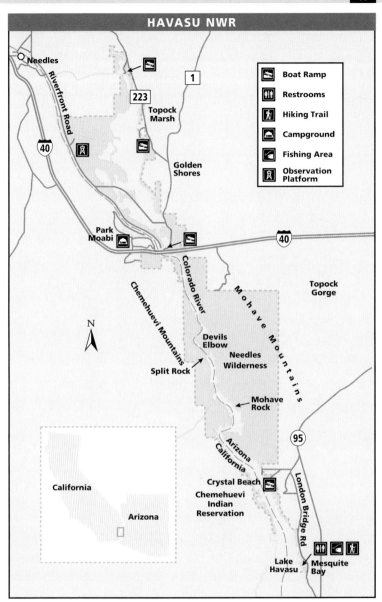

HAVASU NWR

Needles

1

223

Topock Marsh

Golden Shores

Park Moabi

40

Colorado River

Chemehuevi Mountains

Mohave Mountains

Topock Gorge

Devils Elbow

Needles Wilderness

Split Rock

Mohave Rock

95

Arizona California

N

California

Arizona

Crystal Beach

Chemehuevi Indian Reservation

London Bridge Rd

Lake Havasu

Mesquite Bay

Boat Ramp

Restrooms

Hiking Trail

Campground

Fishing Area

Observation Platform

northern section is composed of a flooded flat marshland, Topock Marsh—a 4,000-acre mosaic of ponds, lakes, and marsh fed by an extensive system of water diversion channels. Surrounding these wetlands are 5,000 acres of forested flats and farm fields.

The middle ground is dominated by Topock Gorge on the Colorado River, flanked on the Arizona side by Needles Wilderness Area and on the California side by Havasu Wilderness Area, a total of about 30,000 acres. Here, rugged desert mountains dominate, capped by the Needles, the dramatically sharp volcanic spires that gave a name to the California town just northwest and to the surrounding wilderness area.

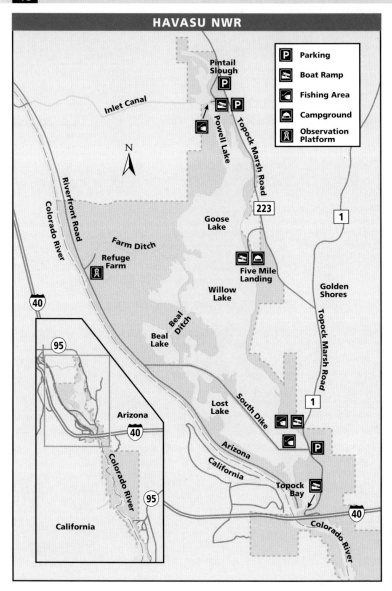

HAVASU NWR

P	Parking
	Boat Ramp
	Fishing Area
	Campground
	Observation Platform

Pintail Slough

Inlet Canal

Powell Lake

Topock Marsh Road

N

Colorado River

Riverfront Road

Farm Ditch

Refuge Farm

223

1

Goose Lake

Five Mile Landing

Golden Shores

Willow Lake

40

Beal Ditch

Beal Lake

95

Arizona

40

Colorado River

95

California

Lost Lake

South Dike

Arizona

California

1

Topock Marsh Road

Topock Bay

40

Colorado River

In the southern sector, Topock Canyon broadens into a wide valley just north of the booming community of Lake Havasu City, a popular water recreation area packed with boaters throughout the summer.

Winter lows dip to just below freezing on occasion, while summer highs have hit a stunning 128 degrees. Rainfall is scant, averaging 4 inches annually, half coming in intense summer thunderstorms and half in gentle winter rains.

■ **PLANT LIFE** More than 200 plants make their home in the varied biomes of Havasu, including an amazing 43 members of the sunflower clan—from the Mojave aster to rabbit brush.

Wetlands Huge expanses of cattail and alkali and American great bulrush dominate the wetlands of Topock Marsh. They grow so profusely that refuge staff must periodically burn off or otherwise retard their spread to maintain open waters within the marshes. At the edges of the marshes are a variety of sedges, from purple nut to yellow nut to spike, and various rushes. All of these are considered emergent plants—that is, emerging from water.

Forests The woodlands found on the valley floor at Topock Marsh are not forests in the usual sense—a better description would be thickets. These are dominated by dense stands of invasive salt cedar (see sidebar in Bosque del Apache NWR). Mixed in with the vast tracts of tamarisk are occasional Fremont cottonwood and Goodding willow trees, original riparian trees of the Colorado River valleys that are almost entirely absent from the area today. The refuge has an active revegetation program, raising tree seedlings in its plant nursery at Topock Farm. Biologist Matt Connolly is experimenting with generating multiple tree shoots from single willow and cottonwood branches laid horizontally on the ground and covered with dirt, which, if successful, will greatly increase restoration efforts.

Arid lands The refuge's mountainous midsection, Topock Gorge and the flanking Needles and Havasu Wilderness Area, are dominated by upland desert flora. Located at the overlapping edges of the Sonoran and Mojave deserts, these arid places support barrel and beavertail cactus, palo verde trees, brittlebush (producing a brilliant yellow flower in March and April), and catclaw acacia. The latter is a shrublike tree growing to 10 feet in height with small olive-green leaves and an abundance of small curved spines, giving rise to its nickname, the "wait-a-minute bush." As in *Wait a minute* —before you try to pet this cat!

Farmlands To provide food for waterfowl, the refuge maintains a 210-acre farm in Topock Marsh, where Bermuda grass is grown for geese, and some moist-soil units, where native foodstocks are raised.

■ ANIMAL LIFE

Birds Havasu's marshes and associated woodlands, river canyon, and desert terrain have been good to birds and bird lovers: Of the 297 species of birds found here, 81 are nesters. Perhaps most prominent are winter concentrations of waterfowl, wading, and shorebirds. A dazzling 27 species of ducks, geese, and swans come to Havasu, including the magnificent tundra swan visiting here in fall and winter.

An early-spring drive around the Topock Marsh, on both sides of the river, can turn up bluewinged teal, cinnamon teal, eared and Clark's grebes, blackcrowned herons, white pelican, and white-faced ibis. A short excursion to Teal Slough may give

Great blue heron

you sights of killdeer, western sandpiper, long-billed dowitchers, cinnamon teal, barn swallows, and great blue herons. This heron is a remarkable creature: a tall wader (more than 4 feet) with long yellow legs, a bluish-gray body, and a white head topped by a rakish black pompadour. Great blues do not like to be disturbed and will croak at you if they feel uneasy. Northern harriers skim low over fields and marsh, hovering delicately, while red-tailed hawks can be spotted throughout the refuge year-round.

In spring or fall as many as 10,000 white pelicans may descend on Topock Marsh, settling down in its lakes like a miniature navy. Present year-round are red-winged blackbirds, singing loudly from perches on cattail stalks, and marsh wrens. Bald eagles show up occasionally in autumn.

The marsh also provides shelter for two endangered birds, the Yuma clapper rail and the southwestern willow flycatcher. A small gray-green riparian-loving bird, the willow flycatcher has confounded ornithologists by nesting in the extensive tamarisk thickets infesting Topock Marsh. They normally set up housekeeping only in dense willow groves, a habitat that has undergone dramatic declines in the Southwest over the past century, contributing to the parallel decline of the bird. Some 25 pairs nested at Havasu in 1999, perhaps the largest group left in the wild.

In the drylands flanking the marshes, expect sightings of both mourning doves and the less common Inca dove. The Inca has reddish wing ends in flight and white edging on its tail, and it calls with a monotonous *coo-hoo* or *no-hope*. Also in the shrub near the marshes you can easily spot plentiful loggerhead shrikes and northern mockingbirds with their flashy black and white flight coloration.

Lastly, inhabiting the refuge's desert terrain year-round are Gila woodpeckers and greater roadrunners.

Mammals   Among the refuge's 46 mammal species is a stable herd of desert bighorn sheep in the Topock Gorge area. Present but much less likely to be seen are bobcat, coyote, and kit fox, which feed on cottontail and black-tailed jack rabbits. Various mice and packrats are common here.

Western diamondback rattlesnake, tongue extended

Reptiles and amphibians
Havasu's desert lands hold some 39 species of reptiles, including the western diamondback rattlesnake, also found in Topock Marsh. You may spot a coach whip (red racer), a slender pinkish snake growing to more than 4 feet. While not poisonous, red racers are extremely aggressive, going so far as chase people! If handled, they won't hesitate to bite. The common wetlands toad is the green toad, which is actually colored mostly brown with green mottling.

ACTIVITIES

■ **CAMPING:** Camping is allowed at select locations within Topock Gorge. Dispersed primitive camping is also permitted within the Needles Wilderness Area (but not within 1 mile of the river). Commercial campgrounds are located in Golden Shores near Topock Marsh. Park Moabi Campground is just off I-40 on the west side of the Colorado River.

■ **SWIMMING:** Swimming is most often pursued in Lake Havasu off Mesquite Bay and the Castle Rock area, as are skin- and scuba-diving.

■ **WILDLIFE OBSERVATION:** An observation tower on Topock Farm unit provides good views of feeding wildlife. Another tower, on the Levee Road south of the farm, overlooks Beal Lake. Two pairs of nesting great horned owls can be viewed at 5 Mile Landing in the massive old salt cedar trees. These owls are over 2 feet tall with prominent eartufts. Males emit five or six resonant hoots: *hoo!, hu-hu-hu, hoo! hoo!*

Walking out on New South Dike offers good birding possibilities, with cottonwood and willows attracting passerine songbirds and shallow marshes drawing waterfowl and grebes.

If you're boating through Topock Gorge, keep an eye peeled for the nesting peregrines at the Devil's Elbow, the 45 to 50 desert bighorn sheep often spotted above the Devil's Bend, and the nesting Clark's grebe along the water's edge.

■ **PHOTOGRAPHY:** Outstanding shots of the spires in the Needles Wilderness Area can be taken at sunset from the Colorado River Bridge or from east of the refuge off I-40 at daybreak. The roads about Topock Marsh offer excellent scenes of marshes and associated wildlife. Boating through Topock Gorge leads to both wildlife and landscape images well worth the voyage.

HUNTING AND FISHING Sport fishing is permitted in all waters open to the public except those designated by sign or barrier as closed. A fishing dock is located at Catfish Paradise on the east side of Topock Marsh, as well as a boat ramp. Another boat ramp is found at 5 Mile Landing. A section of Mesquite Bay, in the refuge's southern sector, off AZ 95, is closed to boating and so has good bank fishing, including a handicapped area (and a restroom).

Hunting for **waterfowl**, **quail**, **mourning dove**, **cottontail rabbit**, and **desert bighorn sheep** (the latter by drawing) is allowed on specific days and times in select areas of Topock Marsh, along the Colorado River. Contact the refuge for details.

■ **HIKES AND WALKS:** A 4-mile birding trail is under construction near Topock Farm. In addition, visitors are allowed to walk all the roads open to the public, as well as throughout the two wilderness areas.

■ **SEASONAL EVENTS:** The refuge has hosted an annual Coot Festival in the early spring in the past. The purpose of the festival was to increase public awareness about the refuge; coots, the honoree, was chosen because literally thousands of these ducklike birds descend on the refuge in the spring. Call in advance for confirmation of an upcoming Coot Festival.

■ **PUBLICATIONS:** Brochure, bird and plant lists, several guides for boating Topock Gorge.

Hopper Mountain NWR Complex and Blue Ridge NWR

Hopper Mountain NWR and Bitter Creek NWR
Ventura and Porterville, California

The wingspan of the California condor (here, banded for research) is immense (up to 9.5 feet).

Soaring on thermal updrafts to 15,000 feet, drifting at speeds up to 55 miles an hour, thousands of California condors once plied the skies from California to Florida—with a wingspan of 9 feet, they are America's biggest birds. By 1982 all that was left were three California condors in captivity and 21 to 24 free-flying birds in the wild mountainous terrain north of Los Angeles.

HISTORY

Having nearly exterminated the condors by taking their feeding grounds, poisoning them with lead (from bullets in the carcasses they ate), shooting them for fun, and collecting their eggs, Americans next decided they wanted to save them. In 1975 the California Condor Recovery Plan was instituted. Its story includes early passionate disagreement about how to save the condors, an accident in which a chick was killed, threats by Earth First to infiltrate the condor-raising facility and let loose all the caged condors, the heart-shattering deaths of the first human-raised condors after they were set free, and, finally, an incipient success story. In March 1999, for the first time in 70 years, 21 condors flew free over the Vermilion and Hurricane cliffs in Arizona, and in California 32 condors soared over Lion Canyon and Castle Crags in the wildest part of Los Padres National Forest and in Big Sur's Ventana Wilderness Sanctuary. With 97 birds in captivity, the total of living California condors was 150, an increase of 500 percent over the lowest number of survivors.

The U.S. Fish & Wildlife Service works at the core of the recovery plan, releasing and monitoring the condors after they have been hatched at the Los Angeles Zoo, San Diego Wild Animal Park, and the Peregrine Fund's World Center for Birds of Prey in Boise, Idaho. Three national wildlife refuges have been established to secure condor terrain—Hopper Mountain, Bitter Creek, and Blue Ridge. Though closed to the public, the last two can be observed from roads or an overlook.

■ **SEASON:** The three refuges are closed to the public.

■ **ADDRESS:** Hopper Mountain NWR Complex, P. O. Box 5839, Ventura, CA 93005

■ **TELEPHONE:** 805/644-5185

TOURING CONDOR VIEWING SITES

■ **BY AUTOMOBILE:** In addition to viewing two of the refuges (described in sections on the refuges), there are several accessible potential viewing sites, by car, by hiking, or mountain bike, where a condor might appear. One site is in the rugged Sierra Madre, located about 20 miles west of Bitter Creek NWR in the Los Padres National Forest. From Los Angeles (4-wheel-drive only), drive north on US 101, or from San Francisco south on US 101, to Santa Maria. Turn east on CA 166 to Cuyama Valley, then south on Cottonwood Canyon Road to Bates Canyon campground. Continue on dirt road about 6 miles to Sierra Madre Ridge. Swing east (left) at the fork and follow signs to McPherson Peak. An alternate route (4-wheel drive necessary) follows CA 166 as above but turns right on Sierra Madre Road (#32513) directly opposite the Rockfront Ranch. Drive 35 miles of rugged dirt road along Sierra Madre Ridge to the top of McPherson Peak.

To reach the Castle Crags condor-observation area, drive south on US 101 from San Francisco or north on US 101 from Los Angeles. At Santa Margarita, turn east on CA 58 about 30 miles. Turn right on Pozo Road past the La Panza California Department of Forestry fire station. Turn left on U.S. Forest Service Road #30S14 (4-wheel drive only). Drive 0.25 mile to the signed California condor observation lookout; it offers a spectacular vista of the surrounding region.

■ **BY FOOT:** From Santa Maria, turn east on CA 166 to Cuyama Valley. In New Cuyama, turn right on Perkins Road and drive about 3.5 miles to the end of the road and park. Hike about 1 mile on U.S. Forest Trail #26W01, take right at fork in trail and hike 6 miles on trail #27W04 to Painted Rock campsite, adjacent to Lion Canyon.

To reach the campsite from McPherson Peak, follow above instructions to the peak. Continue on Sierra Madre Ridge Road beyond McPherson Peak (do not take left road up to the peak). The road continues to a locked U.S. Forest Service gate. Park and hike or backpack about 7 miles to the Painted Rock camp, on left side of road (follow sign).

■ **BY BICYCLE:** Mountain bikes are permitted on the hiking portion of the trail to the Painted Rock campsite and on any roads open to cars. Warning: Dirt roads are often hazardous or impassable in wet weather, even with 4-wheel-drive. Avoid hiking during or soon after storms or in the heat of summer. There is no water on the trails or at the camp. If you're backpacking you should allocate a gallon of water per day per person. Day hikers should carry at least two quarts.

Hopper Mountain NWR
Fillmore, California

■ **ADDRESS:** Hopper Mountain NWR, c/o Hopper Mountain NWR Complex, P.O. Box 5839, Ventura, CA 93005-0839

■ **TELEPHONE:** 805/644-1732

SAVING THE CONDORS The early disagreement about how to save the condors goes to the heart of how we imagine the wild. By 1947 the declining numbers of the condors was well known. The Sespe Condor Sanctuary was established that year and in 1951 expanded to 83 square miles (53,000 acres). In 1952 the San Diego Zoo obtained permission to take condor eggs and adults from the wild to establish a captive breeding flock, but its permits were revoked after protests by the National Audubon Society, who argued that to cage a wild thing is to destroy what it stands for and that, given protection, the species could survive; and only wild birds were worth saving. Domesticated through capture, condors would no longer be a symbol of anything but defeat; and there was little hope that they could ever return to the wild.

By 1980 the birds had continued to disappear, and the California Department of Fish and Game approved a USDF&W proposal for a 35-year research program and captive breeding. But the death of a condor chick being handled in the wild caused the revocation of all permits. A year later permits were reissued, and in 1982 the first condor chick was captured, one of only three condors in captivity. Wild condors by then numbered 21 to 24, the lowest condor population reached. The plan was to leave a few condors in the wild, but in the winter of 1984-85 six wild condors disappeared. The service then received permission to capture all wild condors. On Easter Sunday, April 19, 1987, the last free-flying condor was trapped.

In the meantime, the captive-breeding program proved a success. By

WHAT TO SEE

In the rugged, mountainous terrain of Ventura County, the Hopper Mountain refuge is the center of hope for the California condors. Here, in a refuge closed to the public, is the facility where condor chicks are prepared for release into the wild. The chicks arrive at three months of age after being incubated at the Los Angeles Zoo, the San Diego Wild Animal Park, or the Peregrine Fund's World Center for Birds of Prey in Boise, Idaho. During the first few weeks after hatching, the chicks are fed by biologists wearing hand puppets that resemble a condor's head; this is done so that the chicks don't associate food with people. After arriving at the Hopper Mountain facility, the chicks are fed through feeding chutes, another tactic that helps prevent them from associ-

Male condor

1991 the captive condor population totaled 52 birds, and in 1992 the first two captive-reared birds were released in the Sespe sanctuary. Six months later two men were observed shooting at the female (one of the marksmen was convicted and hit with a $1,500 fine). By October the male condor was found dead, poisoned from ethylene glycol, a component of antifreeze.

The condor's death rate during the first two years of release was a disheartening 46 percent—6 of the 13 condors died, most from collisions with power lines. Those that didn't die were recaptured because of behavior that would eventually get them killed. The condors, intelligent and curious, had no fear of humans because they had no parents to teach them to be afraid. They would soon learn that visiting humans would get them food, and they would end up like the Yosemite bears.

From 1993 on, the condors were given aversion training—mild electric shocks from perching on a telephone pole in their training pen and wildlife biologists running at them to scare them. By March 1999, 88 condors had been released, and their survival rate jumped to 77 percent. The biologists' goal is to establish three healthy, separate populations, one in southern California, one in Arizona, and a breeding population in captivity. Can the California condors survive without us? No. Can they survive with us? The question remains, but the prognosis is hopeful. For those who love the wilderness, to see a condor in flight is to see the triumph of the wild.

ating people with food. They live in six nest caves constructed of "simrock" meant to replicate the wild condor's nesting sites. While at the facility, the birds are given aversion training to keep them off telephone poles and wires in the wild and to instill a fear of people in them.

The 3.8-square-mile (2,471-acre) refuge, ranging in elevation from 1,600 feet to 3,900 feet, was established in 1974. Its grasslands are historic condor foraging habitat, and the refuge includes a freshwater marsh and 350 acres of an oak and California walnut woodland. The native California walnut produces nuts that are hard to crack, but its rootstock is genetically programmed to survive in California soil. Commercial walnut ranchers in the state graft English walnut scions to California walnut rootstock. The refuge's chaparral and coastal sage scrub habitats are home to both white and black sage, ceanothus, and chamise. Two rails, the Virginia and sora, visit the marsh, and black bears, mountain lions, bobcats, and rattlers have been spotted on the refuge. One day a wild condor may again soar over this refuge, the best hope for the survival of its species.

Bitter Creek NWR
Maricopa, California

GETTING THERE

To see the refuge, drive south from Bakersfield on CA 99 and exit west onto CA 119. In Maricopa drive south 4.3 mi. on CA 166 and turn left (east) onto Klipstein Canyon Rd. Shortly after entering the refuge, turn west on Cerro Noroeste Rd. Complete the loop by turning north on CA 166. Look for rifts and displacements caused by the San Andreas Fault.

■ **ADDRESS:** Bitter Creek NWR, c/o Hopper Mountain NWR Complex, P.O. Box 5839, Ventura, CA 93005-0839
■ **TELEPHONE:** 805/725-2767

WHAT TO SEE

The last wild, free-flying condor was trapped on the Bitter Creek refuge and taken into captivity on April 19, 1987, two years after the refuge was established in 1985 as part of the California Condor Recovery Program. County roads loop through and around the 22-square-mile (14,057-acre) refuge (which is closed to the public), where a captive-bred condor reintroduced to the wild may be seen sailing along the high ridgelines in this dry, golden land of hills, piñon pine, juniper, and scrub oak in the arid foothills—ranging in elevation from 1,600 feet to 5,000 feet—abutting Los Padres National Forest.

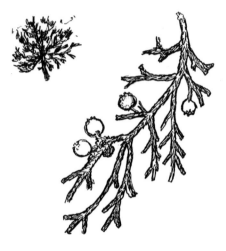

California juniper

California scrub oak, one of about 16 species of oaks growing in the state (the numbers depend on how the trees are classified), is an evergreen shrub, densely branched with pale gray-green leaves. A common plant in the chaparral community, it likes the hot, dry summer foothills and sometimes grows near the California juniper, another drought-resistant inhabitant of the piñon-pine–juniper community. The single-needle piñon pine, a slow-growing tree to around 30 feet, supplied nuts to Indians, who gathered the cones, dried them, and arranged them around a fire. The heat opened the cones and released their seeds, making them easy to gather. The pine can be found on ridgelines and rocky slopes; the juniper prefers rocky, coarse soils.

The San Andreas Fault marks the struggle between the Pacific Plate and the North American Plate. As the Pacific Plate moves north at a rate of 2 inches a year, it sometimes locks against the North American Plate. When stress causes the two to break apart, an earthquake results. The Carrizo Plain to the northwest of the refuge is a place to see the results of the collision of these two mighty forces. The plain was formed as subsistence caused by the San Andreas Fault, which runs through Bitter Creek, depressed the narrow valley. Tule elk and pronghorns are being introduced into the Carrizo Plain in hopes the animals will provide carcasses for the condors and eliminate the necessity for artificial feeding (biologists now leave carcasses for the condors).

Blue Ridge NWR
Porterville, California

GETTING THERE

For an overview of the wild refuge, drive north from Bakersfield on CA 65. Before

Mountain lion

reaching Porterville, turn east on CA 190 toward Springville. In Springville, turn north on Balch Park Rd. and continue around 20 mi. to a fire lookout.

■ **ADDRESS:** Blue Ridge NWR, c/o Kern Complex, P.O. Box 670, Delano, CA 93216-0670

■ **TELEPHONE:** 805/725-2767

WHAT TO SEE

This remote forest of yellow pine (also called ponderosa pine) and lovely incense cedar in the southern Sierra Nevada was a traditional summer roosting site for condors, but by 1985 only two condors were observed in the 1.4-square-mile (897-acre) refuge, which had been established three years earlier, in 1982. The refuge, which is closed to the public, is part of the 17-square-mile (11,000-acre) Blue Ridge Wildlife Habitat Area, protected in hopes that the condors will one day again soar overhead there. Reintroduced condors were documented flying near Springville and possibly onto Blue Ridge in the fall of 1998. Around 107 species of birds migrate through Blue Ridge, including blue grouse, mountain quail, and band-tailed pigeons.

Black-tailed mule deer, mountain lions, and bobcats are among the 24 mammals living on Blue Ridge, which ranges in elevation from 3,000 feet to 7,000 feet.

A ubiquitous tree of the California forests, the yellow pine grows from San Diego County to British Columbia at elevations of 1,000 feet to 9,000 feet. Like the Jeffrey pine, for which it is sometimes mistaken, it has needles that grow in bunches of three, but unlike those of the Jeffrey, the yellow pine's cones prickle when you pick them up. The Jeffrey's cones are smooth to the touch. The Jeffrey's reddish-brown bark grows in jigsaw-puzzle platelets and smells of vanilla. The yellow pine's bark is yellow-tan and does not have the distinctive scent of the flavoring. The Jeffrey is usually found at higher elevations than the yellow pine.

Incense cedar is one of California's most beautiful trees. Its lacy, scale-shaped needles form flat sprays that look like gently waving fans, and its red bark is sometimes mistaken for that of a redwood. It grows together with yellow pines at elevations of 1,000 feet to 8,000 feet and reaches a height of 150 feet.

Humboldt Bay NWR
Loleta, California

Pacific black brant

Bathed in the fog, clouds, and drizzle that so often visit this northern coast, the refuge appears in all shades of gray: gray-green across the marshes, gun-metal gray along Hookton Slough, pearl gray glinted with white on the bay. Birds wing in great flocks over the bay during winter. Humboldt Bay is a major stopoff on the Pacific Flyway. Migrants fly here to rest and feed as they head to their Arctic nesting grounds. As many as 50,000 to 100,000 birds (primarily shorebirds) feed in the mudflats of the bay.

HISTORY

As the glaciers of the last great Ice Age melted around 10,000 years ago, water inundated the valley that is now Humboldt Bay, creating a rich mix of marsh and tidal flats that support more than 200 bird species. The 4-square-mile (2,596-acre) Humboldt Bay NWR was established in 1971. The refuge, which welcomes some 16,000 visitors annually, is planning to expand to 15 square miles (9,554 acres) of wetlands, salt marshes, grassland, open bay, and mudflats.

GETTING THERE

Drive north from San Francisco on US 101 past Ferndale and Loleta. Exit at Hookton Rd. and take the overpass to the left across the highway. At the end of the overpass, turn right on Ranch Rd. and continue into the refuge. From Eureka, drive south on US 101. Take the Eel River Dr. exit, turning right at the end of the offramp onto Eel River Dr. Turn left immediately onto Ranch Rd., continuing to the refuge.

To reach the Hookton Slough trailhead, take US 101 south from Eureka and exit on Hookton Rd. Dr. 1.2 mi. west on Hookton Rd. and follow signs to the parking lot on the north side of Hookton Rd.

■ **SEASON:** Refuge open year-round.

■ **HOURS:** Open sunrise to sunset. Refuge office open Mon.–Fri., 7 a.m.–4 p.m.

■ **ADDRESS:** Humboldt Bay NWR, 1020 Ranch Rd., Loleta, CA 95551
■ **TELEPHONE:** 707/733-5406

WHAT TO SEE

■ **LANDSCAPE AND CLIMATE** This coastal refuge ranges in elevation from sea level (or slightly below—it has diked tidelands) to 30 feet, and receives 40 inches of rain that falls throughout the year. Temperatures are moderate and vary little from winter to summer. Average lows and highs in January are 42 to 53 degrees F.; in July, 53 to 60 degrees.

■ **ANIMAL LIFE**

Birds A northern harrier skims low over the ground, eyes peeled for lizards, frogs, mice, and small birds, taking them by surprise. Also called a marsh hawk because of its preference for flying over open marshes, the harrier nests from Alaska to southern California, then flies in huge groups—at times more than 100 birds—to winter in southern Mexico or fly on through Central America to over-winter in South America.

On a typical winter day, up to 100,000 migratory waterbirds may visit to feed and rest in Humboldt Bay, which ranges in size from 0.5 to 4 miles wide and 14 miles long. The two shallow tidal basins of the bay are connected by a relatively narrow channel. The rich eelgrass beds in the bay—the largest remaining beds south of Washington's Willapa Bay (except in Mexico)—attract as many as 32,000 Pacific black brant at one time. The brant are common in the refuge winter and spring with peak concentrations mid-March to late April. Some of brant banded in the refuge have been seen as far away as Alaska, Canada, Mexico, and Russia.

The great blue heron, with a wingspread of 7 feet and standing 4 feet tall, is the largest of the wading birds. In fields it catches insects and rodents; in the water, it preys on fish by standing motionless until a hapless fish swims by. If it catches a fish too large to swallow whole, it tosses the fish into the air, then snaps its bill up and down to soften the fish before swallowing it head first.

Mammals Harbor seals, black-tailed deer, and seven species of bats visit the refuge.

Fish The eelgrass beds also provide spawning and feeding areas for fish—more than 110 species of fish have been recorded in the area, including everything from soupfin sharks to threespine sticklebacks. Both coho and chinook salmon are seen in the bay as well.

Coho salmon

ACTIVITIES

■ **HIKES AND WALKS:** To explore this fascinating mix of marsh, mudflat, and bay, hike the refuge's two trails. The 1.75-mile Shorebird Loop Trail circles Triangle Marsh (trailhead at headquarters), former ranchland being restored to wetlands. Cattle graze along the trail, shortening the grass so that fresh sprouts preferred by waterfowl can grow. The trail, open weekdays year-round, offers some of the refuge's best shorebird viewing. The 3-mile round-trip Hookton Slough Trail, open year-round seven days a week, sunrise to sunset, follows a tidal slough. Pelicans and cormorants dive for fish; harbor seals swim in from the bay, also searching for fish. At high tide, sand dabs, sole, halibut, salmon, and steelhead swim into the slough. At low tide, migratory shorebirds swarm over the mudflats, eating clams, worms, and crabs.

■ **SEASONAL EVENTS:** Godwit Days is held annually in mid-April. Highlights are a tour of the refuge, trips to view pelagic birds, and night strolls to look for owls.

SATELITTE REFUGE

■ **Castle Rock NWR** Castle Rock is a tiny rock in the Pacific Ocean with more nesting seabirds on it than any place south of Alaska except for California's Farallon Islands. A half-mile offshore from Crescent City (just 26 miles south of the Oregon border), the 14-acre refuge is home to some 75,000 seabirds—99 percent of them are common murres (the largest breeding population in California). Of the estimated population of 32,000 Aleutian Canada geese, 28,000 have been seen in the Crescent City and Castle Rock area, flying out to feed in mainland fields at dawn and returning at dusk.

At various periods in the past, speculators eyed Castle Rock as a potential rock quarry, guano mine, and tourist attraction until it was rescued by The Nature Conservancy, which bought it in 1979 and sold it to the U.S. Fish & Wildlife Service.

Castle Rock's sheer cliffs jut 335 feet above sea level, while its east side, descending gradually, is riddled with the birds' nesting burrows. A sandy beach serves as a haul-out site for California and Steller sea lions and harbor and northern elephant seals.

The refuge, closed to the public, can be viewed from a boat (keep a minimum distance of 500 feet) or from shore with the help of a good spotting scope.

■ **ADDRESS:** Castle Rock NWR, Crescent City, California, c/o Humboldt Bay NWR, 1020 Ranch Rd., Loleta, CA 95551-9633

■ **TELEPHONE:** 707/733-5406

Castle Rock

Imperial NWR
Yuma, Arizona

Refuge wetland, Imperial NWR

Although tamed in an engineering sense, the mighty Colorado River still flows powerfully inside rough canyon walls at Imperial NWR, emerging in shallow basins dotted with pocket marshes and wetlands. Here, clouds of waterfowl gather in winter, enjoying the warm, clear weather and abundant food stocks. A few feet above waterline, the desiccated landscape rolls and breaks toward stony peaks, and earthen badlands painted in pastels shimmer in the heat.

HISTORY

The prehistoric record at Imperial is extensive. Many archeological sites, some containing petroglyphs, are scattered about the refuge, but none is easily accessible. The mighty Colorado River served as a trade conduit for many centuries before modern human occupation, in spite of periodic violent flooding. Flooding was controlled in the 20th century with the construction of a series of upstream dams.

Established in 1941, Imperial NWR takes its name from nearby (downstream) Imperial Dam, an irrigation structure erected in 1937. The refuge covers 25,125 acres. Its southerly location makes it a popular destination for sun-seeking "snowbirds"; some 30,000 people visit in winter. In summer visitors come to pursue water sports.

GETTING THERE

This is extreme southwestern Arizona. From Yuma, head north on US 95 for 22.5 mi., passing the Yuma Proving Grounds artillery display. Continue 2.5 mi. farther north on US 95, turn west (left) onto Martinez Lake Rd., and proceed 10 mi. to Martinez Lake. Look for the refuge sign on your right and follow this gravel road 3.5 mi. to the Visitor Center.

■ **SEASON:** Open year-round.

■ **HOURS:** Refuge open 24 hours daily. Visitor Center open year-round, week-

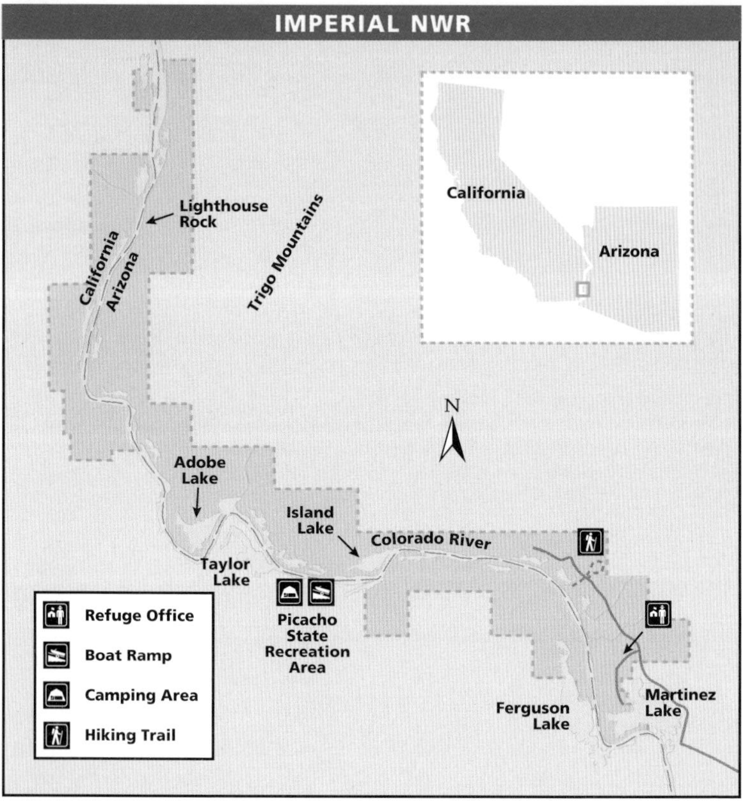
IMPERIAL NWR
California
Arizona
N
Lighthouse Rock
California
Arizona
Trigo Mountains
Adobe Lake
Island Lake
Colorado River
Taylor Lake
Picacho State Recreation Area
Ferguson Lake
Martinez Lake
Refuge Office
Boat Ramp
Camping Area
Hiking Trail

days 7:30 a.m.–4 p.m. (toilets open 24 hrs.), and weekends Nov. 15 to March 31 from 9 a.m. to 4 p.m.

■ **FEES:** Free entry.

■ **ADDRESS:** Martinez Lake, P.O. Box 72217, Yuma, AZ 85365

■ **TELEPHONE:** 520/783-3371

■ **VISITOR CENTER:** Good facility with new exhibitions, screened picnic area, nature bookstore.

TOURING IMPERIAL

BY AUTOMOBILE: A gravel road (Red Cloud Mine Rd.) runs 6 miles from the Visitor Center to a refuge boundary. Branching off this road are four scenic overlook points above the Colorado River: Palo Verde Point at 1.3 miles, Mesquite at 2.2 miles, Ironwood Point at 3.1 miles, and Smoke Tree Point at 4.2 miles. Ordinary vehicles can travel as far as Ironwood Point; beyond that, a high-clearance, 4-wheel-drive vehicle is recommended. Red Cloud Mine Rd. continues north out of the refuge across the Yuma Proving Ground and Bureau of Land Management (BLM) land to dead-end at the boundary of the refuge's northernmost wilderness section. Another road from the Visitor Center runs a short distance down to the river to Meers Point and a boat launching area.

■ **BY FOOT:** Almost all of Imperial refuge is open to hikers (farm units are closed), but there is only one designated footpath, Painted Desert Trail. It winds through the refuge's harsh but fascinating desert uplands.

■ **BY BICYCLE:** Biking is restricted to the refuge's public roads.

■ **BY CANOE, KAYAK, OR BOAT:** Because the Colorado River is a naviga-ble waterway, both powerboats and self-propelled watercraft are allowed here. The marshy backwaters, however, are no-wake zones. A commercial company, Yuma River Tours (520/783-4400), conducts guided wildlife tours by boat. Martinez Lake Resort (520/783-9589) rents canoes and will deliver them and you to the upstream edge of the refuge, allowing an easy downriver paddle or multiday outings.

WHAT TO SEE

■ **LANDSCAPE AND CLIMATE** The Colorado River flows through the refuge from north to south in a narrow canyon, and any green vegetation is limited to a band paralleling the river. Move a few feet up in elevation, and the desert takes over. It is a truly parched landscape, where the shape and color of bare rock dominate.

At Imperial, large patches of "desert pavement"—areas of ground covered with a layer of small rocks and pebbles—support little or no vegetation. You may also notice odd curving or straight lines crisscrossing this pavement. These are pathways created by the refuge's many wild burros.

The jagged Chocolate Mountains rise along the west bank; the color of these peaks ranges from brown to a purple haze. To the north, on the east bank, are the Trigos, while lower foothills flank the refuge's eastern boundary. Rock, rock, and more rock in all colors and hues: pink, lavender, black, tan, and red. It's as if the world has just been formed and its palette of earthen colors were still young and forming.

The refuge, designed to protect the riverine environment and adjoining lands, is linear in shape, running 30 miles north to south but only a handful of miles east to west. You're in Arizona on the river's eastern bank; California, on the western bank. Waters backed up behind Imperial Dam have spilled into lowland basins at various points flanking the river, creating a series of large ponds and marshes running 30 miles upstream. These ponds range in size from a half-acre to more than 700 acres.

Low elevation, the Sonoran Desert habitat, and the southerly locale combine

HORNED LIZARD A favorite discovery of children growing up in the hot sandy wastes of the Southwest was the "hornytoad," a fierce-looking critter resembling a miniature dinosaur. This 3-to-7-inch-long reptile would flatten itself out and puff up with air, causing its sawtoothed backbone, head horns, and short body spines to stand at attention. Still, its belly skin was very soft in the hand, and most children didn't fear it. The highlight of every encounter occurred when the hornytoad had exhausted all visual defenses and would spurt a bit of blood out of its eyes. That always won a quick release!

With body coloration almost always perfectly matched to the local ground's predominant color, these lizards can be tough to spot. Their favorite food is ants, and often a darting movement to snap up a snack is the only thing that gives their presence away.

Found in deserts, grasslands, shrublands, and dry woodlands from Arkansas to California and British Columbia to Guatemala, the 14 hornytoad species are a common (though declining) denizen of the region and one of its more interesting inhabitants.

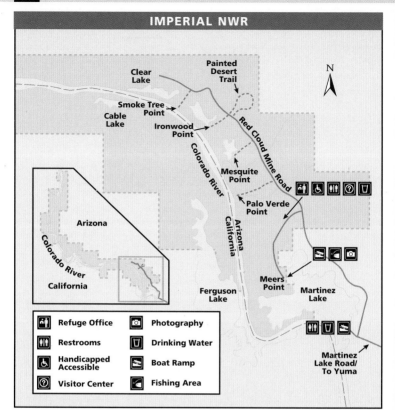

IMPERIAL NWR

Painted Desert Trail

Clear Lake

Smoke Tree Point

Cable Lake

Ironwood Point

Red Cloud Mine Road

Colorado River

Mesquite Point

Palo Verde Point

Arizona

California

Colorado River

Arizona

California

Meers Point

Ferguson Lake

Martinez Lake

Martinez Lake Road/ To Yuma

Refuge Office	Photography
Restrooms	Drinking Water
Handicapped Accessible	Boat Ramp
Visitor Center	Fishing Area

to produce intense heat at Imperial. Expect temperatures to exceed 90 degrees from mid-April through October, with truly hot days topping 120 degrees!

■ PLANT LIFE

Marshes Refuge marshes along the edges of the Colorado River and its floodbasins cover a large area and provide critical habitat for wildlife cover, reproduction, resting, and feeding. Growing right at the water's edge are cattail, three-square bulrush, river bulrush, arrowweed, and phragmites.

On slightly raised ground, Fremont cottonwoods (see sidebar, Bill Williams NWR) and Goodding willow are found, isolated in large expanses of salt cedar (see Tamarisk sidebar, Bosque del Apache NWR). Refuge staff is actively clearing the invasive salt cedar and replanting with native cottonwood and willow, but reversing this situation will take a Herculean effort.

Arid lands Some 68 percent of Imperial refuge is classified as desert uplands, and so its predominant vegetation is of Sonoran Desert lineage. However, this portion of the Sonoran Desert is much drier than that in central and eastern Arizona, and vegetation is far sparser. The primary bush here is creosote (see sidebar, Bitter Lake NWR), growing alongside the spindly ocotillo, brittlebush (a low plant covered with brilliant yellow flowers in early spring), and various cacti. A common cacti is the beavertail, which has fleshy green pads that do indeed look like a beaver's tail. From March through June, hot pink flowers adorn the beaver tail, ripening into fruits favored by wildlife and making a tasty jelly.

Low trees—most often screwbean and honey mesquite, or ironwood—dot the arroyo floors. When winter and spring rains come, wildflower blooms in the desert uplands can be remarkable. Along the Painted Desert Trail, look for scorpion weed (purple), evening primrose (yellow), and chuparosa (red-orange).

Farmlands The refuge also has 360 acres or so in farm production, growing sedges, rushes, millet, wheat, and barley for wildlife consumption. The farm unit is off-limits to the public.

■ ANIMAL LIFE

Birds Imperial's southerly latitude and wetlands draw some sandhill cranes and large numbers of waterfowl during the winter, in particular Canada geese and green-winged and cinnamon teals, northern shoveler, and ruddy ducks. The ruddy, with its cinnamon back, white cheek patch, black head, and blue beak, is easily distinguished. Note, too, its stiff, upright tail. In flight the ruddy's feathers make a buzzing sound.

A wide variety of wading birds and shorebirds is also present (many year-round; others, in all but hottest summer), including great blue heron, dowitchers, yellowlegs, sandpiper, black-necked stilts, white-faced ibis, avocets, various egrets, American coots, and American white pelican.

Say's phoebes are seen at Imperial in every season but summer; black phoebes are present year-round among the refuge's 16 species of flycatchers. This is also a fine place to scope out hummingbirds in winter, with Anna's, black-chinned, and Costa's all on the scene. Look in the uplands for these smaller birds.

The desert uplands support other species, including the frequently spotted Gambel's quail, phainopepla, greater roadrunner, and verdin. The verdin is a small (4 inches) and predominantly gray bird, best distinguished by its bright yellow head. Roadrunners rely on their blazing foot speed to evade predators and capture prey. The roadrunner can easily chase down lizards and will also take on rattlesnakes, jumping into the air to avoid their strikes until the snakes are exhausted and defenseless. Then they use their formidable beaks to seize their prey.

Gambel's quail

Other common refuge birds include the marsh wren, crissal thrasher, loggerhead shrike, and northern rough-winged swallow. Look for swallows dipping and darting over the river or in canyons, where they feed on concentrations of small insects.

Raptors are also plentiful at Imperial. The river attracts bald eagle, osprey, and, most commonly, northern harriers; and desert uplands are home to red-tailed hawk, Harrris's hawk, and a rare peregrine falcon or two.

Spring and fall migrations also bring songbirds through the refuge, including the blue grosbeak with its dull blue color and two contrasting reddish-tan wing bars.

Hardcore birders also enjoy the challenge of spotting a southwestern willow flycatcher or a Yuma clapper rail here. Both are endangered species. The rails hide in the dense cattail marshes and are most often recognized by their voices (a clattering *kek-kek-kek-kek* or *cha-cha-cha* than by sight. The California black rail, a species of concern, is found in bulrush patches. All told, some 271 bird species have been recorded at Imperial to date.

Mammals The refuge's highest-profile mammals—500 to 600 wild, or feral, burros—are, paradoxically, unwelcome inhabitants. These hardy animals are descended from domestic burros that were lost or abandoned in the area. They are reproducing so successfully that their browsing on trees and other vegetation has a deleterious effect on the refuge's natural ecosystem.

Imperial hosts a healthy population of desert bighorn sheep that favors the refuge's rough, mountainous terrain. Also spotted frequently is coyote (see sidebar, Ash Meadows NWR). A black-tailed jackrabbit or cottontail will frequently bound away through the desert scrub.

Reptiles and amphibians Reptiles thrive in the desert environment. Among the refuge's many species are desert tortoise, zebra-tailed lizard, chuckwalla, desert iguana, and western whiptail lizards. The whiptail is an 8- to 12-inch slender lizard with a light tan/gray body and faint-to-distinct stripes and dots, and gray-green tail. Out and about from April to October in daylight, they are especially active during the April

Western whiptail lizard

mating season and are often seen on the Painted Desert Trail.

Fish The Colorado River and its associated marshes provide refuge for a number of endangered swimmers, including razorback sucker and bonytail chub. Refuge staff is creating a pond system free of nonnative fish to better care for the native species, which are often outcompeted physically by introduced fish species.

ACTIVITIES

■ **CAMPING:** Camping is not allowed on Imperial refuge, but just outside its western boundary, on the west side of the river in California, there is camping at Picacho State Recreation Area.

■ **WILDLIFE OBSERVATION:** The observation tower adjacent to the Visitor Center, open during daylight hours, provides a good view of the farm/moist-soil units, a favorite feeding area for cranes, waterfowl, and wading birds in winter.

A short, unnamed trail runs across a raised dike from Mesquite Point through dense riparian vegetation to the Colorado River, providing the refuge's only on-river access other than by boat or the boat ramp at Meers Point. Many birds can be observed in the vegetation flanking the dike and river's edge.

Odd as it sounds, the best place to see desert bighorn sheep is from the waters of the Colorado River. Boaters often spot them on the hills flanking the river in the Smoke Tree area upstream from the Visitor Center. Sheep are also seen occasionally from the summit of the Painted Desert Trail on the cliffs to the east.

Good places to spot lizards and snakes are in the sandy washes along the Painted Desert Trail or other more isolated arroyos and rock outcroppings. The Palo Verde Trail provides good duck viewing.

■ **PHOTOGRAPHY:** A river outing provides a unique vantage point for photography at this refuge. Prime subjects include marsh scenes, river cliffs, and birdlife. Be sure to walk the Painted Desert Trail for fine shots of the Colorado River Valley, desert landscapes, and flora.

Blue grosbeak

■ **HIKES AND WALKS:** Painted Desert Trail loops 1 mile up a gentle canyon, over a ridge, and back down another canyon, providing a fine backcountry introduction to Imperial's desert upland plants, wildlife, and landforms—from sandy arroyos to pastel-colored stone stubs and badlands and jagged cliffs. From the trail's high point, hikers enjoy splendid views of the Colorado River Valley. An interpretive leaflet keyed to markers along the trail is available at the trailhead. Allow an hour for a leisurely walk. The trailhead is located 2.8 miles from the Visitor Center on Red Mine Road.

There is also a short trail at Mesquite Point running to the Colorado River bank.

■ **BOATING:** Rental boats and other equipment are available from Martinez Lake Resort. There are no dedicated swimming areas, but people do swim off their boats.

■ **PUBLICATIONS:** Bird list, brochure, hiking leaflet.

HUNTING AND FISHING Quail, rabbit, fox, coyote, **mule deer** (archery and firearm seasons), **bighorn sheep, waterfowl,** and **dove** can all be hunted on the refuge.

Bass, crappie, sunfish, and **catfish** are most often taken by anglers. Bank fishing and a boating ramp are located at Meers Point on Lake Martinez, 1 mile from the Visitor Center.

Kern NWR
Delano, California

San Joaquin kit fox

More than most California refuges, Kern NWR has been affected by the perennial maneuvering among cities, farmers, and northern and southern California for the state's finite supply of water. Situated in the arid southern reaches of the San Joaquin (pronounced Wah-KEEN) Valley (where only 6 inches of rain fall annually), the refuge, until 1994, was allotted only enough water by the local irrigation district to flood 3 square miles, a pittance when you're trying to replace the historic 1,563 square miles (1 million acres) of marsh that once filled the southern San Joaquin Valley, the largest wetlands in the West.

In 1994, the Central Valley Improvement Act was passed. Its purpose was to compensate for loss of habitat in the Great Central Valley that occurred with the federal Central Valley Project, which dammed rivers in the Sierra foothills and in the Sierra Nevada. (This project is not to be confused with the State Water Project, which includes the aqueduct carrying water from northern California to farmers in the Great Central Valley and to southern California. How much water should go south is another perpetual skirmish in the California water wars.)

Mitigation mandated by the Central Valley Improvement Act now guarantees that Kern NWR will receive an assured water supply, enough to flood 11 square miles (7,040 acres), allowing the refuge to take its place with the Sacramento and San Luis refuges as a major stop for migrating birds in the Great Central Valley.

HISTORY

A vast inland marsh once spread over the lower San Joaquin Valley, so large that travelers had to bypass the marsh by taking to the foothills. The Kern River split into several channels and flowed into Buena Vista Lake. The Kern, Goose, and Tulare Lake basins were filled by the Kern, Kings, and Tule rivers, along with overflow from the 1,563-square-mile (1,000,000-acre) San Joaquin Marsh, the largest freshwater marsh west of the Mississippi. Then the rivers were dammed, the water was taken for irrigation, and the marsh disappeared. With it went the birds that had used the marsh during their migration along the Pacific Flyway. Less than 8 percent of the lower San Joaquin's marshlands remain, much of them in the Kern and Pixley national wildlife refuges. The 16.6-square-mile (10,618-acre) Kern refuge was established in 1960. Limited by the lack of a reliable water source, the refuge in 1994 then received an assured supply of water as mitigation for the federal Central Valley Water Project. New marsh areas have been created, a Visitor Center has been built, and the 5,000 or so annual visitors are expected to increase with new viewing opportunities.

GETTING THERE

From Sacramento (driving south) or Los Angeles (driving north), take I-5 to CA 46 and exit east 5 mi. to Corcoran Rd. Turn north 10.6 mi. to intersection of Garces Hwy. and Corcoran Rd. From Bakersfield, drive north on US 99 to Delano. Exit south on CA 155 (Garces Hwy.). Drive 19 mi. west to the refuge intersection at Corcoran Rd. and Garces Hwy.

■ **SEASON:** Refuge open year-round.

■ **HOURS:** Open dawn to dusk 7 days a week. Visitor Center open Mon.–Fri., 8 a.m.–4:30 p.m.

■ **ADDRESS:** Kern NWR, c/o Kern Complex, P.O. Box 670, Delano, CA 93216-0670

■ **TELEPHONE:** 661/725-2767

WHAT TO SEE

■ **LANDSCAPE AND CLIMATE** The many farm crops surrounding the refuge are deceptive: The lower San Joaquin Valley is a desert, receiving around 6 inches of rain annually. The plant communities that live at Kern, which has no irrigation system, reflect more accurately the Saharan climate (the Sahara receives 4 to 8 inches of rain annually). Saltbush, a family of plants native to California and Australia, includes more than 100 evergreen and deciduous species, 12 of them growing in the California deserts. Most have gray-green foliage and grow in saline and alkaline soil under full sun and drought conditions. (Temperatures at the refuge soar to 110 degrees F. in July and August; the midsummer low is 50 degrees, while January temperatures range from 15 to 65 degrees.)

■ **PLANT LIFE** Bogweed, crown saltbush, and arrowscale are species of saltbush (or

Wildflowers, Kern NWR

atriplex) growing at the refuge. Another drought-tolerant plant is the iodine bush, which, like the refuge's pickleweed, conserves water in a series of succulent sections. Its deep taproots can absorb both salt and water; it drops its top sections to rid itself of some of the salt it has accumulated.

Tumbleweed, famous in song, is another member of the saltbush family, actually a native of Russia brought to Canada accidentally. It took it 25 years to tumble on down to Mexico, distributing its seeds as it rolled.

■ **ANIMAL LIFE** The endangered San Joaquin kit fox likes to eat Tipton kangaroo rats, another endangered species living at Kern. The coyote, which eats them both, is partly to blame for the decline in numbers of kit foxes. Refuge biologists have installed underground dens for the kit foxes, with an entrance small enough to prevent coyotes from entering. Kit fox pups are born February through April after a gestation period of 49 to 55 days. Other predators of the foxes are eagles and large hawks.

Other carnivores on the refuge include raccoons, long-tailed weasels, spotted and striped skunks, badgers, and bobcats.

SATELLITE REFUGE

■ **Pixley NWR** The blunt-nosed leopard lizard likes arid and semiarid plains with scattered low plants—sagebrush, creosote bush, and bunchgrass—terrain like that preserved in the 10-square-mile (6389-acre) Pixley NWR. Although Pixley is closed to the public, CA 43 skirts the west edge of the refuge, where the 9-inch leopard lizards can sometimes be seen catching and eating grasshoppers. One of the refuge's five geographically separate units is a wetland that creates wintering habitat for 2,000 to 3,000 sandhill cranes. Specially arranged tours through the refuge, guided by refuge staff, are available. To visit Pixley, arrange for a tour by calling the refuge office in advance. Around 50 visitors take the tour annually.

■ **GETTING THERE:** From Bakersfield, drive north on US 99 to County Road 22 (first exit after Allensworth). Drive west, then north on CA 43. The refuge is just north of the intersection of the two roads.

■ **ADDRESS:** Pixley NWR, Pixley, California, c/o Kern Complex, P.O. Box 670, Delano, CA 93216-0670

■ **TELEPHONE:** 661/725-2767

Klamath Basin NWR Complex
Bear Valley NWR, Clear Lake NWR,
Klamath Marsh NWR, Lower Klamath NWR,
Tule Lake NWR, Upper Klamath NWR
Tulelake, California

Sunrise over Lower Klamath refuge

Their wings rattling the air across a vast expanse of sky, a thousand tundra swans settle on Tule Lake. Several miles away, two thousand ducks flutter into the sky, then drop back to bob on the rippling waters of Lower Klamath Refuge. Klamath Basin, a crossroads on the Pacific Flyway, is a rest stop for some 80 percent of the birds migrating on the West Coast. To explore the six refuges in the basin, along the California-Oregon border, is to be awed by the vitality and resilience of the two million birds flying through here each year. Each bird has persisted, despite what is seen by many as a concerted effort to destroy the wetlands it needs for survival.

HISTORY

Once a huge, ancient lake filled Klamath Basin. By the time white settlers arrived in the late 1800s, the lake was long gone, leaving its ghostly imprint in a vast wetland of shallow lakes and freshwater marshes filling 289 square miles of the basin. These wetlands, home to six to seven million migrating and nesting birds, were known as the western Everglades and were considered the greatest waterfowl nursery in the United States (Alaska wasn't yet a state).

All that changed forever when the U.S. Bureau of Reclamation began the Klamath Reclamation Project in 1905, draining wetlands for farming. Today two-thirds of the bird populations that used to come to Klamath Basin have disappeared, and only 25 percent of the wetlands remain. (This as a whole is a better record than that of California, which has lost 90 percent of its wetlands.)

To protect what is left, six wildlife refuges were established in the basin, along

AVIAN CHOLERA Bald eagles, smart about conserving energy, avoid the effort of necessary hunting and may even prefer to eat birds something else has killed. That's why they're found in sizable numbers in the Klamath Basin, December through March. A deadly disease called avian cholera struck flocks of wild ducks and geese for the first time In 1944. Although the cholera is not harmful to humans and rarely attacks eagles, it kills ducks and geese within 6 to 12 hours of exposure. It strikes Klamath Basin in October or November with the arrival of the first great flocks of snow geese, which carry the bacteria. The cholera appears to spread when the tule fog hangs low and the birds sleep closer together. (Tule fog is the name given a dense, ground-hugging fog that is responsible each year for chain pileups on the freeways. The fog is formed when cold air is trapped in low spots.) From year to year, the dieoffs, which continue through spring, can be large or small. Whatever is there is meat on the table for eagles and other raptors that inhabit the basin for its easy pickings.

with a preserve administered by The Nature Conservancy and lands under control of the state of Oregon. The Bureau of Reclamation, however, still controls water rights in the basin (the refuges overlie reclamation land); and as elsewhere in the arid west, *water* is what will determine the future of the remaining Klamath wetlands.

GETTING THERE

Begin your visit to the six refuges with a stop at the Visitor Center at Tule Lake refuge on Hill Rd. From Klamath Falls, drive east on OR 140, then south on OR 39. One mi. before reaching Merrill, turn south on Merrill Pit Rd. (at NWR sign). At the end of Merrill Pit Rd. turn left on OR 161 (also known as Stateline Rd.) for 4 mi., then turn left on Hill Rd. to the Visitor Center. (The trip from Klamath Falls is about 22 mi.) From California, drive north on I-5 to Weed, then take CA 97 about 43 mi. north to CA 161 (also known as Stateline Rd.). Turn east on CA 161, which takes you through Lower Klamath NWR. Drive 18 mi., then turn south on Hill Rd. to the Visitor Center.

■ **SEASON:** Open year-round.
■ **HOURS:** Refuge open sunrise to sunset. Visitor Center open, Mon.–Fri., 8 a.m.–4:30 p.m.; weekends and holidays, 10 a.m.–4 p.m. Closed Christmas and New Year's Day.
■ **FEES:** Tule Lake and Lower Klamath auto-tour routes, $3 per car or $12 season pass. Hunting and photo blinds, $5 per day; consecutive 3-day pass, $10; consecutive 10-day pass, $20. Season pass, $50; family season pass, $75. Passes also valid at Humboldt Bay NWR and Modoc NWR.
■ **ADDRESS:** Klamath Basin National Wildlife Refuges, Rte. 1, Box 74, Tulelake, CA 96134; web site: http//www/klamath nwr.org
■ **TELEPHONE:** 530/667-2231

TOURING KLAMATH BASIN

■ **BY AUTOMOBILE:** Thirty-three miles of gravel auto-tour roads are available: Klamath Marsh (10 miles), Tule Lake (9.6 miles), and Upper Klamath (13.5 miles). US 97 skirts the east side of Upper Klamath, and CA 161 cuts across Lower Klamath.

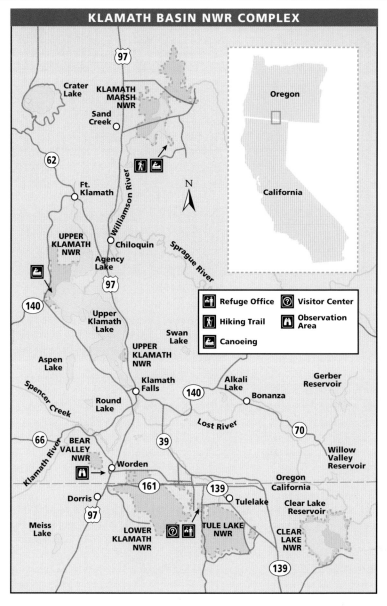

KLAMATH BASIN NWR COMPLEX

■ BY FOOT: Hiking trails near the headquarters and at Klamath Marsh total 10.33 miles.

■ BY BICYCLE: Auto-tour routes and the hiking trail at Klamath Marsh are open to bicyclists.

■BY CANOE, KAYAK, OR BOAT: Only by taking to a boat can you see these immense expanses of water from a floating bird's-eye view, and the Klamath Basin refuges have designed their canoe trails to give you a special perspective into this watery world. Three canoe trails—at Tule Lake (2 miles), Upper Klamath (8.5 miles), and Klamath Marsh (no designated length)—are open July 1 to September 30 unless a marsh has dried out, been drawn down for maintenance, or closed tem-

Klamath Marsh NWR forest

porarily to protect wildlife. The 8.5-mile Upper Klamath canoe trail is open year-round and is by far the most popular of the three trails. Canoes, kayaks, and boats can be rented at Rocky Point Resort, at the northern tip of Upper Klamath Lake (reservations: 541/356-2287).

WHAT TO SEE

■ **LANDSCAPE AND CLIMATE** The tranquil pastoral beauty of the Klamath Basin contrasts with its violent formation. Lying in the eastern Cascade Mountains directly in the great volcanic belt that includes Crater Lake to the north and the Lava Beds to the south, Klamath Basin's volcanic origin is hidden beneath its marshes and lakes. An occasional cliff face, pocked with cavities formed by cooling lava, reminds visitors that this was once a rocky wasteland. January temperatures in the basin range between 4 and 54 degrees. In July temperatures increase, from around 37 to 90 degrees. About 10 inches of rain fall each year—most of it in December through March—with snowfall around 28 inches. Elevation in the refuges ranges from 4,060 feet to 6,595 feet, accounting for the cool temperatures.

■ **PLANT LIFE** The basin is heavily farmed—around half of Tule Lake refuge is leased to farmers—and visitors will see crops of potatoes, sugar beets, onions, grain, and deep green alfalfa growing near the natural plant communities found in the marshes.

Wetlands Tules and cattails (see sidebar on tules, Tule Lake refuge) grow thick in the marshes and wetlands of Klamath Basin. Cattails—their familiar female flowers resembling fuzzy, oversized brown hot dogs—are natural water filters that help clean the marsh of contaminants. In summer, look for the bright yellow flowers of the wocus, or yellow water lily, blooming from mid-June through August. Out of sight underwater, but vitally important as a food source for waterfowl, are sago pondweed (a spindly plant with narrow, flat leaves) and coontail, a bushy, free-floating plant used in aquariums and one of the few vascular plants without roots.

Forest The land around Tule Lake is generally devoid of trees, testament to both the arid climate and the fact that most of the refuge is former lakebed; but at Klamath Marsh, a successional growth of alder and conifers—primarily lodge-pole and ponderosa pine—reminds visitors that the basin is surrounded by parts of five national forests (Winema, Rogue River, Fremont, Klamath, and Modoc), which shelter a wide array of animals, including deer, pronghorn, elk, and bear.

Arid lands The high desert's sagebrush and bunchgrass give way to a flourish-ing juniper forest on the rocky uplands around Clear Lake. The lake's shoreline of tule marsh disappeared when water levels rose after the lake was dammed in 1911. Hidden among the sagebrush are dainty summer wildflowers (look for the orange flowers of Indian paintbrush), appearing much too fragile to survive in the harsh environment.

■ ANIMAL LIFE

Birds Even in the depth of winter, the basin is alive with birds. More than a thou-sand bald eagles winter here from December through February, the largest gather-ing of bald eagles in the Lower 48. Thousands of tundra swans herald the approach of spring as they arrive in February and March, sitting like puffy white balls on the frozen lakes.

The northern migration reaches its peak in March or early April when from one to two million waterfowl—including greater white-fronted geese, northern pintails, and green-winged teal—pass through. March also sees the return of white pelicans to their three breeding colonies in the basin. Spring shorebird migration peaks in April and May.

May and June mark the birth of ducklings as white-faced ibis breed in the marshes. In July northern orioles nest in trees around the refuge Visitor Center; the fall migration of shorebirds also begins in July.

In August and September white-fronted geese arrive, along with double-crested cormorants, herons, gulls, and grebes, all on their fall migration. Sandhill cranes stage in September and October while snow geese fly in during October and November. Fall migration, at its peak in mid-November, ends in December when the lakes and marshes freeze over and most migrants fly south, completing the cycle of the seasons.

Northern pintail

Mammals The basin is home to 78 mammals—big ones such as elk, prong-horn, and black bear—and little ones like the Pacific water shrew, silver-haired bat, and least chipmunk. Your chances of seeing a number of these are good. Mule deer regularly visit the bird feeding station at the Visitor Center to eat the

birdseed, and coyotes (pro-nounced KIGH-oats in these parts) are out early in the morn-ing hunting breakfast. River otter and an occasional long-tailed weasel can be spotted in the marshes; and if you don't actually see a beaver, you can at least observe their industrious efforts as loggers.

Reptiles and amphibians Three species of frog—spotted, western, and Pacific—live in the basin along with seven harmless reptiles (rubber boa, gopher, and common garter snakes among them), but keep an eye out for the eighth, the poisonous western rattlesnake, always recognized by the rattles at the end of its tail.

Fish Fish at Klamath Basin occupy the unfortunate position

Mule deer

of serving as dinner for many of the birds and mammals living here. Kokanee salmon and trout (rainbow, brown, and brook) are a main course for bald eagles. Other fish include the Klamath Lake sculpin and the Pit-Klamath lamprey. Two endangered species, the lost river and shortnose suckers, also swim in these waters.

Invertebrates Human visitors are a potential meal for the millions of mosqui-toes buzzing here June through September. Take mosquito repellent, wear long pants, a long-sleeved shirt, and a hat to protect your head; and, if you're particu-larly attractive to mosquitoes, wear a mosquito net over the hat.

ACTIVITIES

See individual refuges for wildlife observation, hikes and walks, and boating information.

HUNTING AND FISHING Since the Klamath Basin refuges spread over both California and Oregon, pick up hunting regulations for both states, and be sure to check with refuge headquarters before planning a hunt-ing or fishing trip, as regulations can change annually.

At Tule Lake, Lower Klamath, Bear Valley, and Clear Lake, hunting is permitted, but no fishing is allowed.

At Upper Klamath and Klamath Marsh, both hunting and fishing are permitted.

Contact headquarters for specific information on the species of wildlife and fish that may be hunted at each location.

■ **CAMPING:** No camping is allowed on the refuges. Best bet for camping is about 18 miles south of Tule Lake refuge at Lava Beds National Monument; this 43-site campground is rarely full. The refuge Visitor Center has a list of accommodations throughout the area. A primitive camp (around 5 sites) is available at Rocky Point canoe launch, Upper Klamath refuge.

■ **PHOTOGRAPHY:** Bald eagles and hawks use the only tree in sight around Tule Lake for a perch, and one of the basin's eight photo blinds is strategically placed near the tree. The Visitor Center has a list of the blinds, including the wildlife you're likely to see, how to reserve a blind, and suggestions on the best equipment to use in order to take home a spectacular photograph from Klamath Basin. Be prepared to get up early. Most of the blinds are situated for morning photography, and several require you to be there before 7:30 a.m.

■ **SEASONAL EVENTS:** February: Bald Eagle Conference, on President's Day weekend, in Klamath Falls. Intended for families, it offers crafts classes for kids and adults, tours to refuge highlights and nearby attractions, birding in the basin, and, for all ages, bat-house building.

■ **PUBLICATIONS:** *A Birder's Guide to the Klamath Basin* by Steven Summers (Klamath Basin Audubon Society, 1993). *Klamath Basin National Wildlife Refuges* (Klamath Basin Wildlife Association, 1997).

Bear Valley NWR
Tulelake, California

The name isn't right, and it's closed to the public, but Bear Valley NWR maintains an aura of fascination for visitors to Klamath Basin. The refuge is the winter roosting site for 300 to 500 bald eagles—the largest gathering of our national bird outside Alaska. The eagles, arriving in mid-November and leaving by mid-March, roost in the great conifers of Bear Valley's old-growth forest, then fly out at dawn to the basin's other refuges to eat waterfowl, rodents, and fish. The flyout is Bear Valley's big attraction, and you can witness it from the road outside the refuge.

Bald eagle

HISTORY

The name is a bit misleading. Bear Valley is a 6.5-square-mile, 4,200-acre forested hillside of old-growth conifers with an elevation range of 4,090 to 6,595 feet. Established in 1978, its popularity is not vast, but its champions are enthusiastic: About 1,400 visitors watched the flyout in 1997.

GETTING THERE

Drive around 13 mi. south of Klamath Falls on US 97. Just south of Worden, turn west onto the Keno-

Worden Rd. Cross the railroad tracks and turn left onto a gravel road. Continue about 0.5 mi. and park along the shoulder to watch the flyout.

WHAT TO SEE

Rouse yourself before daybreak to watch a hundred bald eagles, their massive wings spreading to seven and a half feet, flying silently overhead as dawn breaks. Look west toward Hammaker Mountain for eagles flying east along the ridges and directly overhead. The biggest concentration of eagles during the flyout, starting about a half-hour before sunrise, occurs in the first hour. Remember: This is January and February, and you should dress warmly. Don't forget your binoculars. If a dawn rendezvous isn't your style, you can watch the eagles later catching their breakfast on nearby Lower Klamath refuge.

American white pelicans

Clear Lake NWR
Tulelake, California

Wind whips across the harsh, desolate high-desert landscape surrounding Clear Lake Reservoir, so remote that only 1,235 visitors found their way there in 1997. In summer, heat soaks into the earth, and all is still. A visit to this bleak land of sagebrush and juniper trees is a chance to see California in all its untamed wildness and marvel at the number of birds and mammals that call it home.

HISTORY

Clear Lake Reservoir, covering half the refuge, supplies water to farmers in the eastern half of Klamath Basin. Established in 1911, the 52-square-mile refuge (33,440 acres) is closed to the public; but Clear Lake can be seen from Forest Road 136, skirting the southern boundary of the reservoir.

GETTING THERE

About 20 mi. south of Tulelake on CA 139, turn east (left) on the signed, gravel forest road (Clear Lake Reservoir Rd). If you reach the right turn to Lava Beds National Monument, you've gone too far. On the gravel road, stay left at first Y, then continue to the northeast. Caution: Heavy rains can turn the refuge road into a quagmire, requiring 4-wheel-drive. The road is not cleared of snow.

WHAT TO SEE

Thrusting its long yellow bill into Clear Lake, the white pelican scoops up a short-nose sucker (an endangered species) and stores the fish in its capacious pouch, to be digested at leisure. Unlike brown pelicans, white pelicans do not fish by flying and diving into the water. Floating high on the water, they simply dip their beaks to catch an unsuspecting passing fish. The lake's rocky islands hold one of the West's few nesting colonies of white pelicans, and some 1,000 of them fledge there each summer. Look for huge white birds, their wingtips extending to 9 feet, flapping their wings for liftoff, then gliding in formation high in the sky. Fellow nesters on the lake's islands are double-crested cormorants, around 5,800 ring-billed gulls, and 3,500 California gulls

On land, a herd of 40 to 50 pronghorns may be seen at any time of year; and flitting about the bushy juniper trees, small mountain bluebirds dine on juniper berries, their blue plumage startling against the snowy landscape of winter. Temperatures in the coldest months drop to 20 to 40 degrees, and a foot or more of snow covers the rock-encrusted desert. In summer, temperatures soar into the 90s. (Hot days and cold nights are typical of this high desert, where the refuge elevation ranges from 4,523 to 4,600 feet.) Carrying water is a necessity when exploring Klamath Basin's semidesert uplands, formed thousands of years ago by the repeated eruptions of nearby Medicine Lake volcano.

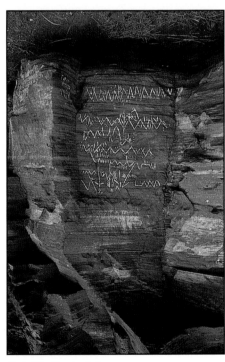

Rock cliff with petroglyphs

This broad, rounded volcano (which is known as a shield volcano) erupted sporadically over a period of more than 500,000 years and is the largest volcano in the Cascade Mountains. (Don't miss a side trip to nearby Lava Beds National Monument, where more than 380 lava tube caves are open for exploration. The tubes formed when hot, fluid lava erupted. As the lava flowed down slope it began to cool and solidify on the sides and top while the molten lava inside the shell continued to flow, draining out and leaving behind a hollow tube.) A short turnoff to the right on the entry road to Clear Lake leads to a lava face called Petroglyph Point, where barn owls, cliff swallows, and prairie falcons roost in myriad holes on the face, formed when a cinder cone erupted from ancient Tule Lake and made an island. No one knows which ancient native tribe carved the petroglyphs. A steep trail leads to the top of the face for an expansive view of the plateau. Caution: Watch for rattlesnakes.

Black-crowned night-heron

Klamath Marsh NWR
Chiloquin, Oregon

A lush field of pond lilies, their bright yellow blossoms reflecting on the rippling water, creates a textured green and yellow carpet spread across Klamath Marsh NWR (formerly Klamath Forest NWR), the northernmost of the marshes in Klamath Basin. Meadows dotted with summertime wildflowers offer expansive views beyond the marsh, and a pine forest snuggled along the marsh's eastern edge shelters Rocky Mountain elk and secretive great gray owls.

HISTORY

Historic home of the Klamath Indian tribes, Klamath Marsh was established as a refuge in 1958 when the first 16,400 acres were purchased from the Klamath Indian tribe with federal Duck Stamp funds. Wet meadows and a natural marsh make up almost 90 percent of the present 63-square-mile refuge, with pine forest covering the remaining acreage, all at an elevation of about 4,500 feet. Annually, around 6,500 visitors explore Klamath Marsh refuge.

GETTING THERE

Drive north on US 97 about 45 mi. from Klamath Falls. Turn east (right) onto Silver Lake Rd. and go approximately 9.5 mi. to just past where the marsh and forest meet. Take the first right onto gravel Forest Service Rd. 690.

TOURING KLAMATH MARSH

■ **BY AUTOMOBILE:** A short auto route of l0.5 miles and an extended route of 13.5 miles are passable in summer. A high-clearance vehicle is recommended, but 4-wheel-drive isn't necessary. Caution: The road is slick after heavy rains and is not plowed clear of the abundant winter snows.

■ **BY FOOT:** A 5-mile (one-way) recreational trail is open to hikers, who may also walk the entire auto loop.

■ **BY BICYCLE:** Mountain bikers can follow the gravel auto-loop route.

■ **BY CANOE, KAYAK, OR BOAT:** Wocus Bay, at the southern tip of the marsh, is open for canoeing or kayaking from July 1 to September 30. No motorized boats are allowed. Check with refuge headquarters before planning a trip, because water levels may be too low for boating in a dry summer—and the canoeing area can be closed at any time to protect wildlife. The canoe launch is approximately 4 miles south on Forest Service Road 690 from its intersection with Silver Lake Road. To rent canoes or kayaks, call Rocky Point Resort (541/356-2287).

■ **BY SKIS OR SNOWSHOES:** In heavy snow years, the 10 miles of Forest Service Road 690 become an ungroomed cross-country ski trail.

WHAT TO SEE

■ **LANDSCAPE AND CLIMATE** Ringed by forest, this natural marsh is unquestionably the prettiest in the six-refuge Klamath complex. Because it lies some 500 feet higher than the other marshes in the basin, Klamath Marsh experiences temperatures about five degrees lower—averaging -1 to 49 degrees in January; in July, the range is around 32 to 85.

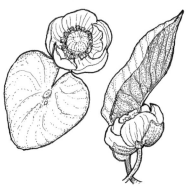

ACTIVITIES

■ **CAMPING:** Camping is not allowed on the refuge, but it is allowed on adjacent national forest land. An overnight camping trip in Winema National Forest is an excellent way to observe wildlife. Klamath Marsh is the only refuge in the basin where you can camp out in the national forest and have a ringside seat to observe wildlife in the refuge across the road. Carry water and bring mosquito repellent.

Yellow pond lily

WOCUS WATERLILIES Even the beaver's appetite for the rhizomes of the Wocas, or yellow pond lily, can't prevent its vigorous growth habits. Once rooted, this perennial spreads thickly, floating on the water's surface, often crowding out other plants. The delicate appearance of the glossy leaves and fragile flowers gives no indication of the plant's enormous rhizome growing underwater, sometimes 16 feet long and 6 inches in diameter.

The Wocus (from the Native *wok,* meaning "seed pods of the wocus") was a major food staple for the Klamath Indians, who gathered the seed pods, which are shaped like acorns matured with a conical head. The head would then be parched over a fire; after the fruit and seeds were separated out, the seeds were pounded and cooked again, then eaten.

Blooming from June through mid-August, the Wocus is now a food for wildfowl and deer, who consume its flowers, leaves, and stems.

In winter, when the trail is open for cross-country skiing, there is opportunity for snow camping and viewing of a completely different group of birds. You won't see many mammals at this time, however: Many of them are hibernating through the winter months.

■ **WILDLIFE OBSERVATION:** The marsh is famous for its 60 pairs of sandhill cranes. Other inhabitants you're likely to see are white-headed woodpeckers (the only woodpecker found in the West with a white head), yellow-headed blackbirds, Steller's jays, and ruddy ducks.

Canoeing or kayaking is a great way to take in the lush scenery in and around the marsh, which shelters 42 species of animals and birds. Take suntan lotion, sunglasses, and a hat to explore the 700 acres of open water and tule and cattail marsh, where you may see pied-billed grebes, cinnamon teal, and black-crowned night-herons. Look for the short-necked heron standing patiently in the water, waiting for a fish or frog to swim by.

■ **HIKES AND WALKS:** The 5-mile recreation trail (serving also as Forest Service Road 690 and the route to the canoe launch) meanders along the east side of the marsh, in and out of the refuge and adjoining Winema National Forest. Here it is particularly interesting to observe the two biomes—marsh and forest. Songbirds keep to their forest home while waterfowl inhabit the marsh.

Tundra swans

Lower Klamath NWR
Tukelake, California

As great billowing masses of birds fly into the Klamath marshes during the spring and fall migrations, the noise is overwhelming: The cackling of thousands of geese combines with the quacks, whistles and cries of ducks numbering in the hundreds of thousands to create a phantasmagoria of motion, color, and noise. Anyone witnessing this astonishing aerial panorama will understand why Lower Klamath is often named one of the 10 top refuges in the United States.

RUDDY DUCKS The ruddy duck struts through the water with its head thrown back as if reaching for its erect tail feathers. Known in various parts of the country as sleepy duck, paddy-whack, stub-and-twist, booby coot, and dumb bird, the ruddy duck lacks the large wing area of geese or swans. It will never soar over the marsh. Because its wings are even smaller than usual for a duck, the ruddy has to work harder at flying than most other ducks. The ruddy's feet are set so far back on the body that it can only take a few steps before it falls over awkwardly on its breast. Functioning like twin outboards, the ruddy's feet make the duck a great swimmer, but a terrible walker.

As the ruddy flies through a freezing fog, its wings gather frost, ice up, and no longer support flight, and the ruddy falls ignominiously out of the sky. Not being able to run, it can't take off even if it deices. The duck needs water. So if you discover a ruddy on your lawn one winter morning, just put it into a box and launch it into a lake, river, or pond. The duck will be just fine.

Leo Smothers, Klamath Basin refuges volunteer

HISTORY

Encouraged by members of the National Audubon Society, who observed the startling decline in birds near the turn of the century, President Theodore Roosevelt established Lower Klamath in 1908 as the nation's first waterfowl refuge. Its 53,598 acres are divided into marsh (56 percent), croplands (28 percent), and uplands (16 percent), all between 4,000 and 4,500 feet in elevation. Lower Klamath and Tule Lake are the basin's most visited refuges. Almost 220,000 people tour Lower Klamath each year.

Ruddy duck

GETTING THERE

From the Klamath Basin NWR Visitor Center on Hill Rd. in Tule Lake, drive north to CA 161, along the Oregon–California border. Turn west on CA 161 and follow it through the Lower Klamath refuge.

TOURING LOWER KLAMATH NWR

■ **BY AUTOMOBILE:** The auto-tour route has two entrances off CA 161. Both entrances link to a loop encircling one of the refuge's marshes. Along the route, interpretive panels describe the habitats—seasonal wetlands, permanent marshes, and dry uplands.

■ **BY BICYCLE:** The auto-tour route is open to bicycles.

ACTIVITIES

■ **WILDLIFE OBSERVATION:** Among the tules, groups of small, chunky brown ducks feed on smartweed. With its erect tail, the ruddy duck is easy to spot. Nibbling at the seeds of smartweed, the ruddy is feeding on one of the food staples in the refuge. Smartweed, recognized by its large lance-shaped leaves (up to 6 inches long), was earlier known as "arsmart," for its tendency to inflame the hindquarters of persons who used it there. To see the male ruddy in its full glory, visit during spring mating season when its plumage turns bright chestnut brown and its beak turns blue.

Tule Lake NWR

Tule Lake NWR

Tulelake, California

It's only when you drive the square corners of the Tule Lake auto route that you realize this crown of the refuges along the Pacific Flyway, once one of the biggest marshlands west of the Mississippi, is actually two man-made sumps created by dikes, receiving drain water from Klamath Basin's agricultural fields. Toxicity levels present in the water from agricultural pesticides and fertilizers are not enough to deter the migratory birds. By November a million ducks, geese, and swans have arrived at Tule Lake and nearby Lower Klamath refuges—tens of thousands of snow geese from Siberia, sandhill cranes, tundra swans from the Arctic, Canada geese, Ross's geese, mallards, wigeons, and the swift-flying green-winged teals.

HISTORY

Like a sea tide, Tule Lake once flowed over the surrounding marshlands when the wet years came and receded during the dry years. Fluctuating water levels created a productive marsh, but it dried up by 1905 after the Reclamation Act of 1902 had put in motion the Klamath Reclamation Project, draining the basin's wetlands for agricultural use. Although Tule Lake was designated a wildlife refuge in 1928, draining continued; and by 1960 Tule Lake was only 13 percent of its original size.

An attempt to restore marshland can be seen at Hovey Point (marker number

TULES The vast beds of hardstem and softstem bulrushes seen in most of the West's marshes got their local name—tule (TWO-lee)—from the Aztecs. Spaniards, moving north from Mexico into California, dropped the "n" from the Aztec "tollin" (a rush) to describe the slender stalks that grow from 3 to 9 feet tall in marshes and muddy ground around lakes and streams. The dense clumps of tules, sprouting from a rhizome, offer cover for river otters, muskrats and raccoons. Marsh wrens, waterfowl, and yellow-headed blackbirds nest in tules, and both Canada geese and white-fronted geese—as well as muskrats—eat the stems and rhizomes. Small tufts of brownish flowers bloom in summer, maturing into nut-shaped fruits that are a staple for marsh birds, ducks, and shorebirds.

Native Americans also ate the rhizomes, grinding them into flour; they also wove baskets from tule stems. Tule sleeping mats helped insulate against the cold ground because of the loose, spongy interiors of the stems.

Caution: If you're driving to the California and southern Oregon refuges in winter, watch out for tule fog. It hangs on the ground, so dense you can't see four feet in front of your nose, and is responsible for any number of fender benders and freeway pileups.

5 on the auto-tour route), a new seasonal marsh that will be drained periodically, and, at times, left as a permanent marsh. Birds have flocked to Hovey Point in both spring and fall, indicating their approval. Wildlife biologists hope the creation of more seasonal marshes will someday see many more birds using Tule Lake.

The refuge—of which more than half is farmland—totals 61 square miles, all between 4,056 feet and 4,600 feet. Tule Lake is the most visited of the Klamath Basin's six refuges, welcoming almost 223,000 annually in recent years.

GETTING THERE

Drive 5 mi. south on Hill Rd. from the Klamath Basin Visitor Center in Tule Lake, CA, and turn left onto the auto-tour route.

TOURING TULE LAKE

■ **BY AUTOMOBILE:** An auto-tour route (9.6 miles one-way) follows dikes along the edges of the north and south sumps.

■ **BY FOOT:** A short but very steep trail (.33 mile roundtrip) ascends Sheepy Ridge behind the Visitor Center. Directly south of the Visitor Center and on the opposite side of Hill Road, a 0.5-mile trail loops through a demonstration wetland known as Discovery Marsh.

■ **BY BICYCLE:** Bicyclists may use the unpaved auto-tour route. For those in good physical shape, it's possible to ride an approximate 38-mile loop around the refuge, with the southern leg following the boundary of Lava Beds National Monument.

■ **BY CANOE, KAYAK, OR BOAT:** A marked canoe trail follows some 2 miles of quiet channels through a 2,500-acre tule and cattail marsh. The trail is open daylight hours, July 1 to September 30, but can be shut at any time because of low water or potential disturbance to wildlife. Check at the Visitor Center.

ACTIVITIES

■ **WILDLIFE OBSERVATION:** Get up early in the morning to see one of the great sights at Tule Lake. On the farm field south of the Visitor Center, as many as 13 coyotes will be busy catching voles in the field, gulping them down in one swallow and trotting along to find the next breakfast tidbit.

Don't miss Hotel Rock en route to the auto-tour route. The rock is a lava face on the west side of Hill Road, pockmarked with cavities created when the lava cooled. Before turning into the tour route, park off the highway and walk north 75 feet. The wildlife service has marked an angled line on the road. Set up a spotting scope (or use binoculars) in line with the marking and scan the cliff face. You'll find a barn owl that makes its home in one of the cavities of the lava face. In summer, cliff swallows nest on the face along with other hotel residents such as prairie falcons and a great horned owl.

Visitors come from all over the world to see the birds at Tule Lake. Drive slowly along the auto route, stay in the car, and you'll see whatever birds are in residence. In June through September, look for ruddy ducks, eared grebes, the ubiquitous great blue heron, Brewer's blackbird, and the California gull. Note the fields of cereal grain and alfalfa on your right—a feast for the birds. The great blue heron, an ashy blue gray, eats fish, grasshoppers, mice, and baby birds. You may spot it standing on one leg in a marsh waiting for a fish to swim by or in the sky, distinguished from the sandhill crane because it flies with its neck folded.

California gull

■ **CANOEING AND KAYAKING:** To find the launch site for the Tule Lake canoe trail, drive north 0.5 mile from the Visitor Center and turn east on East-West Road, driving another 3.2 miles. Just after crossing Lost River, turn right onto a gravel road and continue .25 mile to the junction at the twin pumps. Turn right again and continue .4 mile to the launch site on the right. Early morning and late afternoon offer best chances for viewing ring-necked pheasant bustling through the uplands, redhead ducks among the tules, plus ravens, mule deer, and a host of marsh birds.

■ **HIKES AND WALKS:** The trail up Sheepy Ridge behind the Visitor Center may seem straight up, but the view from the top can't be beat. The ridge separates Tule Lake and Lower Klamath refuges. A free guide, available at the trailhead, is keyed to numbered posts along the trail, where you may see yellow-bellied marmots, gopher snakes, cliff swallows, and American kestrels. Also known as a sparrow hawk, the American kestrel, about the size of a jay, can sometimes be seen hovering in the air while searching for prey or perched on a pole as it looks for lizards and mice. Look for a rusty back and tail.

Upper Klamath NWR
Tulelake, California

Beaver gnawing on log

Klamath Lake is a vacation destination for Oregonians, offering resorts, anglers, and boats; but launch your canoe into the great marsh at the northern end of the lake and you're in a different world. The rustle of tules breaks the deep hush of this water world as your canoe slides through the cattails and bulrushes. The slap of a beaver's tail startles a belted kingfisher into flight, then silence falls again. Floating the sinuous twists of Crystal Creek is entrée into a secret world of animals and birds hidden in this embracing marsh.

HISTORY

Both Upper Klamath and Tule Lake refuges were added to the NWR system in 1928. Located in the center of the basin's six refuges, Upper Klamath sits at about 4,200 feet and includes 23 square miles of territory; all but 30 acres are freshwater marsh and open water. Around 3,000 visitors explore the Upper Klamath refuge annually.

GETTING THERE

From the Klamath Basin refuge headquarters in Tule Lake, CA, drive north on Hill Rd., then west on CA 161, viewing Lower Klamath Marsh on your left. Turn north on US 97, then west on OR 140. Swing north (right) on either Rocky Point Rd. or West Side Rd. to one of the two boat landings. The drive is around 30 mi.

TOURING UPPER KLAMATH NWR

■ **CANOE, KAYAK, OR BOAT:** Exploring Upper Klamath refuge requires a boat, and the four segments of the Upper Klamath Canoe Trail allow you to see as much or as little as you wish. Planning your trip, figure that two physically fit persons can paddle two miles per hour. Here are the options: Launch at Malone Springs boat launch (5.5 miles north of OR 140) to paddle the 2 miles (one-way) of Crystal Creek. Launch at Rock Point boat launch and paddle north to make a 5.1-mile loop around Recreation Creek, Wocus Cut, Crystal Creek, and Pelican Bay. With two cars, you can put in at Malone Springs and take out at Rocky Point (3 miles one-way; no portage necessary). Note: Wocus Cut may be dry by late August. Since the Rocky Point launch has access to Klamath Lake, you're likely to encounter motorized boats on Pelican Bay, the southern loop of the trail.

WHAT TO SEE

The aspen, cottonwood, and willow along the lake's edge offer shelter to flycatchers and warblers. Most birds in the basin stop by Upper Klamath sometime during the year; look for pintails, mallards, gadwalls, and canvasbacks. Other commonly observed species include

Gadwall

white pelicans (nesting in the marsh), Canada geese, bald eagles, and osprey. The secretive yellow rail sometimes winters in the marsh. Difficult to see, the rail stays hidden rather than flying when flushed; it is most active at night.

Modoc NWR
Alturas, California

Fog rises off the Modoc NWR wetlands.

Spread over the northeast corner of California, the Modoc Plateau is a wild and little-visited land formed from 25 to 5 million years ago during the great volcanic eruptions that spread lava across parts of Idaho, Washington, Oregon, and Nevada and into this section of California. The plateau lies on the western edge of the Great Basin desert, the nation's largest desert. There is an exhilarating sense of space and exquisite vistas at the Modoc refuge, situated in the great bowl of this high desert plateau. Pronghorns race across the desert, and sandhill cranes raise their young here.

HISTORY

In 1960 one of the original homesteaded ranches in the area came up for sale. The Davis Ranch included the land lying in the cup of the confluence of the North and South forks of the Pitt River and was dotted with remnant wetlands and natural springs. The family had acquired most water rights in the area, so the new Modoc refuge came with long-standing water rights. The 11-square-mile (7,018-acre) refuge, the former ranch, was established in 1960 to protect migratory waterfowl. It attracts 30,000 visitors annually.

GETTING THERE

From Sacramento, drive east on I-80 to Reno, then north 169 mi. on US 395 to Alturas. At the south end of Alturas, turn east on County Rd. 56—at the Modoc (MOW-dock) County Museum (following signs to the refuge)—and drive about 1 mi., crossing the railroad tracks. Turn south at the first paved road (County Rd. 115) and drive 1 mi. to the refuge entry road (first road on the left). Drive about 0.7 mi. to refuge office.

■ **SEASON:** Refuge open year-round.

■ **HOURS:** Open daylight hours. Headquarters open Mon.–Fri., 8 a.m.–4:30 p.m.

■ **ADDRESS:** Modoc NWR, P.O. Box 1610, Alturas, CA 96101
■ **TELEPHONE:** 530/233-3572

TOURING MODOC

■ **BY AUTOMOBILE:** A 2.5-mile gravel auto-tour route starting at refuge headquarters loops around Teal Pond.

■ **BY FOOT:** The 0.5-mile Wigeon Pond trail circles an interpretive area.

■ **BY BICYCLE:** The refuge has no bike trails. Bicyclists may use the auto-tour route, and public roads at Dorris Reservoir are open to bicycles April–September.

■ **BY CANOE, KAYAK, OR BOAT:** Dorris Reservoir is open to both motorized and nonmotorized boating April–September. The reservoir has two boat launches and two other vehicle access points.

■ **BY HORSEBACK:** An equestrian trail crossing the dam at Dorris Reservoir is open April–September. Riders may also use auto roads at the reservoir during the same period. Parking is available at both the north and south ends of the trail.

WHAT TO SEE

■ **LANDSCAPE AND CLIMATE** The refuge lies in the confluence of the North and South forks of the Pitt River, which drains the plateau and eventually runs southwest to disappear into Shasta Lake, created by the damming of the Sacramento River. The Warner Mountains, an uplifted volcanic fault block to the east of the refuge, are the westernmost range in the basin and range topography of Nevada. Open ponds, marshes, and sagebrush uplands are all found in the refuge, which lies at 4,365 feet and shares the typical temperature range of the high desert: cold winters (0–40 degrees Fahrenheit) and hot summers (40–100 degrees). Rainfall is 12.5 inches annually, putting it slightly above the accepted 10 inches that defines a desert. Total snowfall is around 4 feet, with it being unusual to have more than 6 inches on the ground at any one time.

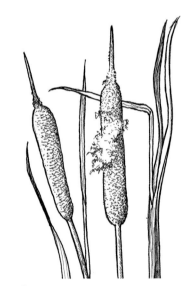

Cattails

■ **PLANT LIFE**

Wetlands Hardstem bulrushes—known in California as tules—provide cover for nesting birds, including Virginia and sora rails. The tules, which can grow to 9 feet, are found in both deep and shallow water and in marshy ground around the ponds. Growing from June through September, the tules' fruit provides food for ducks, shorebirds, and marsh birds. Both geese and muskrats eat the stems. Cattails also grow in the wetlands.

Arid lands Rabbit brush, one of the first plants to appear in disturbed or burned areas in the high desert, is mostly leafless and spreads its golden-yellow blooms along the roadsides during the fall when other plants have ceased flow-

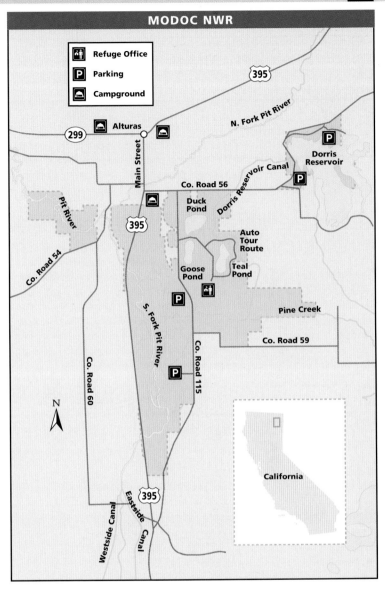

MODOC NWR

Refuge Office
Parking
Campground

395
N. Fork Pit River
Alturas
299
Main Street
Dorris Reservoir
Dorris Reservoir Canal
Co. Road 56
Duck Pond
395
Auto Tour Route
Goose Pond
Teal Pond
Pine Creek
Co. Road 59
Pit River
Co. Road 54
S. Fork Pit River
Co. Road 115
Co. Road 60
N
California
Eastside Canal
Westside Canal
395

ering. If the rabbit brush, which spreads its seeds by wind, is not in bloom, it can be recognized by its spreading branches, which give the appearance of a broom. Look for it in open areas. Several species of the plant grow in the western deserts; the Mojave Desert species is also called rubber brush because of its high rubber content.

The western juniper presents a conundrum to refuge managers. A thirsty and robust tree, it can suck dry seeps and springs, but its berries are a favorite of Townsend's warblers during winter when they move down from higher elevations. Mountain and western bluebirds, jays, and robins, along with coyotes and deer mice, also feast on juniper berries. The fast-spreading junipers, however, invade the sagebrush grasslands needed by the sage grouse, pronghorn, and deer.

SANDHILL CRANES Coyotes and sandhill cranes engage in a running battle of wits. If the coyote wins, a sandhill colt, not yet ready to fly, becomes dinner for the coyote, who views the young birds as meat on sticks. If mother and father sandhill win, their colts may reach the age where they can fly to safety.

The cranes rely on their acute vision to see predators approaching in the distance. Their preference for nesting is in open fields and wet meadows that allow them to see trouble coming and that have a nearby marsh offering escape and cover. If a coyote appears, the colt lies flat while the parents dash off, feigning injury to lure the coyote away from the nest. If approached closely, the colt disappears into the marsh, moving low to the ground through cover, and may pop up on the other side of the marsh.

The sandhills are tall, brownish-gray birds with bright red bald patches atop their heads. They fly with stately wingbeats, their long necks extended. The cries of several hundred migrating cranes sounds like dozens of iron wheels turning on dry axles. The sandhills' dance is fascinating to watch; with wings extended, a crane will bow to another crane, make stiff-legged hops or giant leaps into the air, and carefully toss sticks into the air. Most of the dancing occurs in spring for courtship, but any disturbance may engender a dancing display. When a pair mates, it remains together for life. The cranes breed in northeast California and east and central Oregon and Washington. The Modoc refuge supports the largest breeding group in California.

Junipers are fire-sensitive, and controlled burns are sometimes used to thin them.

Sagebrush dominates the sagebrush steppe, sometimes reaching heights of 9 feet and growing in dense stands. Its deep root system (to 10 feet) helps it survive in areas of limited rain.

■ ANIMAL LIFE

Birds A warm-water spring at the edge of Teal Pond prevents the edge of the pond from freezing over, a small geological anomaly in the snow-covered winter refuge that has attracted a dozen bald eagles. The eagles hang out in the willows and cottonwood growing at the edge of the pond and can usually be seen from November to March.

Among the 246 bird species spotted at Modoc, at least 76 species nest on the refuge, including four of the five grebes observed there. The eared grebe in its breeding plumage is one of the more exotic birds to be found at Modoc. Its red eye is surrounded by a silky tuft of golden feathers, and a black crest looking like a Mohawk haircut sits atop its head. Its black plumage fades to mottled gray and white in winter. Found at Modoc from April to September (the Modoc Plateau is one of its chief breeding grounds), the grebe performs a fascinating courtship ritual. The couple swims side by side, suddenly throwing back their heads, then face each other and finally rush side by side through the water. The western and Clark's grebes, also with red eyes, can be distinguished by their long necks, white on the underside and black on the back, and their mottled black and gray plumage. Similar in appearance, the western grebe has a greenish yellow bill while the Clark's grebe's bill is bright yellow. Both practice the same courtship ritual as the eared grebe.

Sandhill crane

Mammals Twelve species of bats—along with gophers, squirrels, mice, rabbits, and rats—visit Modoc. Larger mammals include porcupines, coyotes, raccoons, minks, badgers, mountain lions, bobcats, mule deer, and pronghorns. The pronghorns are North America's fastest animals, but they don't like to jump. Arriving at a fence, they try to crawl under it. The fencing of the West aided in the decimation of these beautiful animals, which can sometimes be seen during the summer on the refuge or surrounding lands.

Reptiles and amphibians The Great Basin spadefoot toad survives in hot, dry areas by using its strong spade-shaped foot to dig itself into the ground. It uses the horny scrapers on its hind feet to dig backwards into a cavity that allows it to beat the heat. Six species of lizards—including the sagebrush, western collared, and side-blotched—live at Modoc along with seven species of snakes, including the western rattlesnake. Watch for it in the crevices of rocks and sheltered under vegetation.

Fish Nine species of native fish are found on the refuge, including the Pit-Klamath brook lamprey, Goose Lake redband trout, and Sacramento squawfish. Nonnatives include brown and rainbow trout, largemouth bass, and channel catfish.

ACTIVITIES

■ **CAMPING:** Lava Beds National Monument, with its fascinating collection of 200 lava tubes and caves open for exploration, is about 60 miles northwest of Alturas. The monument has a 40-site campground.

■ **SWIMMING:** Dorris Reservoir is open to swimming. To reach the reservoir, continue on County Road 56 past the turn to the refuge. Parking is on the west and north sides of the reservoir.

MODOC HUNTING AND FISHING SEASONS

Hunting
(Seasons may vary)

	Jan	Feb	Mar	Apr	May	Jun	Jul	Aug	Sep	Oct	Nov	Dec
geese	■									■	■	■
duck	■									■	■	■
coot	■									■	■	■
gallinule	■									■	■	■
snipe	■											

Fishing

	Jan	Feb	Mar	Apr	May	Jun	Jul	Aug	Sep	Oct	Nov	Dec
largemouth bass		■	■	■	■	■	■	■	■	■		
channel catfish		■	■	■	■	■	■	■	■	■		
redband trout		■	■	■	■	■	■	■	■	■		
rainbow trout		■	■	■	■	■	■	■	■	■		
brown trout		■	■	■	■	■	■	■	■	■		

The hunting area is open during the first weekend of hunting season and every Saturday, Tuesday, and Thursday thereafter. Dorris Reservoir is open to fishing during daylight hours except during waterfowl hunting season. For more information on the current hunting and fishing regulations for Modoc NWR, including license requirements, seasons, and bag limits, consult refuge office.

■ **WILDLIFE OBSERVATION:** The spring and fall migrations bring Canada geese (white-fronted geese are present only in spring), mallards, teal, gadwalls, wigeons, and pintails to Modoc. As many as 700 tundra swans arrive along with sandhill cranes, waterbirds, shorebirds, and warblers.

In summer, nesting birds include ducks, geese, willets, avocets, black-necked stilts, and killdeer. Other summer residents are white pelicans, double-crested cormorants, egrets, terns, gulls, and herons.

■ **PHOTOGRAPHY:** One photography blind is set up for good shots of waterfowl and raptors. Don't miss a photo of the bald eagles in the willows and cottonwood by the hot spring.

■ **HIKES AND WALKS:** A kiosk off US 395 south of Alturas offers good views across a grain field where pronghorns can often be seen from April–October. Hiking at Dorris Reservoir is permitted throughout the winter, although the area is closed to horses and bicycles.

Sacramento NWR Complex
Sacramento NWR, Sacramento River NWR, Colusa NWR
Willows, California

A refuge visitor takes a photograph from the observation platform at the Sacramento NWR Complex.

A plane flies overhead, and 2,000 snow geese flutter into the sky. Their discordant cries, sounding much like the barking of a pack of hounds, break the early-morning stillness. Nearby, 500,000 ducks float on the marshes, some diving for food, others sheltering among the tules. The seven national wildlife refuges of the Sacramento Valley—one of the most important wintering areas for waterfowl on the Pacific Flyway—provide shelter and food for millions of waterfowl arriving from their summer homes in Alaska, Canada, and Siberia. Three of the refuges—Sacramento, Sacramento River, and Colusa—are open to the public for viewing of this overwhelming gathering of birds.

HISTORY

With the coming of the rains in late November, the once vast grasslands of the Sacramento Valley began to grow, covering the valley floor with a velvety carpet of green. Rivers flowing out of the Sierra Nevada ran swift with storm runoff and overflowed, filling the spreading seasonal wetlands—freshwater marshes and vernal pools—in time for the arrival of millions of wintering waterfowl. By early summer the grass was dry, transforming the green to a carpet of bright golden tan, the color that still defines summertime California.

Early travelers saw less beauty in the Colusa Plains, where the Sacramento refuges are now located, calling them "a swamp . . . a vast, treeless prairie . . . worthless alkali." There is little to recognize now in these early descriptions. The grasslands are 99 percent gone, replaced by farm fields made green with irrigation water pumped from the rivers that are now dammed and no longer overflow to fill the bordering wetlands (except in El Niño flood years). The refuge marshes, which replace the natural seasonal wetlands, are all man-made and as carefully managed as the agricultural fields that surround them.

GETTING THERE

Begin your exploration of the refuges at the complex's Visitor Center. From San Francisco drive north on I-80. Take the I-505 cutoff to Redding north to I-5. About 18 mi. north of Colusa, take the Norman Rd.–Princeton exit and turn right. Drive north on County Rd. 99W (the frontage road) to the entrance to the Sacramento NWR, where you will find the Visitor Center. From Redding drive south on I-5. About 7 mi. south of Willows, take the Norman Rd.–Princeton exit. Cross the freeway and turn north on County Rd. 99W to the refuge entrance.

■ **SEASON:** Refuges open year-round.

■ **HOURS:** Open sunrise to sunset.

■ **ADDRESS:** Sacramento NWR Complex, 752 County Rd. 99W, Willows, CA 95988

■ **TELEPHONE:** 530/934-2801

TOURING SACRAMENTO NWR COMPLEX

■ **BY AUTOMOBILE:** Nine miles of auto-tour routes allow visitors to explore Sacramento and Colusa refuges.

■ **BY FOOT:** There are three hiking trails totaling 3.7 miles on the Sacramento, Colusa, and Sacramento River refuges.

WHAT TO SEE

■ **LANDSCAPE AND CLIMATE** Three of the refuges—Colusa, Delevan, and Sacramento—lie in the Colusa Basin near the base of the Sutter Buttes, an unusual landmark in the unending flatness of the Sacramento Valley. The buttes rise 2,132 feet above the valley floor and are the only geological feature that interrupts the valley flatlands. The refuges lie directly in the center of the Sacramento Valley (the northern half of the Great Central Valley), encircled by the Cascades to the north, the Coast Range to the west, and the Sierra Nevada to the east. The Sacramento River flows south through the valley; a sixth refuge, the Sacramento River NWR, protects riparian woodland along 90 miles of the Sacramento River in several non-contiguous units between Red Bluff and Princeton.

The valley shares California's Mediterranean climate—rain in the winter and spring (an average of 19.5 inches annually), cold winters (January, 34–64 degrees Fahrenheit) and hot, dry summers where the thermometer routinely approaches or exceeds 100 degrees (July, 58–104 degrees). An inversion layer hangs over the valley, trapping cold air flowing off the mountains in winter and creating the dense, ground-hugging fog—

Smartweed

called tule fog—responsible for the nearly annual chain collisions on the freeways. In summer the inversion layer traps the valley's smog.

■ PLANT LIFE

Wetlands The refuges' wetlands are divided into seasonally flooded marsh, watergrass (or millet) marsh, and permanent ponds. More than 350 plant species are known to grow on the refuges, but, typical of the northern Sacramento Valley, 43 percent are not native. Plants common to California's wetlands can be found throughout the refuges—cattails, tules, and a number of rushes, including tuberous and salt-marsh bulrush and Baltic, common toad, congested toad, and Pacific rushes.

The faint odor of methane emanating from the marshes is caused by the decaying plant and animal matter. Bacteria living in the thick, black muck release the gas that gives the marsh its odor. Plants living in the marsh have adapted an interesting method of coping with oxygen-poor soils. The floating primrose (yellow flowers) has air-filled tubes that run from its shiny green leaves to their roots, forming a tube through which the plant can breathe. Cattails and bulrush have air-filled cells around their breathing tubes that provide support for their tall stems.

Swamp smartweed, growing in the quiet water of sloughs and ponds, is a member of the smartweed family; its broad leaves were used in early days on human behinds for treating piles, as poultices for external bleeding, and for itchy skin diseases. The name comes from its old nickname, arsmart, because of what it did to the behind.

Open waters Goodding's black willow and narrowleaf willow (recognized by its grayish linear leaves) are the most common small trees on the refuges, growing along streams. The large valley oak with its massive spreading limbs is present along with western sycamore, box elder, blue elderberry, wildrose, and blackberry vines. Another common riparian tree, Fremont cottonwood, can be found throughout the refuges. The beautiful California wild grape is a woody vine that grows to 30 feet, climbing into trees in riparian habitat by tendrils opposite its large, lobed leaves that look much like those of cultivated grapes. Its purplish fruit grows in clusters but doesn't have much pulp.

The refuges' vernal pools offer a spectacular flood of color during spring bloom with yellow goldfields, white smooth-stemmed popcorn-flowers, and three species of downingia—Hoover's, harlequin, and folded. The harlequin downingia often forms blue rings around deeper pools or turns shallow pools into a solid mass of blue. (See sidebar on vernal pools in Merced NWR.)

■ **Grasslands** The grasses growing on the refuges come from such faraway places as Eurasia, Africa, Europe, and South America. Hairy orcuttgrass is a rare native growing on the dry beds of vernal pools. Another grass

American coot

associated with vernal pools is Lemmon's canary grass, found in shallow pools in upland grassy fields. Ithuriel's spear (grass nut), one of the brodiaeas, flowers in purplish white clusters from April to June. It takes its name from Milton's *Paradise Lost*. Ithuriel was the angel commissioned by Gabriel to search through Heaven for Satan, who had tried to sneak into the Garden. Since the slightest touch of Ithuriel's spear exposed deceit, his quest was successful.

One of California's most exquisite wildflowers is the mariposa lily. The plant grows from an underground bulb and has long, linear leaves, but its bowl-shaped flower, usually white and splotched with intense color at the inner base of its bowl, gives the plant its reputation.

■ **ANIMAL LIFE**

Birds Some of the most spectacular concentrations of waterfowl on the continent can be seen at the Sacramento refuges. Two million ducks and three-quarters of a million geese migrate to the refuges—about 44 percent of waterfowl traveling the Pacific Flyway winters in the Sacramento Valley. Many of the ducks were bred and raised in the prairie pothole region in the Midwest, and most of the geese arrive from the Canadian Arctic, Alaska, and Siberia. As the Klamath Basin freezes over and its waterfowl fly south, there may be more than 2 million birds on the Sacramento refuges. Since 1937 approximately 270 species of birds have been observed on the refuges.

The rare tule goose, a subspecies of the white-fronted goose, can be seen along with snow, Ross', Pacific white-fronted, and Canada geese. Tundra swans appear occasionally, and 20 species of ducks, a number of them remaining to nest on the refuges, frequent the area.

Birds of prey arrive to feed on the waterfowl, including eight species of hawks and two eagles, the bald and golden. Barn, western screech, short-eared, and great horned owls all nest on the refuges; and northern pygmy, northern saw-whet, and long-eared owls occasionally pass through.

The tiny rufous hummingbird (3.5 to 4 inches), a rare visitor to the refuges, migrates between southeast Alaska and Mexico. Two other hummingbirds, Anna's and Allen's, nest on the refuges.

Mammals When a small, black-and-white animal turns its backside to you and lifts its tail, you had better not be too close or you will end up smelling like a skunk. Unlike many other mammals that use their scent glands to establish territory or for social communication, striped skunks use theirs to repel predators. They can spray their foul odor at will from their anal glands to distances of 9 to 13 feet. Known by the nickname of "black-and-white woodpussy" (because of their vague resemblance to cats), striped skunks are among the most widespread of California mammals, living everywhere except the Mojave, the High Sierra, and Colorado Desert. The striped skunk's smaller relative, the spotted skunk, sometimes puts on a show to scare off intruders (although it is not necessary as its scent is equally obnoxious); it stamps its feet or does a handstand, its tail and hind legs straight up in the air. Despite the fact that they are elegant and beautiful animals—and quite friendly—another reason to avoid skunks is that they are a source of rabies.

The Sacramento refuges are home to 28 other mammals, including black-tailed deer, beavers, red and gray foxes, coyotes, and six species of bats.

Reptiles and amphibians The pond turtle's carapace (or shell) blends perfectly with the fallen logs on which it likes to bask—its colors are dark brown, olive, or blackish with spots or lines of brown or black. A silent, hidden approach is necessary for viewing the pond turtle— California's only abundant native turtle—because it slips into the water at the

Striped skunk

approach of humans or predators. Look for pond turtles from February through mid-November on partially submerged logs, mats of cattails, rocks, or open mud banks. They hibernate underwater in bottom mud.

Gopher snakes are found on the refuge, living everywhere in California except the High Sierra. These large yellowish or cream-colored snakes kill their prey by constriction and shelter in rodent burrows and under rocks and fallen logs, coming out when the weather is pleasant. If annoyed it hisses loudly, vibrates its tail, and sometimes flattens its head. Because of this behavior, it is sometimes mistaken for a rattlesnake and killed, leaving one less snake to rid your garden of gophers. A rattler can always be distinguished by the rattles at the end of its body. If winters are cold, gopher snakes will hibernate, often with other species of snakes.

Fish Native chinook salmon return to breeding streams off the Sacramento River, and the river is also home to white crappie, largemouth bass, native steelhead, and yellow and brown bullhead.

ACTIVITIES

See entries under individual refuges.

■ **PUBLICATIONS:** *Birding Northern California* by Jean Richmond; Mt. Diablo Audubon Society. *California Mammals* by E. W. Jameson Jr. and Hans J. Peeters; University of California Press. *Common Riparian Plants of California* by Phyllis M. Faber and Robert F. Holland; Pickleweed Press. *Poisonous Plants of California* by Thomas C. Fuller and Elizabeth McClintock; University of California Press.

Wetlands scene, Sacramento NWR

Sacramento NWR
Willows, California

The showpiece of the six Sacramento Valley refuges, the Sacramento NWR is a rich complex of man-made marshes so integrated into the landscape that they appear natural. Streams lined with a luxuriant growth of willow and cottonwoods meander through the refuge, and a beautiful row of Red River eucalyptus trees lines the entry to the refuge. (The eucalyptus, whose towering, graceful shapes can be seen throughout California's foothills and valleys, arrived in California from Australia; they have become a point of contention in some areas, where they are cut down because they are an introduced species.) Visiting the Sacramento NWR in December or January, when hundreds of thousands of ducks and geese swirl overhead, is one of the peak experiences for refuge visitors.

HISTORY

The lands that are now the Sacramento NWR were considered worthless by early settlers, dismissed as "goose-lands" and "so flat that the water does not run off it readily, and it is alkali." The first attempt to farm the land in the 1870s failed (geese ate the wheat, and there was no summer water), but by 1910 farmers realized that the layer of hardpan underlying the topsoil that prevented water from draining made a perfect paddy for growing rice, which became the dominant crop in the area. During the Great Depression the ranch that is now the refuge failed and was transferred in 1937 to the federal government, becoming the Sacramento Migratory Waterfowl Refuge (now the Sacramento NWR).

Wood duck

By the late 1930s the vast seasonal marshlands fed by the Sacramento River during spring runoff were mostly gone. What remained of the marshes, the winter home of 80 percent of the birds using the Pacific Flyway, had been drained, contoured, and turned into orchards and rice paddies. The birds continued to arrive, crowding into what wetlands were left and dining on the farmer's rice. Helping the farmers was the chief impetus for the establishment of the new refuge, which was intended to provide a place for the waterfowl and help keep them out of the rice paddies and grain fields.

There were no remaining natural wetlands on the property. Members of the Civilian Conservation Corps constructed the entire network of permanent ponds and seasonal marshes, flooded with water purchased from local water districts.

The 16.8-square-mile (10,783-acre) refuge, a showplace in the valley, welcomes around 60,000 visitors annually.

GETTING THERE

From Sacramento drive north on I-5. About 18 mi. north of the turnoff to Colusa, take the Norman Rd.–Princeton exit and turn right to County Rd. 99W (the frontage road). Drive north on County Rd. 99W to the refuge entrance.

■ **SEASON:** Refuge open year-round.

■ **HOURS:** Open sunrise to sunset. Visitor Center open Oct.–March, Mon.–Sun., 7:30 a.m.–4 p.m. Open same hours April–Sept., weekdays only.

■ **FEES:** A fee of $3 per car is paid at the unstaffed entrance kiosk, where a teller machine that takes credit cards will give change in dollar coins.

■ **ADDRESS:** Sacramento NWR, c/o Sacramento NWR Complex, 752 County Road 99W, Willows, CA 95988

■ **TELEPHONE:** 530/934-2801

TOURING SACRAMENTO

■ **BY AUTOMOBILE:** A 6-mile auto-tour route on the Sacramento refuge meanders by marshes and streams and includes a viewing platform at the halfway point.

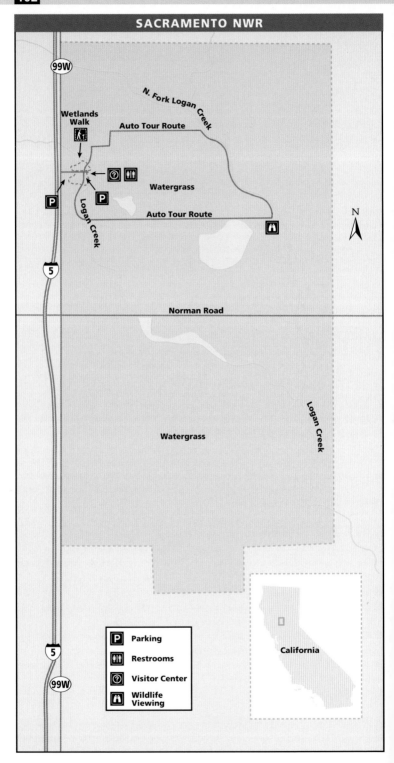

FRESHWATER MARSHES A marsh is low—or not there at all—on most lists of scenic splendors, but these humble bodies of shallow water are among the most productive ecosystems on earth. Confusion about marshes usually begins with deciding what to call them. Here is a run-down on the characteristics of different types of marsh that you will encounter in your exploration of our national wildlife refuges.

Wetlands is the term used to describe all marshes, swamps, and flood-plains.

Moist-soil areas are meadowlike areas that are seasonally flooded but dry quickly. Look for wildflowers, rushes, and spike rushes.

Shallow marshes are usually 1 foot to 2 feet in depth with vegetation that includes smartweed and arrowhead. Their fluctuating shoreline shrinks as summer heat evaporates some of their water.

Deep marshes average around 3 feet in depth and contain the plants most often associated with marshes—cattails, tules, and bulrushes.

Swamps differ from marshes by having trees and shrubs growing in them.

Bottomlands flood, often deeply, when rivers overflow but dry out quickly because of easy runoff.

Lakes and reservoirs are deep enough bodies of water that plants do not grow in them (except around shallow edges).

Tidal saltwater marshes are a mix of saltwater and freshwater; their depth changes with incoming and outgoing tides.

In addition to providing a home and food to a wide variety of inver-tebrates, fish, birds, and mammals, marshes serve the important function of filtering pollutants out of the water and of recharging groundwater aquifers. The cattails that grow in the marshes also are excellent filters of pollutants. Ninety percent of California's marshes have been drained and plowed under. The next time you see one, instead of driving by, stop and get acquainted with one of these rapidly disappearing little gems of nature. Their subtle beauty is sure to charm you.

■ **BY FOOT:** The 2-mile Wetlands Walk loops around shallow marshes, along Logan Creek, and by vernal pools and permanent deep ponds. The trailhead is next to the Visitor Center, and a cutoff at the halfway point allows visitors wishing a shorter walk to return to their cars.

■ **BY BICYCLE:** Bicyclists can use the auto-tour route. Note: The route is grav-eled and somewhat difficult for bicycles. It is recommended that you lock your bikes and walk the trails.

ACTIVITIES

■ **WILDLIFE OBSERVATION:** The best months for viewing waterfowl are November and December, although birds begin arriving in October and com-plete their departure in February. Look in the flooded marsh for snow and Ross' geese, northern shovelers, teal, bufflehead, ruddy ducks, and ring-necked ducks. March through May sees the arrival of shorebirds probing the mudflats of the receding seasonal marshes for invertebrates. Look for sandpipers, black-necked stilts, avocets, and curlews. In summertime (June–August), watch for song-birds—warblers, tanagers, and orioles—and herons, egrets, and grebes. Remember the midday heat, and visit early morning or late afternoon. Deer, otter, and muskrats may be seen. Fall marks the beginning of winter migration, but wait for winter to see the great flocks of birds that make this refuge a must stop on every bird lover's itinerary.

■ **PHOTOGRAPHY:** The Sacramento refuge has two roomy photo blinds. Both require wading through marsh water to reach and entry before sunrise. The blinds are available Tuesdays, Thursdays, and Saturdays from October to March for a fee of $10 a day. Reservations begin in August, and photographers are limited to four days per week. The blinds have logs in front of them on which birds sometimes perch. A telephoto lens is needed for good photographs.

■ **HIKES AND WALKS:** While on the Wetlands Walk, look up tree trunks for the nest boxes that have been placed for wood ducks. These artificial nests are intended to replace natural tree cavities that have disappeared with the loss of riparian habitat. The nests are also used by owls, honeybees, and woodpeckers.

Mallards

Sacramento River NWR
Willows, California

It is only on the Llano Seco Unit of the Sacramento River NWR that visitors can acquire an acute sense of the unvarying flatness of the Sacramento Valley. The area of Llano Seco (pronounced YAH-no SEK-oh) open to the public is a 0.9-square-mile (600-acre) marsh engineered out of a field of rice stubble in 1993 and, consequently, without trees to obstruct the view of the flatness. A raised platform allows a view of the marsh and, across the road, of the totally flat farm fields that extend one after the other to the Sierra Nevada foothills.

Where the riparian forest along the edges of the Sacramento River has been left untouched, the vegetation is so thick it appears to be a jungle. Wild grapevines coil up trees, then hang down in great loops, completely enveloping the trees. Towering cottonwoods, sycamores, and oaks branch together, forming a cool canopy that shades the ground below. The hush, broken only by birdsong, is immense. The Sacramento River NWR stretches out along 90 miles of the river between Red Bluff and Princeton, a series of disconnected patches of riverine

POISON OAK Brush against a patch of poison oak the first time, and nothing will happen. But make that mistake a second time, and you will very likely be in misery from one to three days later. Poison oak is a beautiful plant with glossy green leaves growing in groups of three. (They look like oak leaves.) In fall the leaves turn a stunning bright red or orange before dropping. Unfortunately, this pretty bush—or vine (it loves to climb into a nearby tree)—is California's most prevalent poisonous plant. It contains urushiol, a toxic allergen present on the leaves and stems. The slightest touch will cause around 70 percent of the population to develop a miserable, itching rash if for a second time they touch the plant or anything that has come in contact with the plant.

The only sure way to avoid getting poison oak is to avoid all contact with it and with anything that has touched it. (If you are out hiking in poison oak country, do not hug your dog, for he has no doubt run through some poison oak.) Wearing long pants and long-sleeved shirts can help. Wash them in hot water as soon as you get home. Also shower as quickly as possible using strong soap to remove any urushiol and cool water so you won't open your pores.

If these admittedly dubious precautions don't help and you find yourself watching a rash appear that soon turns into blisters oozing a liquid that eventually dries into a brittle crust, then grit your teeth and be prepared for two or three weeks of agonizing itching. (Don't scratch.) If your case of poison oak is severe enough, a doctor will give you a shot of cortisone; but most sufferers apply calamine lotion.

Seasonal advice: Winter hikers, take care. Poison oak is just as poisonous in winter, but, without its leaves, it appears as an innocuous bare woody stalk.

habitat. The restoration of these units imitates what was there before Shasta Dam stopped the natural flow of the Sacramento—marshes that attract thousands of waterfowl and a dense forest used by songbirds. Llano Seco is the only unit open to the public.

HISTORY

The Llano Seco Rancho was the last Mexican land grant in California to remain under single ownership. It was bought in 1861 by J. Parrott, a prominent San Francisco banker. The rancho became one of the most profitable grain and livestock ranches in California, and an irrigation system installed in the 1920s allowed the ranch to expand to dairy, almonds, rice, corn, and alfalfa.

Poison oak

The 23-square-mile (14,940-acre) refuge was established on part of the rancho in 1989 to preserve and restore riparian habitat. It welcomes around 22,500 visitors annually.

GETTING THERE

From Chico, drive west on CA 32 (8th St.). Where the road makes a 90-degree turn to the right, turn left instead and drive south 4.7 mi. Turn right onto Ord Bend Rd., drive 3.1 mi. through Dayton and turn south on Seven Mile Ln. Continue 2.1 mi. and turn west into the refuge.

■ **SEASON:** Refuge open year-round.
■ **HOURS:** Open sunrise to sunset.
■ **ADDRESS:** Sacramento River NWR, c/o Sacramento NWR Complex, 752 County Rd. 99W, Willows, CA 95988-9639
■ **TELEPHONE:** 530/934-2801

TOURING SACRAMENTO RIVER

■ **BY FOOT:** A 0.66-mile trail leads to a second viewing platform. The first platform is at the parking lot and is wheelchair-accessible.

ACTIVITIES

■ **WILDLIFE OBSERVATION:** In summer the marsh is allowed to dry out, and wildlife is spare. Visit in December or January to view sandhill cranes and waterfowl. The two observation platforms offer an excellent view of the adjoining marsh.

■ **HIKES AND WALKS:** When completed, the Sacramento River NWR will be the largest riparian restoration program in the country and will have doubled riparian habitat in the Sacramento Valley. (The list for habitat loss in California is endless: 99 percent of the grasslands gone, 94 percent of the wetlands, and 89 percent of riparian habitat.) The Llano Seco marsh has meandering streams within it and islands of various sizes and shapes. Unless one is aware that it once was a rice field, the marsh appears totally natural.

> **HUNTING AND FISHING**
> Both spaced blinds and free-roaming areas are available. Waterfowl such as **geese**, **duck** and **coot** may be hunted Sept. through Jan. (**White-fronted geese** may not be shot after Dec. 14.) **Snipe** may be hunted Sept. through Jan., and **pheasant** hunting is permitted Nov. and Dec. An area for pheasant hunting only is reserved in Colusa NWR.

Best viewing at the refuge occurs from mid-November through January, when peak waterfowl migrations occur. Thousands of ducks—gadwall, mallard, shoveler, pintail, and green-winged teal—can be seen. Peregrine falcons and bald eagles migrate through along with white-crowned sparrows and American avocets. Redwinged blackbirds and ring-necked pheasants are year-round residents; and yellow-headed blackbirds nest in the marshes near the second viewing platform.

Colusa NWR
Colusa, California

Surrounded by rice fields, winter wheat, and orchards, the Colusa refuge enjoys the magnificent backdrop of the Sutter Buttes. In the middle of the vast flatlands of the Sacramento Valley, the buttes soar 2,132 feet above the valley floor, the only vertical relief in the entire valley. Colusa refuge lies in the flatlands west of the Sacramento River, its man-made marshes mimicking the historic seasonal marshes that appeared each winter with the coming of the rains.

Lesser snow geese

HISTORY

The refuge was established in 1945 under the authority of the Lea Act and Migratory Bird Conservation Act. The Lea Act became law to alleviate severe crop losses farmers were experiencing because of depredation by wintering ducks and geese. The act authorized the acquisition of habitat for the waterfowl in order to help keep them off farmlands. The 6.3-square-mile (4,040-acre) refuge draws around 15,500 visitors annually.

GETTING THERE

Return to Norman Rd. from the Sacramento NWR and drive east to Princeton. Drive south to Colusa, turn west on CA 20, and follow directional signs to the refuge.
- **SEASON:** Refuge open year-round.
- **HOURS:** Open sunrise to sunset.
- **ADDRESS:** Colusa NWR, c/o Sacramento NWR Complex, 752 County Rd. 99W, Willows, CA 95988
- **TELEPHONE:** 530/934-2801

WHAT TO SEE

Long frequented by hunters, Colusa has a 1-mile Discovery Walk (open to hikers) that passes a dense riparian slough and a marsh. An auto-tour route of 3 miles meanders through freshwater wetlands. Bicyclists may ride the auto-tour route. Note: The road is graveled, making it difficult going for bicycles. The spectacular gathering of winter waterfowl in the Sacramento Valley can be seen on the refuge, where more than 350,000 ducks and some 150,000 geese spend the winter. Look for snow and Ross's geese along with pintail, green-winged teal, shovelers, mallards, and gadwalls. The influx of winter migrants includes white-faced ibis, white-crowned sparrows, American avocets, and yellow-rumped warblers.

Like all refuges in the Sacramento complex, Colusa's marshes are heavily managed. Wetlands are drawn down in late March and April to allow the sprouting of plants that will eventually feed the waterfowl, and are then reflooded beginning in August.

Garter snakes are one of the two reptiles commonly found in California's riparian habitat (the other is the state's only native turtle, the pond turtle). The Colusa refuge has a high density of giant garter snakes, which reach 27 feet in length and live only near permanent fresh water. They feed on fish, frogs, birds, and small mammals. Excellent swimmers, they wait motionless underwater until an unwary fish swims too close. Their method of repelling attackers is unique: They curl around the predator and defecate. A noxious-smelling secretion from their musk glands is mixed with the feces. The snake hopes this combination will convince the predator that it is not a tasty meal.

Giant garter snake

A population of about 40 black-tailed deer live on the refuge along with raccoons and black-tailed jack rabbits. Year-round bird residents include ring-necked pheasants, herons, egrets, and red-winged blackbirds.

The Sutter Buttes, near the refuge, are a point of major interest. This former volcano began forming around 1.5 million years ago with the intrusion of molten igneous rock. As surface water penetrated downward, turning to steam as it hit the hot rocks buried several thousand feet below the surface, a series of volcanic eruptions occurred, creating the buttes. The volcanic rocks of the buttes are similar to those found at the Cascade volcanoes, an indication that the buttes may be the southernmost point of the Cascade Mountains, even though the flat valley floor separates them by more than 100 miles.

SATELLITE REFUGES

■ **Delevan NWR, Butte Sink NWR, and Sutter NWR** Delevan, Butte Sink, and Sutter are satellite refuges in the Sacramento refuge complex. All have re-created marshes and are similar in appearance to the Sacramento and Colusa refuges. Butte Sink is totally closed to the public; Delevan and Sutter refuges are open for hunting.
■ **ADDRESS:** c/o Sacramento NWR Complex, 752 County Rd. 99W, Willows, CA 95988
■ **TELEPHONE:** 530/934-2801

Salinas River NWR
Castroville, California

Black-necked stilts foraging for food

The Salinas River flows south to north through the broad Salinas Valley (made famous by John Steinbeck) and continues past Monterey to empty into Monterey Bay and the Pacific. Shifting sand dunes and a secluded beach mark the river's exit into the ocean. This is the Salinas River NWR, a tiny, pristine corner of the California coast in an area where 90 percent of the Salinas Valley's marsh and wetlands has been plowed under by farmers and filled and built on by developers.

HISTORY

The Salinas River refuge was established in 1973 with a transfer of land from the U.S. Army and the U.S. Coast Guard. The small 0.6-square-mile (367-acre) refuge welcomes around 8,000 visitors annually.

GETTING THERE

From Monterey, drive north on US 1 about 11 mi. to the Del Monte exit (just south of the Salinas River). Turn left on Del Monte (it becomes a dirt road) and follow it to the refuge parking lot at the end of the road. Note: The dirt road becomes impassable after rains. Cars have been broken into at the parking lot. Take all valuables with you and leave nothing in the car that might be attractive to a thief.

■ **SEASON:** Refuge open year-round.
■ **HOURS:** Open daylight hours.
■ **ADDRESS:** Salinas River NWR, c/o San Francisco Bay Complex, P.O. Box 524 Newark, CA 94560-0524
■ **TELEPHONE:** 510/792-0222

WHAT TO SEE

■ **LANDSCAPE AND CLIMATE** Hiking the 0.5-mile Ocean Beach Trail offers a rare chance to see (but not to walk on) a coastal dune community—foredunes, coastal scrub dunes, and all the plants that create a colorful display of spring wild-flowers. Walking on the dunes is off limits because of the endangered plants growing there. The foredunes are constantly moving as sand deposited by the Salinas River is picked up and blown by the wind.

When visiting the refuge expect warm to hot and dry summers (40–102 degrees Fahrenheit) and moist, mild winters 20–81 degrees F.). Fog often bathes the coast during summer. Around 20 inches of rain falls annually at Salinas River, with January and February the wettest months.

■ PLANT LIFE

Few plants are equipped to survive in this volatile environment. They cope by sending down long taproots and growing low to the surface, creating a cover that helps stabilize the sand. Sand verbena forms a mat 2 to 3 feet across. Two varieties grow at Salinas River. The yellow-flowered verbena blooms from May to October. A second variety of verbena has rose-colored flowers blooming in dense clusters. Another pink bloomer is the sea rocket, and the beach evening primrose adds its bright yellow four-petaled flowers to the mix. The beach morning glory's rosy purple blooms add yet another hue to this colorful scene.

Behind the foredunes, coastal scrub dunes—less affected by windblown sand movement—are more stabilized and display two common California wildflowers, blue beach lupine and red-orange Monterey paintbrush. Gilia, a member of the phlox family with blue-purple blooms, is an endangered species found on the refuge as is the Monterey spineflower. The coast and dune buckwheats are host to the endangered Smith's blue butterfly. Plants in the scrub dunes begin to reach up rather than out—mock heather grows to a compact 2 feet in height. Its bright green leaves shade to tinges of rust as they mature; in late summer the mock heather's small, yellow flowers form a crown over the plant. The flowers give way to a fluff of cream–tan seeds.

American kestrel

■ ANIMAL LIFE

Birds The snowy plover is a rotund little bird with a tan back and white breast that looks as if its head is connected to its body without benefit of a neck. If the female is disturbed on her nest, she dashes across the sand, head down and tail depressed, then squats in the sand. The snowy plovers' coloration matches the sand so perfectly that it is almost impossible to see them unless they move. The plover's eggs are the same sand color speckled with black—also impossible to see. Like the least tern, snowy plovers lay their eggs in a depression in the dry sand above high tide line. And like the least tern, they are endangered because most of the California beaches have been taken over by people. Note: It is especially important to stay on the designated paths at Salinas Beach because it is so easy to step on a snowy plover egg without realizing it is there.

By visiting the refuge in winter, you my see wintering populations of dunlin, black-necked stilts, sanderlings, dowitchers, American avocets, and phalaropes. From 500 to 3,000 ducks (depending on the water supply) winter at Salinas River. Main species are the ruddy duck, mallard, green-winged and cinnamon teals, gadwall, and northern pintails.

HUNTING AND FISHING Hunting for **ducks**, **geese**, **coots**, and **common moorhens** is permitted in the refuge's hunting zone daily in Oct. and Nov.

Surf fishing is permitted at the beach.

Four species of raptors nest on the refuge—short-eared owls, northern harriers, black-shouldered kites, and American kestrels—and others hunt there—peregrine falcons, red-tailed hawks, golden eagles, and merlins.

San Diego NWR Complex

Sweetwater Marsh NWR, Tijuana Slough NWR,
San Diego NWR
Imperial Beach, California

Tijuana Slough NWR coastal marsh

Riding the bike path that follows the edge of the South San Diego Bay Unit of the San Diego NWR Complex, it is almost possible to forget that a million and a half people are living all around you. In one of the three most highly developed coastal areas in California (San Diego joins Los Angeles and the San Francisco Bay area), three national wildlife refuges preserve a small corner of the spreading coastal estuaries that once flourished wherever a California river rolled into the Pacific. The refuges are Tijuana Slough NWR, Sweetwater Marsh NWR, and the South San Diego Bay Unit of the San Diego NWR (dedicated in 1999, this new addition provides habitat for thousands of resident and overwintering waterfowl and shorebirds, protects the bay's remaining eelgrass beds, and supports the largest contiguous mudflat in southern California).

The Tijuana refuge, which was established in 1980, was designated in 1982 as part of the National Estuarine Research Reserve System, a series of 21 national sanctuaries chosen for their importance as estuaries. Only four other sites exist on the West Coast—at Elkhorn Slough on the Central California coast (3.5 miles east of Moss Landing), South Slough on Oregon's Cape Arago (5 miles south of Charleston), Padilla Bay in Washington's Puget Sound (5 miles north of OR 20 between Burlington and Anacortes, WA), and Kachemak Bay on the Kenai Peninsula in south central Alaska. Tijuana Slough, Sweetwater Marsh, and the South San Diego Bay refuges are designated as Globally Important Bird Areas by the American Bird Conservancy. In addition, the South Bay refuge is designated as a Western Hemisphere Shorebird Reserve site.

HISTORY

The Tijuana River rises in Mexico, and three-fourths of its watershed is in our southern neighbor, making the Tijuana Estuary one of the few wetlands in the United States draining the waters of two countries. The estuary has also remained in a reasonably natural state despite the heavy development around it—and it supports six endangered species. The estuary is Southern California's only coastal lagoon not bisected by roads and rail lines. Recognition of these factors led to the estuary being named a part of the National Estuarine Research Reserve system.

GETTING THERE

From San Diego, drive south on I-5 toward Imperial Beach and the Mexican border. Turn west on Coronado Blvd. (Do not turn onto the exit that says Coronado Bridge or you will find yourself on Coronado Island.) Coronado Blvd. becomes Imperial Beach Blvd. Continue west, then turn south on 3rd St. and east on Caspian Way. Entrance sign to headquarters for the San Diego NWR Complex, the Tijuana Slough NWR, and the Tijuana Estuary Visitor Center is on the right off Caspian Way. Tijuana Slough and Sweetwater Marsh NWRs are within easy driving distance of each other.

■ **SEASON:** Refuges open year-round.
■ **HOURS:** Open daylight hours. Visitor Center open 10 a.m.–5 p.m.
■ **ADDRESS:** Tijuana NWR, 301 Caspian Way, Imperial Beach, CA 91932-3149
■ **TELEPHONE:** 619/575-2704

TOURING THE SAN DIEGO COMPLEX REFUGES

■ **BY FOOT:** The Tijuana Slough refuge has 3 miles of trails, the McCoy Trail (0.25 mile), the Grove Street Trail (0.25 mile), the River Mouth Trail (2 miles), and the North Beach Trail (0.5 mile).

The Sweetwater Marsh refuge has 1.5 miles of trails, Center Trail (0.25 mile), Coyote Trail (0.25 mile) and a third trail, also 0.25 mile closed annually April 15–August 15. Spurs on each of the trails add to the mileage.

■ **BY BICYCLE:** The Bayshore Bikeway runs around 10 miles from 13th Street in Imperial Beach to Coronado, partly encircling the South San Diego Bay refuge.

■ **BY HORSEBACK:** The Sunset horse trail crosses Border Field State Park and a corner of Tijuana NWR. Horses can be rented at Sandi's Horse Rentals, 2060 Hollister St., San Diego 92154. Telephone: 619/424-3124.

WHAT TO SEE

■ **LANDSCAPE AND CLIMATE** San Diego's balmy year-round weather puzzles newcomers, who wonder where the weather is. January averages 45 to 65 degrees F.; July, 64 to 73 degrees. Only 9.5 inches of rain fall annually. Tijuana Slough NWR lies north of the mouth of the Tijuana River, which rises in Mexico and until the building of a fence was a favored crossing point for undocumented immigrants. Sweetwater Marsh NWR is on San Diego Bay at the outlet of the Sweetwater River. The bay has been enclosed from Coronado Island to Imperial Beach with a dredge and fill operation that joined natural islands, creating the Silver Strand, a causeway connecting the two cities. Entrance by water to the bay is north of Coronado Island. The refuges are flat—sea level to 25 feet—and the estuaries lack a large, open body of water. Tijuana Slough comprises a series of channels with a relatively narrow mouth to the Pacific.

■ **PLANT LIFE**
Coastal Salt marshes are among the most productive ecosystems on earth. Because they mix fresh and salt water, they support plants and organisms that exist

in each habitat. Plants in the salt marsh grow in a definitive order—from those that do not mind being submerged in water much of the time to those that prefer a drier environment. Cordgrass grows at the lowest level of the marsh. It spreads by underground roots (rhizomes), growing to 4 feet. Its flowers are dense but colorless, blooming on a 5-foot to 6-foot stalk from July to November. Salt-marsh plants are able to separate salt from the water and excrete it through their leaves. Cordgrass is called the "hotel" of the marsh because so many creatures live in it. It is particularly important to the light-footed clapper rail, which uses it as nesting material and cover.

Growing higher in the marsh are pickleweed and saltwort. Pickleweed rids itself of excess salt by storing it in the joints of its stems, which dry up and break off after it rains. Pickleweed blooms from April to September, and its picklelike joints are food for the endangered Belding savannah sparrow. Saltwort grows from Los Angeles County to Mexico and has long, narrow leaves that resemble pickleweed. Spikes of small violet flowers bloom on the sea lavender plant from July to December. The plant's large leaves are often covered with excreted salt. Alkali heath, a bushy, low-growing plant, has small pale pink flowers, blooming from June to October. Another perennial is sea blite, growing in a many-branched clump with small, unnoticeable flowers. It disappears when the ground is dry for a long period.

Moving to the highest elevations in the salt marsh, we find perennial glasswort, a type of pickleweed, and shore grass and salt grass, both creeping perennials.

Because it is picky about where it lives, the salt-marsh bird's beak is on the endangered plant list. A small annual, growing 4 to 12 inches in height, it prefers a narrow strip just above high-tide line, where it grows with neighboring saltgrass. Several species of bees are the only insects that know how to crawl down into the tube of the flower to pollinate it. Its tubular flowers (with a slight stretch of the imagination) look like a white version of the beak of a tufted puffin.

The toyon (Christmas berry or California holly) grows as a rounded tall shrub or low tree, flowering from late June to November. Its red berries, known as

Clapper rail in marsh at high tide

Christmas decorations, may last until spring. The plant is used extensively in California landscaping and gave its name to Hollywood.

The bush-sunflower has showy yellow flowers, blooming from February to June, and grows near the coast from San Diego north to Santa Barbara County. Drought tolerant and fast growing, it controls erosion and provides cover.

■ ANIMAL LIFE

Birds Staying hidden in thick stands of cordgrass has not prevented the light-footed clapper rail from landing on the endangered bird list. As California's estuaries are being filled in, the clapper rail population continues to decrease. Tijuana Slough has the second biggest population of clapper rails in California (the largest is at Huntington Beach). This secretive gray-brown bird, chiefly made up of bill, neck, and legs, stays hidden in cordgrass and moves to higher ground to conceal itself in pickleweed with the influx of high tide. The rail is one of five endangered birds (others are the California least tern, California brown pelican, least Bell's vireo, and, listed by the state as endangered, Belding's savannah sparrow) found on the refuges along with more than 370 other bird species.

Least Bell's vireo

Belding's savannah sparrow nests in beds of pickleweed, feeding on seeds and insects. It may be seen running along the banks of streams or through the marsh. Belding's sparrow is one of 16 subspecies of savannah sparrows. It can commonly be seen at all times of the year, sometimes foraging among kelp washed up on the beach, looking for sandflies and washed-up seeds.

Brown pelicans use the estuary along with least terns, and in the riparian areas least Bell's vireos, black phoebes, Bewick's wrens, and bushtits may be seen.

Mammals Coyotes, jackrabbits, cottontails, California ground squirrels, skunks, long-tailed weasels, and opossums are all present.

Fish Twenty species of fish use the estuaries, including barred sandbass, mullet, and California halibut. The halibut feeds lying flat on the floor of the ocean. To accommodate this prone lifestyle, one eye has migrated to the topside so two eyes look out from one side of the fish, something in the order of a Picasso cubist rendering. Other sea dwellers seen in the estuary include bat rays, cusk eels, stingrays, longjaw mudsuckers, and combtooth blennies.

Estuaries are fish nurseries. Fish breed and give birth in the shallow waters and in turn become food for the young of fish-eating bird species.

Invertebrates The white or gray round sand dollar that beachcombers like to collect is actually the sand dollar's skeleton (called the "test"). Tiny hairs on the test of the living sand dollar move trapped food particles toward its mouth. When the weather turns rough, the sand dollar (about 3 inches in diameter) uses its movable spines to bury itself into the sand, then flattens down to avoid the strong currents.

The yellow shore crab likes muddy areas and will take a nip if you approach it too closely. This testy crustacean hides under rocks and in crevices during the day and comes out at low tide at night to feast on algae.

Other invertebrates present in the estuaries include hermit crabs and ghost shrimp and the littleneck, jackknife, and purple clams. The most visible are the millions of California horned snails that cover the mudflats at low tide.

ACTIVITIES

■ **SEASONAL EVENTS:** The two-day San Diego Bay Bird Festival, held at the end of January, offers bird walks in the Tijuana River Valley and along the beach. Both the Sweetwater Marsh and Tijuana Slough visitors' centers offer activities during the event.

■ **PUBLICATIONS:** *Seashore Life of Southern California* by Sam Hinton, University of California Press, 1989. *A Flora of San Diego County* by R. Mitchel Beauchamp, Sweetwater River Press, 1986. *Walking San Diego* by Lonnie Hewitt and Barbara Moore, The Mountaineers Press, 1989.

> **HUNTING AND FISHING**
> There is no hunting or fishing allowed on Sweetwater Marsh NWR refuge.
>
> Fishing is permitted year-round at Tijuana Slough NWR, but hunting is not allowed. Anglers fish for a variety of species, including **surf perch, corbina, leopard sharks** and **halibut**.

Sweetwater Marsh NWR

Sweetwater Marsh NWR
Chula Vista, California

A jackrabbit may hop across the road as a bright red trolley carries visitors into Sweetwater Marsh refuge, away from the constant clamor on Interstate 5, just a

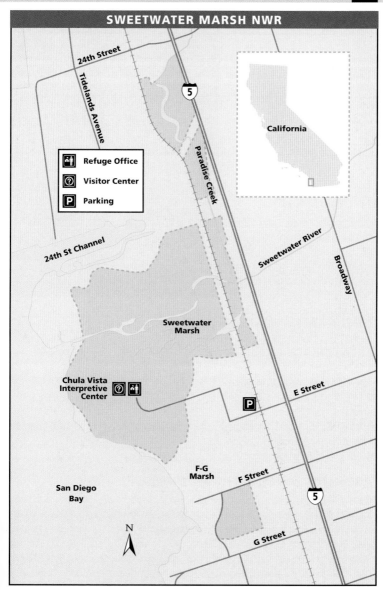

SWEETWATER MARSH NWR

- 🛉 Refuge Office
- ⓘ Visitor Center
- 🅿 Parking

24th Street

Tidelands Avenue

5

Paradise Creek

California

24th St Channel

Sweetwater River

Broadway

Sweetwater Marsh

Chula Vista Interpretive Center ⓘ 🛉

🅿

E Street

F-G Marsh

F Street

San Diego Bay

5

N

G Street

block from the edge of the refuge. Birdsong and the cries of gulls tell visitors that they are in one of San Diego's last wild places.

HISTORY

Sweetwater Marsh NWR was established in 1988 as mitigation for a proposed hotel, flood-control channel, and the completion of CA 54, all of which would remove more of the dwindling San Diego wetlands. Environmental organizations, including the National Audubon Society and the Sierra Club, sued, resulting in a settlement that allowed the U.S. Fish & Wildlife Service to acquire the refuge land. The refuge serves as an outstanding example of how governmental agencies can work together to conserve natural resources in crowded urban environments. Sweetwater Marsh is in the city of Chula Vista, which has built and operates a first-class museum and Visitor Center on the refuge. A number of live birds, fish, amphibians, and invertebrates are displayed in glass cases, and interactive exhibits invite visitors to partic-ipate. The 0.5-square-mile (316-acre) refuge welcomes 50,000 visitors annually.

Salt-marsh bird's beak

GETTING THERE

Drive south on I-5 from San Diego toward Chula Vista and exit west on E St. The Visitor Center parking lot is at the end of E St. No cars are permitted on the refuge, but a free shuttle bus, running about every 20 min-utes, takes visitors to the Visitor Center.

■ **SEASON:** Refuge open year-round.

■ **HOURS:** Refuge and Visitor Center open Sept.–May, Tues.–Sun., 10 a.m.–5 p.m.; also open Mon., same hours, June–Aug.

■ **FEES** $3.50 adults, $2.50 seniors, and $1 youth ages 6–17. Free first Tues. of month.

■ **ADDRESS:** Sweetwater Marsh NWR, c/o Tijuana Slough NWR, 301 Caspian Way, Imperial Beach, CA 91932

■ **TELEPHONE:** 619/575-1290

TOURING SWEETWATER MARSH

■ **BY FOOT:** This is a small refuge, making it easy to walk all three trails (0.25 mile each) in one visit. Six thousand years ago Native Americans who practiced the La Jolla cultural pattern lived by the marsh in small groups, moving often as food supplies shifted location. They ate shellfish, seeds, and acorns and used the marsh plant known as sea blite. Like pickleweed, sea blite has the ability to excrete salt from its leaves. The Indians steeped the entire plant in water to extract a rich black dye that they used to dye fibers for creating designs in their baskets. A related plant, desert blite—also called inkweed—grows in salty soils in the desert.

WHAT TO SEE

■ **LANDSCAPE AND CLIMATE** This small (0.4-square-mile, 279-acre) marsh appears fragile against the onslaught of development around it. The only nearby undeveloped area—lying on the refuge boundary to the east and south—is privately owned and is scheduled for development (housing, shops, theaters, restaurants, and a hotel). Coronado Bridge soars across San Diego Bay to the north and, across the bay, the Silver Strand buffers the South San Diego Bay from the open ocean. Sweetwater Marsh NWR protects part of the 9 percent of San Diego Bay's wetlands that have not yet been filled in.

ACTIVITIES

■ **WILDLIFE OBSERVATION:** Begin an exploration of the refuge from the observation platform at the Visitor Center. (Binoculars can be rented for $1.) Of the 220 bird species spotted on the refuge, three are endangered. Both the light-footed clapper rail and Belding's savannah sparrow nest in the marsh: the clapper rail deep in the cordgrass (the nest it has constructed floats up and down with the tide) and the savannah sparrow in pickleweed, where it feeds on seeds, insects, and the tips of pickleweed. The savannah sparrows like the banks of streams running through the marsh. The California least terns return to a few sites in Southern California each spring to nest and raise their young. Look for them attempting to catch small fish in the sloughs and bay.

Among shorebirds that may be seen at the marsh is the lesser yellowlegs, which breeds in Alaska north to Hudson Bay and winters along the Southern California coast. Shorebirds have been clocked flying at around 45 mph. The lesser yellowlegs is known to fly 1,900 miles in six days—or 316 miles per day for almost a week.

Six hawks frequent the refuge—red-shouldered, red-tailed, northern harrier, sharp-shinned, Cooper's, and ferruginous—along with nine species of gulls.

KELP HARVESTING During World War I a gunpowder manufacturing plant was operated on what is now Sweetwater Marsh NWR. The Hercules Gunpowder Factory, built in 1916, harvested the rich beds of kelp off San Diego and extracted acetone from the kelp. The acetone was used in the manufacture of gunpowder. The factory operated for four years, then shut down, but the harvesting of the kelp beds continued.

Kelp provides food and habitat for sea otters and other marine mammals, and for fish and invertebrates; but its use in more than 100 manufactured products has fostered the giant kelp-harvesting industry off the Southern California coast. This seaweed's most important component, used in fertilizers and soaps, may be algin. It is used to prepare commercial ice cream to prevent large ice crystals from forming. It is also used in paints, polishes, and antibiotics, and to thicken such products as latex.

By harvesting only the top 4 feet of kelp, the remaining plant receives unexpected sunlight and continues to grow. It uses rootlike fibers to fasten itself to rocky surfaces as much as 100 feet below the surface and reproduces itself by releasing spores that attach themselves to rocks and grow into tiny male and female plants. The male plants release sperm that fertilizes the female plants and starts their growth. The young plants grow at a rate of up to 2 feet a day and continue to sprout new shoots for up to 10 years.

Giant kelp

■ **PHOTOGRAPHY:** A photo blind off Coyote Trail looks onto mudflats and tideland with chances for shots of brants, loons, and mergansers. Use a telephoto lens and be prepared to wait.

■ **HIKES AND WALKS:** The refuge's short trails all have spurs that increase their length. On Center Trail, look for western fence and legless lizards.

■ **SEASONAL EVENTS:** The refuge celebrates National Wildlife Week in October.

Heermann's gull

Tijuana Slough NWR
Imperial Beach, California

So close to the border that undocumented immigrants once trekked north through the refuge (a fence at the border has moved the entry points farther east), Tijuana Slough NWR has the Pacific Ocean for a backdrop and a state park and naval landing field as neighbors. It shares management of its Visitor Center with the state of California, is designated as a Globally Important Bird Area by the American Bird Conservancy, and has, along with Seal Beach NWR farther north, one of the best native gardens on the coast.

HISTORY

Tijuana Slough NWR was established in 1980 to protect wildlife living in the dwindling coastal estuaries. Its marshes occupy 70 percent of the rehabitats, 20 percent; and uplands and open water, 5 percent each. The 1.7-square-mile (1,056-acre) refuge draws around 50,000 visitors annually.

GETTING THERE

From the Visitor Center, drive east on Caspian Way and turn south on 5th St. Access to the tidal ponds and marsh is at Grove Ave. and at Iris Ave. To explore the beach, return to Imperial Beach Blvd. and drive west. Turn south on Seacoast

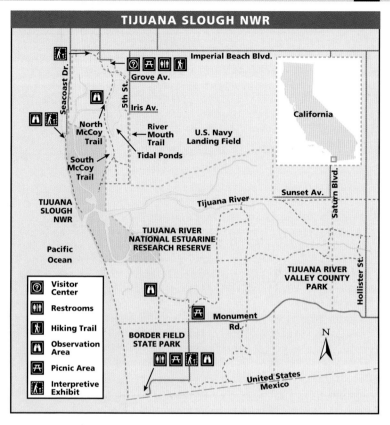

TIJUANA SLOUGH NWR

Imperial Beach Blvd.

Grove Av.

Seacoast Dr.

5th St.

Iris Av.

North McCoy Trail

River Mouth Trail

U.S. Navy Landing Field

Tidal Ponds

South McCoy Trail

California

TIJUANA SLOUGH NWR

Tijuana River

Sunset Av.

Saturn Blvd.

Pacific Ocean

TIJUANA RIVER NATIONAL ESTUARINE RESEARCH RESERVE

TIJUANA RIVER VALLEY COUNTY PARK

Hollister St.

Monument Rd.

BORDER FIELD STATE PARK

N

United States
Mexico

	Visitor Center
	Restrooms
	Hiking Trail
	Observation Area
	Picnic Area
	Interpretive Exhibit

Dr. South. Access is at the end of Seacoast. (Because the dunes are closed to foot traffic, visitors are asked to walk on the ocean side of the dunes.) To visit the southeastern section of the estuary, drive east on Imperial Beach Blvd., turn south on Saturn Blvd. and west on Sunset Ave.

■ **SEASON:** Refuge is open all year except for Thanksgiving Day, Christmas Day, and New Year's Day.

■ **HOURS:** Visitor Center: 10 a.m.–5 p.m. 7 days a week. Refuge open till sundown.

■ **FEES:** None.

■ **ADDRESS:** 301 Caspian Way, Imperial Beach, CA 91932

■ **TELEPHONE:** 619/575-3613

TOURING TIJUANA SLOUGH

■ **BY FOOT:** A 5-acre native plant garden surrounds the Visitor Center and is an excellent place to become acquainted with the refuge. In 1980 volunteers began clearing the garden site—an industrial dump littered with asphalt, trash, and old cars. By 1989 planting began, and the area is now verdant with native plants that survive California's Mediterranean climate of low winter rains and long dry summers. Wildlife has returned to the area, including skunks, opossums, cottontail rabbits, and many bird species, as well as lizards, insects, and spiders.

■ **BY BICYCLE:** Don't miss the bike path. The scenery is spectacular, and there are good views of the dune area of the refuge. The refuge has salt pans, poorly drained areas where salt concentrations can reach three times that of ocean water.

GRAY WHALES A West Coast tradition brings thousands of people to the coast each year to watch the passing of the gray whales. Swimming a round trip of some 12,000 miles a year at the sedate rate of 3 to 4 miles an hour, the whales migrate between Baja California, where they breed and give birth, and the food-rich Bering and Chukchi seas off the northwest coast of Alaska.

To feed their enormous bulk (they grow to 50 feet in length during their 50-year life span and weigh about 50 tons), the whales eat about 2,600 pounds of small crustaceans a day, foraging at the bottom of the sea. Gray whales are toothless. They use their baleen—140 to 170 plates of long, fingernail-like material hanging down from their upper jaws—to trap the tiny invertebrates they eat.

Because they migrate only a half mile or so offshore, gray whales are the most conspicuous of the Pacific whales. Whereas land mammals exchange only around 10 percent to 20 percent of the air in their lungs each time they breathe, gray whales expel around 80 percent. The exhaled air, which looks like a water spout, is usually warmer than the surrounding atmosphere and condenses rapidly, creating the jet of steam that is often the first indication that one of these ancient mammals is passing.

More than 11,000 gray whales follow the migratory path along the west coast, so chances of seeing them are good. Many whale-watching excursions leave from towns along the coast, and the whales can be seen from any number of headlands and beaches.

To see extensive salt-evaporation ponds, pick up the bike trail at 7th St. and Boulevard Ave. (Return to Imperial Beach Blvd. from the refuge, drive east on it and north on 7th.) Owned by Western Salt Company, the ponds are used to extract salt by moving the increasingly salty water from pond to pond as the water evaporates.

■ **BY HORSEBACK:** The horse trails are extensive, passing through not only the refuge but the National Estuarine Research Reserve areas and the Border Field State Park. The beach horse trail runs from the south bank of the Tijuana River almost to the Mexican border.

WHAT TO SEE

■ **LANDSCAPE AND CLIMATE** The collision of the Pacific and North American plates has created a steeply uplifted coastline along California, completely unlike the broad coastal plains of the East Coast. California's estuaries tend to be small, tucked in between the Coast Range and the Pacific. Tijuana Slough's size continues to decrease as sedimentation is deposited from river runoff and, at the same time, catastrophic beach erosion has shifted the shoreline landward. In 1997 construction was completed on a dredging operation that created almost two acres of new wetlands and opened the Oneonta Slough to tidal lagoons southeast of the Visitor Center. Around 12,000 cubic yards of sand were dredged from the new tidal link and deposited near the mouth of the river to help restore the area's beaches.

ACTIVITIES

■ **WILDLIFE OBSERVATION:** Strolling the riparian area of the native plant garden may give glimpses of songbirds. Best viewing is in spring and fall. Wading birds, raptors, and shorebirds are present year-round. Brown pelicans appear in summer and fall, terns and least clapper rails in summer, and geese and ducks in winter. With the coming and going of the tides, visitors can usually find birds to watch in the early morning and late afternoon.

■ **PHOTOGRAPHY:** With a telephoto lens and very fast film, you may be able to catch the brown pelicans in flight or diving into the Pacific after fish. Because cars are not permitted on the refuge to serve as a blind, photography requires more patience—sitting quietly until the birds resume their activities.

■ **HIKES AND WALKS:** Don't miss River Mouth Trail (trailhead at 5th and Iris streets), a 2-mile, one-way loop leading to the mouth of the Tijuana River, with great birding. The helicopters practicing takeoffs and landings at the Navy landing field will remind you that civilization is next door.

■ **SEASONAL EVENTS:** The refuge celebrates National Wildlife Week in October.

Burrowing owl

San Diego NWR
Jamul, California

Under the summer sun, California's Coast Range turns a tawny gold. Coastal live oaks interrupt the panorama of dry hills with patches of somber green. This quintessential California landscape is rapidly disappearing in southern California's San Diego County as development sweeps east from the coast. A stunning section of this landscape—steep hills, a river that flows year-round, and gray-green Diegan coastal scrub—is preserved in the Otay-Sweetwater Unit of the San Diego NWR.

HISTORY

The 9-square-mile (5,700-acre) refuge was established in 1996. (The newest addition to the refuge, the 3.4-square-mile (2,200-acre) South San Diego Bay Unit, was added in 1999 and brings the size of the refuge to 12.4 square miles.) The refuge attracts around 2,000 visitors annually.

GETTING THERE

From I-5, I-15, or I-805 in San Diego, turn east on CA 94 (Martin Luther King Jr.

Freeway). Continue on CA 94 as it is renamed to Campo Rd. at Rancho San Diego and continue southeast. In Jamul (Ha–MOOL) turn left (northeast) onto Lyons Valley Rd. The refuge office is on the north (left) side of Lyons Valley Rd. at 13910 in a small office complex.

■ **SEASON:** Refuge open year-round.

■ **HOURS:** Open sunrise to sunset. Office open 7:30 a.m.–4 p.m.

■ **ADDRESS:** San Diego NWR, 13910 Lyons Valley Rd., Suite R, Jamul, CA 91935

■ **TELEPHONE:** 619/669-7295

WHAT TO SEE

Although the refuge is not officially open, a number of hiking and horse trails crisscross the area. The refuge can also be seen from Campo Highway, which traverses the refuge, and during guided birding hikes. The refuge office has a schedule for the hikes.

■ **PLANT LIFE** When you smell a sagelike or minty odor, you are near the Diegan coastal scrub community of plants. They are small- to medium-sized and often drop their leaves during a drought. Three sagebrushes—black, white, and purple—can be found in Diegan coastal scrub. Mixed in with it are the San Diego sunflower, deerweed, poison oak, and California encelia. The encelia is a sprawling woody shrub about 4 feet in height with broad leaves 1 to 2 inches long. Springtime brings blooms of yellow rays and purplish brown centers.

Look for lemonade berry on north-facing slopes. An evergreen shrub, its leaves are toothed, and its flattened reddish berries are covered with a sticky secretion. Soaking the berries produces a drink something like lemonade. (Note: Lemonade berry is in the rhus family, which includes poison oak, and persons susceptible to poison oak may react to other members of the family.) Lemonade berry's whitish rose flowers can be admired by all without touching. The plant blooms in winter as soon as the rains begin.

Purple sage

San Diego barrel cactus, cholla, and coastal prickly pear also grow in a rare segment of maritime succulent scrub within the refuge. The refuge was established to protect these disappearing habitats. Some 70 percent to 90 percent of southern California coastal sage scrub have been destroyed. In San Diego County 61 percent of riparian woodland is gone. Both riparian woodlands and forests (denser vegetation than the woodlands) can be seen on the refuge. Look for willows, western sycamores, cottonwoods, and Mexican elderberry. Some 94 percent of San Diego County's grasslands have also been lost.

Coyote

■ ANIMAL LIFE

Birds The refuge's grasslands are used by many of the refuge's more than 200 species of birds—including burrowing owls, flycatchers, the American kestrel, and red-tailed hawks.

Mammals Mammals include raccoons, badgers, the western spotted skunk, gray foxes, coyotes, bobcats, and opossums. Capt. John Smith, the founder of Virginia, wrote the first description of an opossum in 1603. It "hath a head like a swine, a taile like a rat, and is of the bignes of a cat. Under her belly she hath a bagge wherein she lodgeth, carrieth and sucketh her young." The mother opossum can have up to 25 babies but averages 13 teats, so the earliest born survive by clamping onto a nipple. Around seven or eight babies survive to weaning as the remainder die from starvation or exposure. The survivors can sometimes be seen riding on their mother's back.

The word coyote comes from the Aztec word *coyotl*. Found only in the West during the 1800s, coyotes moved north to Alaska shortly after 1900 and found their way to Costa Rica as well. The song of the coyote singing to the full moon is one of the West's great sounds. Listen for it on the far hills of the San Diego NWR.

Reptiles Reptiles using the grasslands include the red diamond rattlesnake, coast horned lizard, and coachwhip.

San Luis NWR Complex
San Luis NWR, Merced NWR
Los Banos, California

White-fronted geese, Merced NWR

From the sky, the necklace of wetlands once strung out along the entire 400-mile-long Great Central Valley now appears as mostly string with very few beads left. Flying in from Alaska and Canada to winter in the valley, more than 14 million waterfowl first see the Sacramento refuges, 60 miles south of the mountains, then Stone Lakes, another 75 miles, then the San Luis refuges, an additional 80-mile hop, and, finally, 120 miles away, to the southernmost refuges at Kern. A half-million of these birds winter in the Grasslands Ecological Area, which includes the San Luis refuges. These lands, like all the national wildlife refuges in the valley, have been re-created on former wetlands long since drained, dried, and plowed under to grow rice, grain, and fruit crops.

HISTORY

The historic tule marshes of the San Joaquin Valley were so vast that they brought early explorers to a halt. The intricately linked wetlands prevented trailbreakers from crossing the 40-mile-wide valley. (The early Spanish explorer Juan de Anza was among those forced to turn back to Monterey.) The marshes were a portion of the more than 6,250 square miles (4 million acres) of wetlands in California's Great Central Valley that were filled as rivers overflowed each spring with snowmelt pouring out of the Sierra Nevada.

Spanish land grants covered much of the San Joaquin (Wah-KEEN) Valley. Great herds of cattle raised for their hides roamed the grasslands along with deer, tule elk, and antelope. Both the cattle and wild animals were slaughtered in vast numbers to feed the 49ers who came to California for gold. By the 1870s the land was overgrazed, droughts occurred, and the price of beef fell. The valley became an area of intensive agriculture, and the wetlands were gradually filled in.

Today these wetlands have almost disappeared. All but 5 percent have been transformed into farmland, shopping malls, and subdivisions. The largest remaining historical wetland acreage is in the San Joaquin Valley's Grasslands Ecological Area in Merced County. The San Luis, Merced, and (former) Kesterson national wildlife refuges are within this 250-square-mile (160,000-acre) grassland. An easy drive from each other, the refuges can be visited in a day.

GETTING THERE

From San Francisco, cross the Bay Bridge, and drive south, then east on I-580. Stay on I-580 as it swings south to join I-5. Drive south on I-5, then east on CA 152 to Los Banos. Begin your visit with a stop at refuge headquarters on CA 152 in Los Banos—947 West Pacheco Blvd. Suite C. From Sacramento, drive south on US 99. Turn south on CA 165 to Los Banos. From Los Angeles, drive north on I-5. Turn north onto CA 165 to Los Banos.

■ **SEASON:** Refuges open year-round.

■ **HOURS:** Open one-half hour before sunrise to one-half hour after sunset. Refuge headquarters open Mon-Fri., 8 a.m.-4:30 p.m.

■ **ADDRESS:** San Luis NWR Complex, 947 W. Pacheco Blvd., Suite C, P. O. Box 2176, Los Banos, CA 93635

■ **TELEPHONE:** 209/826-3508

TOURING SAN LUIS NWR COMPLEX

San Luis NWR has three auto-tour routes, including a 5-mile, one-way Tule Elk loop and a Waterfowl tour loop of 9.7 miles. Passing the turnoff to the Tule Elk loop, the Waterfowl loop joins and then follows the curve of the San Joaquin River. Both routes are open all year, 7 days a week. Entrance road to the two loops is off Wolfsen Rd. The 2.5-mile West Bear Creek loop passes Raccoon and Valley marshes and Sacaton Pond. The entrance is off CA 165.

Merced NWR has one 5-mile, one-way loop tour. The entrance is off Sandy Mush Rd.

■ **BY FOOT:** In the San Luis refuge, there are 3 miles of trails. On Merced NWR there are 0.6 mile of hiking trails. Hikers in San Luis must stay on the hiking trails.

■ **BY BICYCLE:** Bicycles are allowed on the auto-tour routes.

WHAT TO SEE

■ **LANDSCAPE AND CLI-MATE** It is not difficult to imagine the vast inland sea that once covered the Great Central Valley, depositing marine sediments of gravels and sands later themselves covered by alluvial deposits that washed out of the Sierra, creating a valley of such flatness that the laser-guided farm machinery used to level the

California poppy

fields seems almost redundant. The elevation within San Luis and Merced refuges varies only 25 feet, from 65 to 90 feet at San Luis, and from 90 to 115 feet at Merced. Thick tule fog that clings to the ground may be present in winter (heaviest from December to February), lowering visibility to a few feet. (Warning: Tule fog causes chain pileups on the freeways each year. Drive carefully.)

Winters are cold, with the January thermometer readings from 15 to 75 degrees F. Rainfall, limited because the refuges are in the rain shadow of the Coast Range, averages 10 to 11 inches a year (deserts get 10 inches or less annually), falling from November to April. Summer heat can be blistering. July temperatures range from 46 to 111 degrees.

■ PLANT LIFE

Wetlands Water plantain grows on both refuges—two native species and one introduced. Arrowhead plantain, a native, has arrow-shaped leaves and an interesting flower structure. Male flowers with stamens grow only on the upper part of the flower while female flowers that produce the seed grow only on the lower part of the flower cluster. The giant bur reed has similarly shaped leaves, but they are longer and more narrow. The bur reed has the same flower structure, but the male flower quickly dries up while the female flowers produce many burs, each containing one seed. Other wetland plants are swamp timothy, spike rush, and California bulrush.

Grasslands Although introduced annual grasses have taken over much of California's remaining grasslands, the Grasslands Ecological Area is one of the best places to see the state's native grasses. Seventeen are found on the refuges. Perennial bunchgrasses were the most common natives, flowering and maturing from April to June. They grow in dense clumps of stems, leaving space between each clump, which allows room for invasive annual grasses to take hold. Squirreltail, knot grass, and alkali grass are among the natives growing on the refuges.

At the height of wildflower season—usually in late April—the grasslands take on the aspect of a brilliantly flowered carpet. Blue dicks are among the first flowers to bloom, often in February. They have long, naked stems topped with bluish-

Tricolored blackbird

violet flowers in dense heads. Following soon after are the yellow Johnny-tucks (butter-and-eggs), growing to about a foot in height, often in great masses. The elegantly shaped orange-flowering fiddlenecks got their name because the top of the flower stem curves around like the neck of a violin. Blue lupine and California poppies add to the colorful meadows. Two unusual plants, one native and one introduced, also grow on the refuges. The native jimsonweed, with large white trumpet-shaped flowers, was used by Native tribes in puberty ceremonies. Containing poisons, it causes hallucinations and finally unconsciousness. The introduced hemlock is the same plant used by Socrates to commit suicide.

Riparian California's riparian habitat has fared even less well than the wetlands.

WHATEVER HAPPENED TO THE KESTERSON NWR? In the early 1980s, the 2-square-mile (1,300-acre) Kesterson Reservoir, a parcel within the 9.2-mile (5,900-acre) Kesterson NWR, situated just west of the San Luis refuge, became notorious for producing badly deformed birds. The refuge was what is known as an overlay refuge, which means that the refuge status is secondary to the primary purpose of the area. Kesterson NWR sat on top of land controlled by the Bureau of Reclamation. Kesterson's troubles began with the attempt to farm marginal lands on the west side of the San Joaquin Valley with imported water. The result was one of the major environmental disasters on a national wildlife refuge.

Hardpan—an impermeable layer of hardened clay particles near the surface—causes groundwater to stand rather than drain, concentrating the pesticides, chemicals, and salts into the roots of plants. One of the minerals dissolving into the water was selenium, a nonmetallic chemical present in particularly high amounts in the soil of the valley's west side.

To solve the problem for the farmers, the federal Bureau of Reclamation began to build a canal known as the San Luis Drain that would carry the accumulated water 188 miles to San Francisco Bay. After only 82 miles were built (at a cost of $40 million), the project came to a halt. Environmentalists protested any further pollution of San Francisco Bay, and money dried up. The uncompleted canal ended up draining into the Kesterson Reservoir, at that time part of the overlay national wildlife refuge. In only two years, water quality in the marsh disintegrated, and by 1984 birds hatched there were deformed. In 1983, a dieoff of 246 birds was discovered, with 106 of them deformed.

Selenium had concentrated in the reservoir's food chain and was causing the deformities. The only solution appeared to be to destroy the reservoir so birds could not come there. In 1986 the drains were closed, and the reservoir was dried out and sealed with $6 million of fill dirt.

That solved the immediate problem of Kesterson Reservoir; but farming in California is big business, and eventually the state reopened a portion of the San Luis Drain. The California Regional Water Quality Control Board established stringent selenium discharge standards, and farmers who exceed the standards face fines.

As for Kesterson Reservoir, it was returned to the Bureau of Reclamation and the remaining noncontaminated 7.2-square-mile (4,600-acre) portion was transferred from the Bureau of Reclamation to the U.S. Fish & Wildlife Service and now exists as a unit of the San Luis NWR.

TULE ELK A herd of tule elk clusters on a point of land that extends into a tule-infested marsh. The herd bull, bedecked with a set of multi-branched antlers, stands to the side of his harem of cows and calves, which nonchalantly feed on a lush stand of bird's-foot trefoil. Suddenly, the bull tilts his head upward until the massive rack nearly touches his rear haunches. Mouth agape, he issues a five-note flutelike bugle which ends with a series of coughing grunts. Almost immediately, the bugle is challenged by a group of rival bulls that encircle the herd. As the nearby bulls continue to bugle, the herd bull paws the dirt and thrashes his antlers, reducing a clump of tules to splintered stalks.

Suddenly, another large bull begins to move stiff-leggedly toward the herd. Immediately, the herd bull confronts the interloper, cutting him off from the herd of cows. Circling the herd, the two bulls walk side by side in the "parallel walk" display. Then the herd bull drops his head, turns to the rival, and the two bulls crash their antlers in an amazing display of strength. Dust flying, the two bulls push each other back and forth across the grassland arena.

Sensing the unguarded herd, the other bulls move in to claim a cow or two as the warriors continue to battle. Sensing the loss of his harem, the herd bull makes a final lunge at his rival and the battle is over. Recovering quickly, the herd bull turns to the encroaching males and issues a victory bugle. His challengers, sensing the herd bull's strength, retreat, knowing that their turn will come as continuing battles will eventually sap the herd bull's strength, and that a new and stronger animal will take over the harem.

Gary R. Zahm, San Luis refuge manager

Only 2 percent remains. The stretches of great, broad-leafed trees growing along California's waterway are one of the most characteristic sights in the Great Central Valley. These thickly wooded bands of trees that follow the rivers' oxbows are about the only thing that breaks the monotony of driving the valley's endless flatlands. Valley oaks are the stately monarchs of the riparian tree belt. The largest of all American oaks, the valley oak spreads massive limbs (the circumference of its trunk has been recorded at 27 feet). Joining the oaks are the Fremont cottonwood, growing to 40- to 90-feet tall, and several species of willow.

■ ANIMAL LIFE

Birds Some 40 percent of the waterfowl that migrate along the Pacific Flyway winter in the Great Central Valley, and of those a half million spend the winter—November through February—in western Merced County within the Grasslands Ecological Area. In March these flocks, which include some 100,000 white-fronted, Ross', and snow geese, head north to their Arctic breeding grounds. Sandhill cranes—typically 14,000, but as many as 19,000—also winter at the refuges. (Viewing for these species is best at Merced.) Twenty species of ducks pass through the refuge, including 12 species that nest in the area. The northern shoveler can be spotted by the broadness of its bill, which looks like a spatula with rounded end. The shoveler's call sounds something like a rattle turned by jerking the hand, and the baby shovelers look rather comical with their outsized bills. Other ducks commonly seen include green-winged teal, mallard, northern pintail, and ruddys.

Tule elk

Four blackbirds—red-winged, tricolored, yellow-headed, and Brewer's (200,000 in mixed flocks, the great majority red-winged)—nest on or utilize the refuges. In the riparian areas look for yellow-rumped warblers, scrub jays, and yellow-billed magpies. With luck, you may see blue- or black-headed grosbeaks or lazuli buntings. All three nest on the refuges.

Mammals Legend has it that only a handful of tule elk remained near Buena Vista Lake by the time the slaughter of the vast, free-roaming herds in California's Great Central Valley came to an end around 1872. Whatever the numbers, the tule elk were at the edge of extinction and were saved only because Henry Miller gave them sanctuary on his ranch near the southern end of the San Joaquin Valley. Their home range was the vast grassland and tule marshes of the Great Central Valley. This gave them their name.

Tule elk, one of four subspecies of North American elk, live only in California and are the smallest of the elk (they are also known as valley elk, dwarf elk, and dwarf wapiti). Tule elk bulls weigh around 600 to 900 pounds, while Roosevelt bulls (California's other native elk) weigh between 1,000 and 1,200 pounds.

The first attempts to corral the remaining elk and transport them to new ranges ended badly with a number of the remaining elk dying after resistance to being captured, but by 1914 a successful transfer was made of 54 tule elk. In 1974 a herd of 18 tule elk was transferred from the San Diego Wild Animal Park to the San Luis NWR. The herd usually consists of around 30 to 60 elk (some are relocated when the herd reaches its capacity of 50 to 60 animals) living in a 1.2-square-mile (780-acre) enclosure that can be seen by following the Tule Elk tour route.

The black-tailed jackrabbit likes open country for its home and has exceptionally long ears, enabling it to hear predators approach, and exceptionally long legs, allowing for a fast escape. The blacktails also use their long ears and legs to help them dissipate high heat. Wiggling their ears moves heat away from their bodies through convection. Cottontail rabbits are also found on the San Luis refuges along with coyotes, San Joaquin kit foxes, and California ground squirrels. The California ground squirrel can be distinguished from other ground squirrels by an absence of stripes and by its large size, gray-brown color, and long

Ground squirrel

fluffy tail. It is the most widespread of California squirrels, living everywhere except the Mojave and Sonoran deserts.

ACTIVITIES

For activities, look under the individual refuges.

■ **SEASONAL EVENTS:** The Wild on Wetlands Weekend, occurring in mid-March, features some 30 different tours—Tule Elk at San Luis Refuge, Birding for Beginners, Wildflowers & Vernal Pools, and View the Slough by Canoe are a few offerings. The Poetry of Place, Botany of the Central Valley, and Nature Photography Techniques are among the nearly 30 workshops. Hunters will like the decoy-carving, duck-calling, and retriever-training demonstrations, while amateur naturalists may attend a wildlife-rehabilitation workshop. For information, call 800/336-6354 or 209/827-4772.

San Luis NWR

Los Banos, California

The sinuous oxbows of the San Joaquin River curve along the refuge's east edge, then twist sedately through the refuge to join Bear Creek, where the river continues its slow journey to the Sacramento–San Joaquin Delta. The river's fringe of woodland is rich with stately oaks and towering cottonwoods, their shade offering the illusion of coolness during summertime when temperatures sizzle; in winter their bare branches are ghostly in the tule fog.

HISTORY

The San Luis refuge was established in 1966. The 40.7-square-mile (26,074-acre) refuge welcomes some 90,000 visitors annually.

GETTING THERE

From Los Banos, drive north 8 mi. on Mercey Springs Rd. (CA 165). Turn right on Wolfsen Rd. To reach the Waterfowl and Tule Elk tour routes, continue 2 mi. on Wolfsen Rd. to the refuge entrance. To reach the Blue Goose and Freitas units of the refuge, drive north on Mercey Springs Rd. (CA 165) from Los Banos and stay on CA 165 past the Wolfsen Rd. turnoff. The Blue Goose and Freitas units will be on your left, the entrance to the West Bear Creek tour route to the right slightly farther on. To reach the Kesterson Unit, continue north on CA 165 and turn west for 6 mi. on CA 140 (4 mi. east of Gustine).

■ **SEASON:** Refuge open year-round.

■ **HOURS:** Open daylight hours. Automatic gate for the San Luis Unit opens a half-hour before sunrise and closes a half-hour after sunset.

■ **ADDRESS:** San Luis NWR, c/o San Luis NWR Complex, P. O. Box 2176, Los Banos, CA 93635.

■ **TELEPHONE:** 209/876-3508

TOURING SAN LUIS

■ **BY AUTOMOBILE:** The Tule Elk tour loops around the tule elk enclosure, providing good chances to see the elk, particularly from the north side (4 interpretive stops and an observation platform); the Waterfowl loop has 6 interpretive stops, an observation platform, information kiosk, and restroom.

Before levees were built to contain California's rivers, the rivers flooded annually, spilling the snowmelt over vast areas, sometimes reaching 10 miles beyond the riverbed. (Sacramento's early houses were built with a cellar at ground level and the first floor 10 feet up to keep its occupants dry.) These seasonal wetlands promoted a luxuriant riparian growth of willow, cottonwoods, and oak, but California's riparian habitat has suffered an even greater loss than its wetlands—only 2 percent of the original riparian habitat remains. On the West Bear Creek

VERNAL POOLS The enchanting beauty of a vernal pool surrounded by rings of flowers in full bloom is one of the spectacular sights of the Great Central Valley's wildlife refuges. Vernal pools (also called hog wallows) appear suddenly during the winter rains—and disappear again within days, weeks, or months, depending on the depth of the depression they fill. They are found anyplace a layer of hardpan, volcanic rock, or any impermeable layer lies under a depression in the surface soil. Dependent on rainwater to fill, they dry out when the rains stop.

Rings of flowers, each in turn dependent on moisture from the pool to bloom, grow in concentric circles of various colors around the pool, blooming in succession as the water recedes. The outer ring may be a circle of white meadowfoam, blooming in early March. Next comes goldfields, small annuals only a few inches high that bloom in March and form broad masses of bright gold. White popcorn flowers germinate under water, then wait as seedlings for the water to recede, allowing them to flower. Look for them in late March and April. Also germinating under water is the beautiful blue downingia, producing a blue "bathtub ring" as the water recedes in April. The last colorful plant to flower in the pools is the purple owl's clover.

The pools support a variety of invertebrates, including several species of fairy and tadpole shrimp. They burrow into the muddy pool bottom or creep along it, surviving from year to year by laying resistant eggs that withstand high heat, cold, and dryness.

Vernal pools can be seen on the Merced NWR along Sandy Mush Road and on the San Luis NWR.

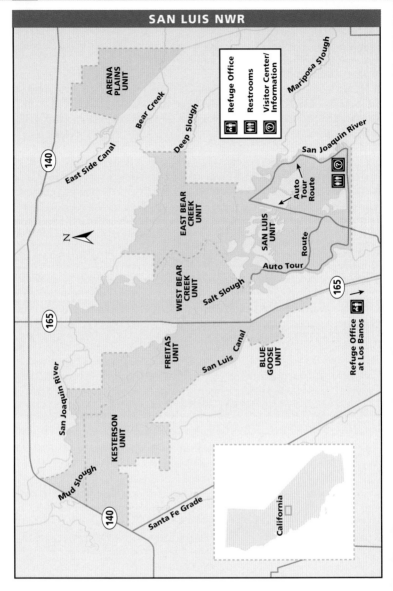

SAN LUIS NWR

Refuge Office

Restrooms

Visitor Center/
Information

ARENA
PLAINS
UNIT

Bear Creek

Deep Slough

Mariposa Slough

East Side Canal

San Joaquin River

140

Auto
Tour
Route

EAST BEAR
CREEK
UNIT

SAN LUIS
UNIT

Route

Auto Tour

WEST BEAR
CREEK
UNIT

Salt Slough

165

FREITAS
UNIT

San Luis Canal

BLUE
GOOSE
UNIT

Refuge Office
at Los Banos

165

San Joaquin River

KESTERSON
UNIT

Mud Slough

Santa Fe Grade

California

140

tour route, it is possible to see a remarkable effort to restore a riparian area. Volunteers and wildlife service personnel have planted 40,000 cottonwood and willow cuttings, oak seedlings, buttonbush, and coyote bush. Soon, a new area of lush riparian growth will be available to wildlife. The West Bear Creek tour route is open only on Wednesday, Saturday, and Sunday during waterfowl hunting season.

■ **BY FOOT:** The .75-mile Winton Marsh loop, open year-round, includes an observation platform with benches overlooking the marsh. The 1-mile Sousa Trail and observation platform, open year-round, provide views of riparian restoration efforts. The 1-mile Chester Marsh Trail is open February 1–October 1. All three trailheads, Chester, Sousa, and Winton, are on the Waterfowl tour route. A short .25-mile trail branches Chester Marsh Trail, leading to a historic site on the San Joaquin River.

■ **BY BICYCLE:** Bicyclists may use the two tour routes and three trails on the San Luis Unit as well as Salt Slough Rd. Note: The auto-tour loops are graveled.

ACTIVITIES

■ **WILDLIFE OBSERVATION:** While driving the auto-tour route, pause and let stillness fall around you. Then you will hear the sounds of San Luis—the flutelike bugling of the tule elk, the booming of the American bittern (known colloquially as the "thunder pumper"), the liquid, bubbling notes of the marsh wren (like the rapid vibration of a string instrument preceded by a pizzicato), and the musical call of the red-winged blackbird. Late August through October is rutting season for the tule elk. Best month for viewing ducks at San Luis is December, especially green-winged teal and mallards.

■ **PHOTOGRAPHY:** A March visit to San Luis will yield gorgeous shots of wild-flowers in rampant bloom.

■ **HIKES AND WALKS:** In addition to the refuge's designated trails, hikers are welcome to explore Salt Slough Road (park at any of the three parking areas along the road), which begins at the northwest corner of the Tule Elk tour route. The slough is a popular fishing area. Check at the information kiosk for directions to the refuge's newest trail, the one-mile Sousa Trail.

HUNTING AND FISHING Waterfowl hunting (**geese**, **duck**, **coot** and **common moorhens**) is permitted Oct. to Jan. Common snipe may also be hunted Oct. to Jan., and pheasant hunting is allowed in Nov. and Dec.

Fishing for catfish, largemouth bass and carp is permitted year-round.

Ross' geese

Merced NWR
Los Banos, California

The exuberantly colored fields of wildflowers on Merced NWR create a spring-time palette of great beauty. Pioneers described the Great Central Valley as so full of wildflowers it was as if a Persian carpet had been laid across the entire 100 miles. A glimpse of what the historic valley must have been is preserved in the Merced refuge. In winter the fields are a tapestry of green and white as thousands of geese feed on the winter grasses.

HISTORY

Merced NWR was established in 1951 with the purpose of growing feed for migratory waterfowl to help keep them on the refuge and prevent them from eating local farm crops. The 11-square-mile (7,034-acre) refuge attracts some 12,000 visitors annually.

GETTING THERE

From Los Banos, drive north on Mercey Springs Rd., then east on Henry Miller Rd. Turn north on Turner Island Rd. and jog right but stay north as Turner Island Rd. becomes Erreca Rd. Turn east on Sand Slough Rd., north on Nickle Rd., and east on Sandy Mush Rd., which cuts through Merced refuge.

■ **SEASON:** Refuge open year-round.

■ **HOURS:** Open daylight hours.

■ **ADDRESS:** Merced NWR, c/o San Luis NWR Complex, P.O. Box 2176, Los Banos, CA 93635

■ **TELEPHONE:** 209/826-3508

TOURING MERCED

■ **BY AUTOMOBILE:** Stop at the observation tower at the beginning of Merced's auto-tour route for an overview of the refuge's extensive marshes and wetlands before driving the 6.6-mile one-way loop. A restroom and information kiosk are near the observation platform. The gravel tour road follows Dead-man Creek, then passes several ponds, wetlands, and Cinnamon Slough. In November the four interpretive stops provide great views of some of the 100,000 geese to be found on the refuge between November and March. The entrance is off Sandy Mush Road.

■ **BY FOOT:** Hiking is not permitted on the auto-tour route. There is an observation platform at the trailhead of the 0.6-mile Meadowlark Trail, accessible from the tour route.

■ **BY BICYCLE:** Bicyclists may use the auto-tour route and Meadowlark Trail.

Lesser sandhill crane

ACTIVITIES

■ **WILDLIFE OBSERVATION:** The largest population of lesser sandhill cranes—as many as 14,000—in the Great Central Valley can be found at Merced.

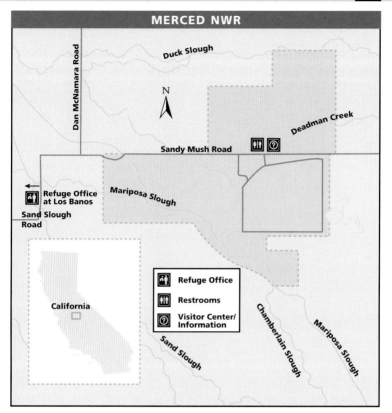

The refuge is also a hot spot for viewing geese: Nearly 100,000 geese—including Ross', snow, white-fronted, and cackling Canada geese—use the refuge croplands and marshes from November to March. In winter and spring the tricolored blackbird can often be seen. A spotting scope is installed on the viewing platform, and interpretive panels explain some of the sights on the refuge.

■ **PHOTOGRAPHY:** Use your car as a blind while driving the auto-tour loop. When the geese are at their greatest concentration (January and February), the large swarming flocks provide excellent shots.

HUNTING AND FISHING
Waterfowl hunting is permitted mid-Oct. until mid-Jan. Check with the refuge for special duck-hunting limitations.

There is no fishing on the refuge.

San Pablo Bay NWR
Vallejo, California

San Pablo Bay NWR

A crisp wind bathes the mudflats as the fog swirls around Mount Tamalpais. Sailboats skim San Pablo Bay, and the receding tide washes the mud with a spray of tiny bubbles as a group of long-billed dowitchers skitters after the flowing water, their slender bills probing the mud. Here at the northern edge of San Pablo Bay, speeding traffic passes one of the few remaining salt marshes in San Pablo–San Francisco bays.

HISTORY

The 20.6-square mile (13,190-acre) refuge, established in 1974, welcomes more than 3,000 visitors annually.

GETTING THERE

From San Francisco, drive north on US 101 and take the Black Point cutoff (CA 37) east to the refuge. From Sacramento, take I-80 west, then turn west toward San Rafael on CA 37 to the refuge. (Note: Take care driving CA 37. The locals call it Blood Alley.)

■ **SEASON:** Refuge open year-round.
■ **HOURS:** Open daylight hours.
■ **ADDRESS:** San Pablo Bay NWR, P.O. Box 2012, Vallejo, CA 94592
■ **TELEPHONE:** 707/562-3000

WHAT TO SEE

In the Tolay Creek Unit (open to the public), the 3-mile Tubbs Island Trail follows Tolay Creek from CA 37 to San Pablo Bay. At the trail intersection several choices are available. To the left Bay Trail skirts San Pablo Bay and loops around, returning to Tolay Creek. A right turn leads to several shorter loops, one passing by Mid Marsh Pond. Hiking the three loops increases the roundtrip mileage to around 7 miles. The trailhead for Tubbs Island Trail is 0.25 mile east of the intersection of CA 37 and CA 121 off a small, ten-car parking lot on the south shoulder of CA 37.

The trail is bordered on the left by hay and oat fields, on the right by a restored marsh. Salt grass, seen growing along the edge of the marsh, has short, yellow-green leaves and is able to rid itself of excess salt through special glands. Pickleweed and fat hen also grow in the marsh. Note: The trail is excessively muddy in winter. Wear rubber boots if you want to walk it during the rainy season.

The California clapper rail and California black rail are illusive, although shorebirds, waterfowl, and other waterbirds are abundant in fall, winter, and spring. The term "skinny as a rail" is commonly believed to refer to a railroad track, but the saying originated from looking at a clapper rail straight on. There isn't much to view of this hen-sized bird that consists mostly of long beak and long legs. The California clapper rail, an endangered species, lives in salt marshes, and its decline parallels the decline of the marshes.

Canvasback duck

More than 20 species of ducks visit the refuge; several of the most common are buffleheads, mallards, lesser scaup, canvasbacks, northern shovelers, and cinnamon teals.

ACTIVITIES

■ **SEASONAL EVENTS:** The annual three-day Flyway Festival, held in late January (call the refuge office in January to have a flier sent to you), features a number of walks and hikes led by naturalists to explore the various marshes in San Pablo Bay. A canoe trip through the estuary wetlands and birding walks are offered, as well as a class on stream bank restoration techniques; participants get hands-on experience weaving and tying branches to create willow revetments that stabilize stream banks. Bay weather in January alternates between fog, sun, and rain. Dress warmly and wear waterproof hiking boots.

SATELLITE REFUGES

■ **Antioch Dunes NWR** Antioch Dunes is the only inland national wildlife refuge that was forced to close to the public because of a whale. As the Mojave Desert went south (it has long since retreated across the Tehachapi Mountains, the traditional division between northern and southern California, around 260 miles from Antioch), it left behind 100-foot-high sand dunes piled beside the San Joaquin River where it pours into the delta on its way to San Pablo Bay and the Pacific. The refuge consists of remnant dunes left after many years of industrial use—the sand was mined for use in making bricks. Some of the early bricks went to rebuild San Francisco after the 1906 earthquake and fire.

The endangered Lange's metalmark butterfly, Antioch Dunes NWR

Forty miles upriver from the ocean is the last place where a humpback whale might be expected to be found, but a young humpback got lost there. And everyone went trampling across the sand dunes to see this astonishing sight, crushing Antioch Dunes' white-blooming evening primroses and sweet-smelling Contra Costa wallflowers (both growing nowhere else) as they surged forward to view the whale, who had promptly been named Humphrey.

The story has a provisionally happy ending. The 55-acre refuge, which was established in 1980 and remained open to the public for only six years, was closed in 1986 following Humphrey's visit. The endangered Lange's metalmark butterfly now feasts undisturbed on its host plant, the endangered Contra Costa wallflower; and the endangered humpback whale, after swimming for days through the delta and up the Sacramento River, was finally enticed back to the Pacific by a boat playing an underwater medley of humpback songs.

■ **ADDRESS:** Antioch Dunes NWR, Antioch, California, c/o San Pablo Bay NWR, P.O. Box 2012 Mare Island, CA 94592-0012

■ **TELEPHONE:** 707/562-3000

■ **Marin Islands NWR** Two little islands, West Marin and East Marin, rise out of San Rafael Bay east of San Rafael. An impressive rookery of great blue- and black-crowned night-herons and both great and snowy egrets is situated on West Marin. The sheltered coves and shallow mudflats of East Marin attract diving ducks and provide feeding sites for the herons and egrets. East Marin consists of a 13-acre island and the tidal mudflats that make up 118 acres of the 131-acre refuge. East Marin is closed to the public to protect the rookery, although you probably wouldn't want to go there anyway because both islands are covered with poison oak. (West Marin is owned by the California Department of Fish and Game.)

Poison oak grows throughout California at elevations below 5,000 feet. Recognized by shiny green leaflets growing in groups of three, poison oak usually grows as a robust bush some 3 feet to 6 feet high; it also climbs tree trunks like a vine, hanging on with delicate aerial roots and draping down over branches. In fall the leaves turn a beautiful red. In winter poison oak sheds its leaves, but the

SAN PABLO BAY HUNTING AND FISHING SEASONS

Hunting (Seasons may vary)	Jan	Feb	Mar	Apr	May	Jun	Jul	Aug	Sep	Oct	Nov	Dec
geese	■									■	■	■
duck	■									■	■	■
coot	■									■	■	■
pheasant											■	■

Hunting for geese, ducks, and coots is permitted by boat access only, and pheasant hunting is permitted in the Tolay Creek floodplain.

San Pablo Bay is open to fishing year-round. Species such as **striped bass**, **sturgeon**, and **shark** should be eaten only occasionally and in limited quantities. Mercury, PCBs, and other chemicals have been found in San Pablo Bay fish. To reduce your exposure to chemicals, eat smaller fish, eat only the fillet portions, do not eat guts, liver, or fat, and bake, broil, grill, or steam fish, allowing chemical-containing juices to drain away.

bare branches are as poisonous as they are in the summer and much more difficult to spot. The poisonous oil penetrates the skin within 10 minutes of contact. If exposed, wash thoroughly as soon as possible, including all clothes, but avoid touching pets that may carry the oil. Helpful advice that is impossible to follow: If you develop the rash, don't scratch. (See also the sidebar in Sacramento River NWR.)

■ **ADDRESS:** Marin Islands NWR, San Rafael, California, c/o San Pablo Bay NWR, P.O. Box 2012 Mare Island, CA 94592-0012

■ **TELEPHONE:** 707/562-3000

Seal Beach NWR
Seal Beach, California

California least tern

Turn in a circle on the observation platform at the Seal Beach refuge, and what you will see is residential development pressed right up to the edge of the Seal Beach Naval Weapons Station, where the refuge is situated. Oil derricks (on the refuge itself), condominiums, apartments, highways, and bridges make the wildness of this saltwater marsh all the more special.

HISTORY

As development has continued to swallow California's open space, the U.S. Navy has found itself in the unusual position of protecting the state's natural resources. The Seal Beach NWR, established in 1972 by President Richard Nixon, occupies 1.4 square miles (917 acres) of the 7.8-square-mile (5,000-acre) Seal Beach Naval Weapons Station, one of the last remaining large open spaces in coastal Southern California.

The weapons station had its start in World War II when the government purchased 5,000 acres for the storage and dispersal of weapons. By 1964, the Navy designated Anaheim Bay and the salt marsh as a Navy Wildlife Refuge and now shares management of the refuge with the U.S. Fish & Wildlife Service. Until 1995, the refuge was closed to the public, but an accommodation with naval security requirements has opened the refuge to visitors—if advance permission is obtained. The refuge, which attracts around 1,200 visitors annually, opens the last Saturday of the month for tours led by the Friends of the Seal Beach National Wildlife Refuge.

GETTING THERE

From Los Angeles drive south on I-605 and merge south onto I-405. Exit at Seal Beach Blvd. and drive left about 1 mi. (second stoplight past Westminster Blvd.)

to the main entrance of the Seal Beach Naval Weapons Station (800 Seal Beach Blvd.). Turn left into parking lot.

■ **SEASON:** Refuge open year-round.

■ **HOURS:** Open 7:30 a.m.–5:30 p.m. The refuge is open to the public for tours only on the last Saturday of the month from 9 a.m. to 1 p.m. (no reservations necessary). Special tours may be arranged with three-week advance notice to the refuge manager, 562/598-1024, or the public affairs office of the Seal Beach Naval Weapons Station, 562/626-7215. Individuals wishing to see the refuge should call the refuge office in Building #226 at least 48 hours in advance.

■ **ADDRESS:** Seal Beach NWR, P.O. Box 815, Seal Beach, CA 90740-0815

■ **TELEPHONE:** 562/598-1024

WHAT TO SEE

The least tern, a small pale gray and white bird with a black cap, black eye mask, and yellow bill, long ago developed the unlucky habit of laying its eggs on the beaches of Southern California. As development engulfed the coast, the least tern has been driven into smaller and smaller habitats. Its former habit of picking up and moving down the beach to lay a second clutch if a predator arrived to eat its eggs is no longer possible—there is nowhere to go. The tern habitat at the Seal Beach refuge is fenced, preventing land-based predators, but the fence doesn't keep out the crows, which in a recent year ate almost all the eggs in 74 least tern nests.

The light-footed clapper rail, brown pelican, Belding's savanna sparrow, and least tern—all endangered—inhabit the refuge with 225 other bird species.

Historically there were 25 square miles (16,000 acres) of salt marsh in Southern California's Los Angeles and Orange counties. Today the Seal Beach refuge encompasses one-quarter of the remaining salt marsh in the two counties and serves as home to 35 species of plants, including cordgrass, pickleweed, alkali heath, jaumea, saltwort, and sea lavender, with its branched clusters of dainty blue violet flowers that remain on the branches when they dry. Cordgrass grows abundantly along the sinuous channels of the marsh, frequently becoming covered by saltwater in the twice daily tidal fluctuations that characterize the marsh. Spreading by rhizomes, it has hollow stems that allow oxygen to reach its roots; its specialized glands eliminate excessive salt.

An auto-tour route of 0.25 mile with several stops along the way leads to a platform overlooking the salt marsh. A walking trail follows the shoulder of the road. Look for cottontails, black-tailed jackrabbits, and California ground squirrels.

A native plant garden at the nature center provides an excellent place to view native plants; it is described in a pamphlet keyed to numbers along the path. The encelia (or bush sunflower) has showy yellow flowers that bloom from February to June. Coyote brush, favored as a fire retardant in hillside homes, is a fast-growing carpetlike plant that attracts butterflies. Fragrant pink flowers bloom from May to August on the California rose, and the vivid blue flowers of the penstemon and yellow flowering heads of the golden yarrow make a rainbow of garden colors.

Sonny Bono Salton Sea NWR
Calipatria, California

Aerial view of Sonny Bono Salton Sea NWR

Something is wrong here. Dead fish line the shore. Man-made dikes hold back the sea. Two crematoriums incinerate diseased birds to carbonized ash and bone. Distraught birds pull out their feathers. This is the Sonny Bono Salton Sea NWR, the country's most troubled national wildlife refuge. Birds come to this artificial sea by the millions each year—some 4 million of them. They have no place else to go. What happens here in the next several decades will to a large extent define how we as a people intend to live with nature.

HISTORY

Before recorded time, the Salton Sink was once the bottom of a prehistoric sea. The Sea of Cortez (which now separates Baja California from the Mexico mainland and is also known as the Gulf of California) flowed north into what are now the Imperial and Coachella valleys lying between the Chocolate Mountains to the east and Superstition Hills to the south. Over eons the Colorado River deposited vast quantities of silt as it flowed into the Sea of Cortez, forming a delta that eventually closed off the northern arm of the sink from the gulf. The Colorado periodically overflowed its natural levees, creating a vast inland sea known as Lake Cahuilla. Eventually the lake evaporated, forming a dry alkaline basin now called the Colorado Desert, the name given to California's section of the Sonoran Desert.

Westerners, as usual unwilling to watch any source of water flow by unused, diverted water from the Colorado at Yuma, Arizona, into Mexico and back into California to provide water for irrigating the Imperial Valley (now one of the country's main suppliers of agricultural products). The Imperial Canal was completed in 1901, but silt buildup quickly forced a relocation of the diversion a short distance downstream.

WHAT KILLS THE BIRDS During the 1990s, around 200,000 birds died at the Salton Sea. Although the number seems large, it pales beside numbers from the Great Salt Lake and from Saskatchewan, where avian botulism killed a half million birds in one year. But attention focused on the Salton Sea in 1992 when 150,000 grebes died and again in 1996 when some 1,500 California brown pelicans and more than 8,500 white pelicans died.

Loss of habitat along the Pacific Flyway has helped create the conditions for disease. Migratory birds are forced to concentrate in smaller and smaller areas, making disease easier to spread. At the Salton Sea, avian botulism strikes in the summer when fish-eating birds stop at the refuge, where the disease is tied to fish carrying the botulism bacteria. Avian botulism is a paralytic, often fatal, disease. The clostridium botulinum bacterium that carries the toxin resists heat and drying and remains viable for many seasons. Contributing factors to outbreaks of avian botulism include water quality, the presence of vertebrate and invertebrate carcasses, and high ambient temperatures. If rotting carcasses are not picked up, maggots become infected with the bacteria and are eaten by birds. Waterbirds and shorebirds are most often affected by the disease.

Avian cholera is a highly infectious disease caused by the bacterium pasteurella multocida. Death can result in 6 to 12 hours after exposure. Two of the country's major focal points for avian cholera are in California—the Central Valley and Klamath Basin. Major dieoffs of waterfowl are common, occurring almost yearly. At the Salton Sea, avian cholera usually strikes in December and January—in wintering areas where the birds concentrate. It is believed to arrive with the white geese. Death can be so quick that birds may literally fall out of the sky with no sign of illness.

The first documented instance of Newcastle disease in wild birds west of the Rocky Mountains occurred in double-crested cormorants in their nesting colony at the Salton Sea in 1997. The disease has many mutations, not all fatal, but a virulent form of the disease strikes suddenly and kills quickly without other clinical signs. It is normally associated with chickens and turkeys.

An unknown disease has appeared at the Salton Sea, killing only eared grebes. The birds pull out their feathers (it is not known if this is a result of the disease) and crowd around the inlets where freshwater is released into the sea. It is, perhaps, the consequence of attempting to live in a body of water degraded with runoff pesticides and an ever increasing level of salinity.

Winter floods in 1905 breached the diversion. For 15 months the entire Colorado River poured through Mexicali and the Imperial Valley into the Salton Sink, creating the Salton Sea. The surface of this 35-mile-long sea now lies 227 feet below sea level.

The Salton Sea NWR was established in 1930 by President Herbert Hoover. Renamed the Sonny Bono Salton Sea NWR in memory of the late member of the U. S. House of Representatives, the 58.8-square-mile (37,659-acre) refuge attracts around 30,000 visitors annually.

GETTING THERE

From Los Angeles, drive east on I-10 past Palm Springs. In Indio, turn south on CA 111 and drive along the east side of the Salton Sea to Niland. Five mi. south of Niland, turn west on Sinclair Rd. and drive 6 mi. to refuge headquarters. To visit the southern unit of the refuge, drive south on Gentry Rd. from refuge head-quarters. Take a sharp right jog, then turn south again on Forrester Rd. Turn west on Bannister Rd., then north on Vendel Rd. to the refuge parking lot.

From San Diego, drive east on I-8, then north on CA 86. In Brawley, follow signs to CA 111 north and follow instructions above.

■ **SEASON:** Refuge open year-round.

■ **HOURS:** Open sunrise to sunset. Visitor Center open Mon.–Fri., 7a.m.–3:30 p.m. Call ahead to see if the Visitor Center will be open on the weekend.

■ **ADDRESS:** Sonny Bono Salton Sea NWR, 906 W. Sinclair Rd., Calipatria, CA 92233

■ **TELEPHONE:** 760/348-5278

TOURING SONNY BONO SALTON SEA

■ **BY FOOT:** Trailhead for the 2-mile Rock Hill Trail is near the Visitor Center. A .5-mile trail on Unit 1 leads to an observation platform.

■ **CANOE, KAYAK, OR BOAT:** Boating is popular on the Salton Sea. There are no boat rental businesses near the refuge, however.

WHAT TO SEE

■ **LANDSCAPE AND CLIMATE** Sonny Bono Salton Sea is the only refuge in the West that has lost ground—literally. Because the Salton Sea is the lowest point in the region, everything flows into it—pesticides, fertilizers, untreated sewage from the New River flowing out of Mexico, heavy metals, water—and nothing flows out.

Blue-footed booby and chick

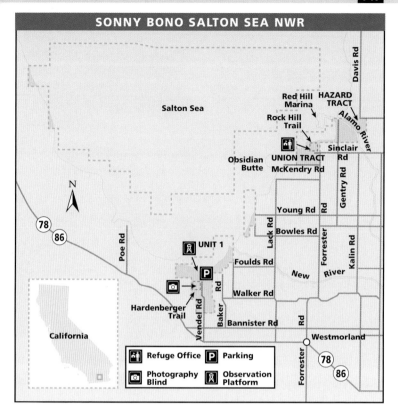

SONNY BONO SALTON SEA NWR

The rising sea level (which was relatively stable during the 1990s) has reduced the refuge's original 37,000 acres to about 1,785 acres remaining above water.

But the increase in size of this accidental sea is the least of its problems. Evaporation from its 380-square-mile surface (35 miles long by 9 to 15 miles wide) continues to increase the saline content of the sea at a rate of 0.5 percent per year (the concentration of pesticides and other pollutants also continues to rise). At century's end the sea's salinity was 44,000 parts per million (20 percent more than the Pacific Ocean's salinity of 35,000 parts per million). If the salinity reaches 50,000 parts per million, no fish will be able to spawn, and an entire ecosystem based on a food chain that includes fish-eating birds will simply disappear.

In a scenario eerily reminiscent of Los Angeles's taking of the Owens Valley water, plans are advancing for San Diego to buy clean water from the Imperial Irrigation District, which controls the waters flowing into the Salton Sea. Agricultural fields would lie fallow part of the year instead of being in production 365 days, causing the Salton Sea to recede and the salinity level to increase even more rapidly in this desert where only 1.5 inches of rain falls annually. (A side effect of the Imperial Irrigation District sale of water is that the refuge would regain some of the land it has lost.) It was estimated that by 2008 fish would no longer be able to spawn in the sea, and the chief living thing to be found in the water would be brine shrimp and possibly tilapia that were able to spawn in the freshwater canals flowing into the sea. Fish-eating birds could no longer depend on the sea for food.

Wildlife biologists agree that the only way to save the Salton Sea is to pump in

The yellow-footed gull's only stop in the United States is at Salton Sea.

less salty water and pump out highly saline water. (Pumping in freshwater would of course be the best solution, but freshwater is tied up in California's complicated water-allotment system.) A proposal to pump water from the Pacific Ocean some 130 miles over the mountains into the sea and pump the highly saline water out to some area willing to accept it has been suggested, an engineering feat posing no technical problems but raising a basic question about the nation's commitment to our wildlife: How much is the continued life of an entire ecosystem worth?

■ PLANT LIFE

Wetlands Cattails and alkali bulrush grow in the refuge freshwater marsh habitat along with swamp timothy and spike rush. Cottonwoods and willow can be found in the riparian areas surrounding the freshwater, but the common tree is the invasive tamarisk. Because it looks something like a cedar, its common name is salt cedar. The tamarisks choke out native vegetation and use copious amounts of water. Because their seeds spread so easily, they are difficult to control.

Arid lands Plants growing in the high heat of the Colorado Desert have evolved to withstand temperatures of 110 degrees F., long periods of no rain, and, near the Salton Sea, high salinity. Pickleweed, growing in abundance at the edge of San Francisco Bay, is also found in abundance at the edge of the Salton Sea, where it tolerates the high salinity. This succulent has a series of jointed sections and absorbs both salt and water. The top joint eventually dies and falls off, allowing the plant to shed salt. The iodine bush, also growing in saline soil near the pickleweed where other plants can't survive, uses the same mechanism for survival: succulent sections that store water and dilute the effect of the salt. Both plants have a long taproot; and, like pickleweed, the iodine bush drops off its top sections.

The honey mesquite, an inhabitant of the alkali sink, has a long taproot that can reach to water some 50 feet underground. In a severe drought the mesquite sheds its leaves, then regrows them when it finds moisture. Displaying daisylike flowers of bright yellow after spring rains, the brittlebush also drops its leaves in extremely dry conditions. Summer usually finds it leafless.

Grasslands Blue and green palo verdes, screwbean, desert thorn, and honey mesquite can be found growing along the edge of refuge croplands leased to farmers growing winter wheat and alfalfa. The crops are intended to keep the birds on the refuge and away from adjoining agricultural fields.

■ ANIMAL LIFE

Birds At any time of the year, the Salton Sea teems with birds (although—unless you enjoy wandering around in 110-degree heat—you may not want to explore the refuge in summer). For those less timid of desert heat, the refuge offers unique birds seen only during the summer at the Salton Sea—nesting gull-billed terns, black skimmers, and Caspian terns right at refuge headquarters as well as rare visitors from Mexico such as magnificent frigatebirds and blue-footed boobies.

The refuge has one of the largest and most diverse bird lists in the country—384 species and counting. Birders will want to visit the refuge to view species such as the yellow-footed gull (present in spring—the Salton Sea is the only area in the United States where it can be seen). For most visitors, the exciting spectacle of 30,000 white pelicans—an estimated 80 to 90 percent of the western population—stopping over (common in spring, summer, and fall) is reason enough to visit the Salton Sea. In winter 90 percent of the nation's eared grebes migrates through the sea during winter months on their way to the Sea of Cortez.

American avocets and black-necked stilts breed in the refuge; thousands of waterfowl winter at the Salton Sea—Canada, Ross', and snow geese, ruddy ducks, pintails, and green-winged teal—and are commonly seen. Seventeen species of gulls have been recorded at the refuge, and on land the endearing greater roadrunner may dash past (common all year)—with Wily Coyote not far behind, of course.

Around 70 to 80 percent of the state's burrowing owls live in Imperial County's low-lying grasslands and semidesert, where they inhabit burrows abandoned by ground squirrels. The burrow entrances are quite distinctive because

Burrowing owls

the owls line them with cow manure, insect parts, cotton, dead frogs, plastic, and tinfoil. Burrowing owls on the refuge have their own "owl condos." More than 50 artificial owl nest chambers, consisting of a tube and plastic box for the nest area, have been placed on and off refuge property. Biologists, having easy access to the chambers, study potential effects of pesticides on burrowing owls, including their fledging success. The tubes also help prevent the owls from damaging the sides of the area's irrigation canals.

Mammals Twelve species of bats inhabit Sonny Bono Salton Sea. The Mexican long-tongued bat uses its long tongue to feed on nectar and pollen. The California leaf-nosed bat, an insect eater, hovers above ground and swoops down to seize its prey. The hoary bat, with a wingspan to 16 inches, is a rare species that migrates to the sea in winter. Another rare species, the spotted bat, curls up its long ears when resting. The smallest bat in the United States, the western pipistrel, has an 8-inch wingspan and a weak, fluttering flight like that of a moth.

Bat

Pocket gophers, the bane of western gardeners, live in burrows and feed on roots. It is not unusual to watch a plant sedately disappear underground. The gopher is dragging it down for a midday feast. Among the larger refuge mammals are coyotes, desert kit foxes, raccoons, ringtail and coatis, badgers, and western spotted and striped skunks.

Reptiles and amphibians

The most irascible member of the desert community has to be the desert diamondback rattlesnake. Approached, it rattles continuously and strikes frequently at anything nearby. Pugnacious and big (to 4 feet), it has the typical beautiful pattern of diamonds down its back and the rattles at the tail end that rightly strike fear into those hearing them unexpectedly (the rattles are meant to warn off intruders). Hunting, the snake locates its victim by odor, using its forked tongue. The snake employs its temperature-sensitive labial pits on either side of its nostrils to sense the approach of its prey and strike. The snake's jaws can separate, allowing it to swallow prey much larger than itself. Watch for rattlers behind rocks and under logs. Never put your hand where you can't see what's there, and watch where you step. If you see a rattler, simply back away. It doesn't really want to bite you because you are too big for dinner.

Fish At least 1 million fish die in the Salton Sea annually, yet enough fish remain to adequately feed 30,000 white pelicans, 12,000 double-crested cormorants, up to 5,000 brown pelicans, and numerous herons, egrets, and Clark's and western grebes. Few species can tolerate the sea's high salinity—several species introduced in the 1950s, including gulf croaker and orangemouth corvina, are greatly reduced or gone, and the tilapia are dying by the thousands, floating on the surface and strewn along beaches. (Sport fishing remains a popular activity at the sea.) Freshwater fish include carp, channel catfish, largemouth bass, and sailfin molly.

ACTIVITIES

■ **CAMPING:** Two campgrounds are available in the Salton Sea State Recreation Area south of Desert Beach near the north end of the sea.

■ **WILDLIFE OBSERVATION:** Best times for visiting Sonny Bono Salton Sea are fall, winter, and spring. For shorebirds, visit in spring. Waterfowl visit the refuge in fall and winter, with 60,000 ducks present on any day from November to February and up to 30,000 Ross', snow, and Canada geese during the same period. More than a million eared grebes arrive in late winter, and various species of songbirds can be seen at all times of the year.

■ **PHOTOGRAPHY:** In Unit 1, a photo blind (a wooden box sized for two people) overlooks a wetland where waterfowl and clapper rails may be present. Arrive in early morning. No reservations. A viewing platform near headquarters may allow good early-morning shots of perching birds.

HUNTING AND FISHING
Waterfowl hunting is permitted from Oct. to Jan.

Shore fishing for **corvina**, **croaker**, **striped mullet**, and **talapia** is permitted on the refuge, but note that because driving is not permitted on the refuge, you will have to walk to the shore. Boat fishing is not permitted.

■ **HIKES AND WALKS:** Rock Hill Trail near headquarters passes a thicket of desert trees and leads to a long dike holding back the sea. The land here is around 8 feet below sea level. The trail continues past marshes to Rock Hill and to great views of the sea and refuge.

■ **SEASONAL EVENTS:** The Salton Sea International Bird Festival is held in February during President's Day weekend. Children's activities, tours, and talks about wildlife on the refuge are offered throughout the weekend. A trade show features books, binoculars, and other items of interest to birders. In October, the refuge celebrates National Wildlife Refuge Week.

■ **PUBLICATIONS:** *California Wildlife Viewing Guide* by Jeanne L. Clark, Falcon Press, Helena and Billings, Montana, 1996.

Stone Lakes NWR
Elk Grove, California

American avocets

The sun sends shafts of sunlight onto the shady path, a kaleidoscope of dark and light, offering cool relief from the blasting, dry heat of the valley summer. The trees tower overhead, cottonwoods, sycamores, valley oak. This rare stand of riparian woodland is dense with undergrowth: bushes, blackberry vines, poison oak, and wild grapevines. It is a reminder of the wild beauty that was once common along the streams and rivers of the Great Central Valley.

HISTORY

The story repeats itself wherever you go in California: At one time the Great Central Valley had more than 6,250 square miles (4 million acres) of wetlands—early travelers described needing a boat to get from San Francisco to Sacramento because the many sloughs and marshes made winter and spring overland travel impossible. By 1985 only 5 percent of the wetlands remained. The Stone Lakes Basin, a remnant of these once vast waterways, was established as a national wildlife refuge in 1994 to protect the area from the burgeoning Sacramento metropolitan area. Only a small portion—1.6 square miles (1,000 acres) of the proposed 28.4-square-mile (18,200-acre) refuge—has been purchased. There are no public facilities yet, but around 7,500 visitors explore the refuge annually during guided tours and other scheduled events. There is no open access to the refuge.

GETTING THERE

From Sacramento, drive south on I-5 and take the Elk Grove exit east. Turn right at stop sign and drive to the refuge gate. The refuge office was scheduled to move in late 1999. Call the California-Nevada FWS office at 916/979-2034 for current location and phone number.

■ **SEASON:** Refuge open only one Saturday per month (for docent-led tours), one Sunday per month, and occasionally for special events.

■ **HOURS:** Tours usually conducted 9 a.m.–noon, but timing varies with season.
■ **ADDRESS:** Stone Lakes NWR, 2233 Watt Ave., Suite 375, Sacramento, CA 95825
■ **TELEPHONE:** Call 916/979-2034 for the new refuge phone number.

WHAT TO SEE

Before most of it was plowed into agricultural fields, the Great Central Valley in springtime was a glory of wildflower bloom—vast fields of golden-orange poppies contrasted against tall stalks of blue lupine and funnel-shaped pinkish white flowers of morning glory spilling over bushes and tufts of grass. (Wild morning glory, by the way, is not the common bindweed, the white-flowered morning-glory lookalike that is almost impossible to eradicate, wrapping around and choking everything it contacts.) Bright red-orange paintbrush and tidytips with their large, pale orange centers tipped with white contrasted with bluish-white brodiaea. A patch of this abundant wildflower garden is preserved at Stone Lakes and makes a springtime expedition to the refuge a special treat. The refuge offers guided walks featuring spring wildflowers and vernal pools.

In winter tule fog hangs low over the valley. Bare branches of the oaks, cottonwoods, and sycamores loom silently through the gray mist, shaking and rattling in the rising wind. Leafless branches on the huge cottonwoods surrounding North Stone Lake reveal the massive stick nests of double-crested cormorants, great blue herons, and great egrets. Some 350 pairs of these large birds nest on the refuge.

Tides originating in the distant Pacific Ocean suck water in and out of the refuge, a tidal change of 6 to 12 inches a day. (The highest point in the refuge is only 16 feet above sea level.) Stone Lakes is a small part of the ecosystem that supports millions of wintering ducks in the Great Central Valley—10 to 12 million ducks arrive in the valley each winter, including 65 percent of all pintails in the United States. Among the several thousand that stop at Stone Lakes are green-winged teal, widgeon, and northern shovelers—along with American avocets, black-necked stilts, greater yellowlegs, sandpipers, and American white pelicans.

Beaver, muskrats, and river otters live in the lakes with Sacramento blackfish, largemouth bass, prickly sculpin, white catfish, Sacramento sucker, and bluegill. Raccoons, gray foxes, striped skunks, opossums, and coyotes inhabit the grasslands and woodlands.

Hawaiian and Pacific Islands NWR Complex

Hakalau Forest NWR, James Campbell NWR, Kealia Pond NWR, Kilauea Point NWR, Hanalei NWR, Midway Atoll NWR, Pacific/Remote Islands NWR Complex

Kilauea Point NWR

The dense greenery of the Hakalau Forest

Hakalau Forest NWR
Hilo, Hawaii

Mist and rain shroud the forest in all shades of gray, and the enveloping canopy of koa and aeohi'a trees closes out the sky, softening the sunlight to fleeting shafts of brightness. Graceful fern fronds brush the forest floor. On the eastern flank of 13,796-foot Mauna Kea, the tallest mountain in the Pacific, lies Hakalau, the United States' only tropical mountain rain forest wildlife refuge. (The country's other tropical rain forests—not preserved as national refuges—are found in Puerto Rico and the Virgin Islands.)

HISTORY

Established in 1985 to protect Hawaii's disappearing forest birds and their forest habitat, the 59.4-square mile (38,033-acre) refuge is divided into two units: the 51-square mile (32,733-acre) Hakalau Forest Unit on the eastern slope of Mauna Kea and the 8.3-square mile (5,300-acre) Kona Forest Unit, added to the refuge in 1997 to conserve endangered plants and birds, particularly the alala (Hawaiian crow). Although open to the public, the rare ecosystem of the Kakalau Forest Unit is explored by fewer than 1,000 visitors a year. The Kona Unit is closed to the public.

GETTING THERE

From Hilo drive west on Saddle Rd. (HI 200). Near the 29-mi. post, turn north on the Mauna Kea Summit Rd. and drive 2 mi. Turn east on Keanakolu Rd. (also known as Mana Rd.) and drive about 16.5 mi. to the locked Maulua gate. Four-wheel drive is necessary to negotiate the two-hour trip on a rutted, unimproved road. Check at refuge headquarters (in downtown Hilo at 32 Kinoole St. across from the post office) for road conditions and reservations (which should be made a week in advance). The Maulua Tract is divided into two areas, the upper (west) end, accessed through the Maulua gate, and the lower (east) end, accessed by crossing the state Piha Game Management Area or Laupaehoehoe Natural Area Reserve. The arduous hike into Lower Maulua follows rough, unmarked trails and takes at least two hours.

■ **SEASON:** The 11.25-square-mile (7,240-acre) Maulua Tract of the Hakalau Unit is open every weekend and holidays to hikers, birders, and photographers. Lower Maulua is open daily.

■ **HOURS:** Maulua Tract is open sunrise to sunset. Both the Hilo and Kona Forest refuge offices are open Mon.–Fri., 7:30 a.m.–4 p.m.

■ **ADDRESS:** Hakalau Forest NWR, 32 Kinoole St., Ste. 101, Hilo, HI 96720-2469; Kona Forest Unit, Hakalau Forest NWR, P.O. Box 244, Honaunau, HI 96726

■ **TELEPHONE:** Maulua Tract, 808/933-6915; Kona Forest unit, 808/328-7366

WHAT TO SEE

■ **LANDSCAPE AND CLIMATE** This magnificent forest tells the story of rain and how it creates an environment. Rain falls heaviest at the forest's lowest elevations (2,500 feet to 4,000 feet in the Hakalau Forest)—at the impressive rate of 250 inches a year. Deep gulches carved by runoff dissect the slopes, covered with bogs

and scrubby forest, all that can grow in such damp conditions. Rain slacks off to a mere 150 inches annually above 4,500 feet, allowing the growth of a luxuriant, close-spaced forest of two native Hawaiian trees. Above 6,000 feet, rainfall tops out at 100 inches a year, and the native forest is edged by abandoned pasture land. During winter months clouds often envelope the rain forest for long periods of time. Heavy rain is interrupted by periods of mist.

At other times of the year, clear morning hours often give way to clouds and rain. Although temperatures in Hilo remain warm all year (averaging 62 to 79 degrees F. in January and 70 to 82 degrees F. in July), the thermometer drops by 3 degrees for each 1,000 feet of gain in elevation.

Feral pigs are a threat to the refuge's native plant species.

■ **PLANT LIFE** The aeohi'a, the most abundant of the Hawaiian native trees, is found in miniature in the lowland bogs, but at higher elevations it stretches to 100 feet, spreading a gorgeous canopy studded with red flowers that resemble pompoms sacred to Pele, the fire goddess. (It was said that if the flowers were gathered en route to the mountain without the correct prayers, a rainstorm would follow, suggesting that quite a few Hawaiians ignored the proper ritual.)

Another forest tree, the koa, with specimens estimated at 300 to 500 years old (their sturdy trunks approach 6 feet in diameter) grows quickly to more than 90 feet.

■ **ANIMAL LIFE** Both trees shelter 14 native birds that have retreated to this last vestige of their native habitat. At that, 8 of the 14 are listed as endangered. The bright orange male aeakepa feeds on insects found among the flowers at the top of aeohi'a trees. It is the only Hawaiian honeycreeper that always nests in tree cavities. Crows—the most ubiquitous of birds in the Western states—have not fared well in the 50th state. The 'alala, or Hawaiian crow, numbers fewer than 20 in the wild. Another rare bird, the aeakiapola'au, lives in the upper forest, feeding on caterpillars and insects living under the bark of trees. The male's plumage is a brilliant yellow with a black mask, and it uses its lower bill to chisel holes in bark. Tip: Best chance of seeing birds in the dense forest is to find a rise above the canopy and look down on the birds as they fly in and out.

Feral pigs eat native plants, spread weeds, and damage the forest floor by their rooting and trampling. They are slated for elimination from the refuge and can be hunted on Lower Maulua only.

Hawaiian stilts

James Campbell NWR
Haleiwa, Hawaii

Passing some of the world's most famous surfing beaches—the Banzai Pipeline, Waimea Bay, and Sunset Beach—while driving Oahu's northern coast hardly prepares one for the tiny corner of old Hawaii now preserved as James Campbell NWR. Trade winds whip across open flatlands where a view of the Pacific is lost behind sand dunes, and birds—all four species of Hawaii's endangered shorebirds—loaf and nest in the flatwater refuge ponds lying next to a sewage plant built on this exquisite coastline.

HISTORY

Driven almost to the point of extinction from loss of their wetland homes and the

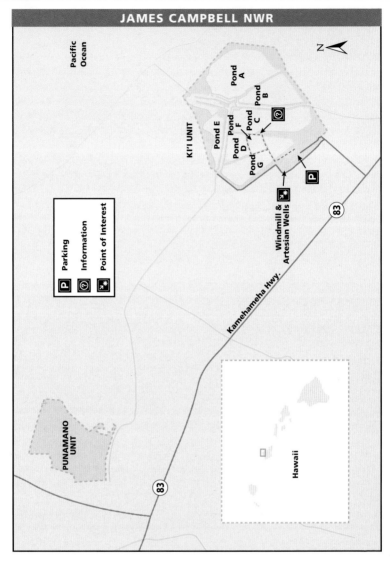

introduction of disease, Hawaii's native birds found one refuge in the settling ponds used to wash sugarcane at the bustling Kahuku Sugar Mill on Oahu's northern coast. When the mill shut down, the ponds dried and birds lost another home. The tiny refuge, only 0.25 square mile (160 acres), was established in 1976 for the purpose of returning the area to bird habitat. It welcomes visitors on a limited basis. Fewer than 575 nature enthusiasts visit James Campbell annually.

GETTING THERE

From Honolulu drive west on H-1. Swing north onto H-2 and take Exit 8 to Wahiawa. Continue through Wahiawa and follow the highway across a plateau through the Dole pineapple plantation. To visit the refuge office, descend the hill to the stop light and turn left toward Haleiwa to the traffic circle. Take the first right on the circle to Haleiwa. Turn right at the Arco station on your right and

The Hawaiian moorhen is one of four endangered bird species on the refuge.

turn into the driveway immediately after the station. Refuge headquarters is on the second floor of the building labeled Excel Surf.

To reach the refuge, continue east on the Kamehameha Hwy. At the Turtle Bay Hilton Resort, check your speedometer and continue 2 mi. to a series of ponds on your left. Turn left at a white, not very noticeable refuge sign, also on your left. Just past the sewage plant veer left onto a gated dirt road.

■ **SEASON:** Refuge open Aug.-mid-Feb.

■ **HOURS:** Office open Mon.–Fri., 7:30 a.m.–4 p.m. Visitors must call the refuge office for an entry permit to the refuge.

■ **ADDRESS:** James Campbell NWR, Oahu NWR Complex, 66-590 Kamehameha Hwy., Rm 2C, Haleiwa, HI 96712-1484

■ **TELEPHONE:** 808/637-6330

TOURING JAMES CAMPBELL

■ **BY FOOT:** Guided walking tours of the refuge are available. A short trail, less than 0.25 mile, leads to a viewing kiosk, then loops around a pond.

WHAT TO SEE

■ **LANDSCAPE AND CLIMATE** James Campbell shares the balmy but breezy climate of the islands. The potentially unpleasant humidity that ranges around 60 percent is alleviated by trade winds blowing fairly regularly during the hot summer season. Temperatures remain steady throughout the year, from 65 to 79 degrees F. in January and 74 to 87 F. degrees in July. Rain falls on the refuge at a rate of 28 inches a year. Like all islands in the Hawaiian chain, Oahu is gradually sinking into the ocean as its great weight causes a sag in the Pacific Plate, which carries all the islands northwest at a rate of around 3 inches a year.

■ **PLANT LIFE**
Wetlands The ponds' low-growing plants provide both cover and food for the waterfowl. As in all of Hawaii, 70 percent of the plants on the refuge are introduced, although four native species can be found in James Campbell. The

English water hyssop is a creeping herb only an inch high with long stems that root at the nodes. Its small flowers are white to pale lilac, and the hyssop, growing in brackish water, is indigenous to various Pacific islands. The English sea purslane (*akulikuli* in Hawaiian), growing in mudflats and coastal wetlands throughout the Pacific, is a succulent whose flowers are pink on the inside and green on the outside. Other natives include the Hawaiian honohono, a creeping prostrate grasslike herb, and a perennial sedge called makai by Hawaiians. Makai is also found in many areas of Asia, the Americas, and Europe.

Among the introduced plants are cattails, pickleweed (growing robustly in Hawaii, it tends to dominate a pond, forcing out other vegetation), and English swamp morning glory.

■ ANIMAL LIFE

Birds Seventy kinds of birds found nowhere else in the world were on Hawaii when Captain James Cook first visited in 1778. Today 25 are extinct and 30 are threatened with extinction.

Four endangered birds endemic to Hawaii (species that evolved and breed in Hawaii and nowhere else in the world) use James Campbell's ponds—the 'alae 'ula (Hawaiian moorhen or gallinule), 'alae ke'oke'o (Hawaiian coot), koloa maili (Hawaiian duck), and ae'o (Hawaiian stilt). Both male and female koloas look like a common mallard, but smaller, and have been interbreeding with mallards dropping by Hawaii during migration. Only Kauai currently has a purebred strain of koloas. The Hawaiian coot, recognized by its white bill and forehead, nests in fresh or brackish ponds in a floating nest constructed from aquatic vegetation. Similar in appearance but with a bright red bill and forehead is the Hawaiian gallinule. The moorhen hides in shoreline vegetation and rarely swims in open water like the coot. The Hawaiian stilt is impossible to miss with its long pink legs and pretty black-and-white plumage. Its distinctive yipping call will alert you to its presence before you see it.

The sadly low average numbers of these endangered birds counted on the refuge in 1998 are a commentary on endangered species: stilts, 100; coots, 250; moorhens, 37; and Hawaiian ducks, 19.

Commonly seen nonnative birds on the refuge include the cattle egret and spotted and zebra doves. The frequently seen black-crowned night-heron is indigenous.

Just a few of the nonresident birds stopping off at James Campbell are the bristle-thighed curlew, pectoral sandpiper, long-billed dowitcher and lesser yellowlegs—as well as several duck species.

Mammals The introduced mongoose preys on the eggs and chicks of shorebirds. An intensive trapping program targeting the mongoose, rats, and feral cats and dogs has reduced but not eliminated these predators.

Mongoose

ACTIVITIES

■ **WILDLIFE OBSERVATION:** Looking out from the viewing kiosk—with its fake owl swaying in the trade winds at the end of a rope—offers an excellent overall view of the refuge. The owl scares off alien birds that were covering the kiosk with white droppings. Walk the loop trail slowly and quietly to observe nesting activities of the birds.

■ **PHOTOGRAPHY:** Stopping at a viewpoint off the Kamehameha Highway from late December through mid-March may offer shots of humpback whales. The refuge has no photo blinds, and wary birds keep their distance. A powerful telephoto lens is needed for close-ups of stilts or moorhens.

■ **HIKES AND WALKS:** Refuge naturalists offer a monthly guided tour during the refuge open season with views of five of the refuge's seven major ponds. The trail around the ponds is exposed. Bring a hat with a chin strap, windbreaker jacket, sunglasses, and suntan lotion. Summer can be hot and muggy if the trades aren't blowing.

■ **PUBLICATIONS:** *A Guide to Pacific Wetland Plants* by Lani Stemmermann, U.S. Army Corps of Engineers, Honolulu District, 1981. *A Pocket Guide to Hawaii's Birds* by H. Douglas Pratt, Mutual Publishing, 1998.

Migrating ruddy turnstones

Kealia Pond NWR
Kihei, Maui, Hawaii

Winds rush through Maui's isthmus and brush Kealia Pond. The Hawaiian stilts shelter next to clumps of vegetation in the largest natural wetland still remaining in Hawaii. Across the narrow land bridge that separates Kealia Pond from the Pacific Ocean, dozens of baby hawksbill turtles erupt from their sandy nests and rush across the beach to the ocean. Set against a backdrop of the 10,000-foot Haleakala Mountains, the pond is a place of changing dimensions, shrinking from 210 to 50 acres as the island's rains decrease during the summer months, expanding as the rains swell the three streams flowing into the pond.

HISTORY

Human engineering of Kealia Pond began long before it became a wildlife refuge. Around 400 years ago, the Hawaiians living near the pond utilized an inlet that connected the pond to the Pacific. Nearshore fish, such as mullet, swam into the pond where they could be trapped and caught.

When the pond dries in summer, shrinking to half its size, it leaves a crust of pure crystalline salt around its perimeter. One meaning of "Kealia" is "the salt-encrusted place," and Hawaiians gathered salt there for centuries. The 1-square-mile (691-acre) refuge was established in 1992 and attracts approximately 3,900 visitors each year.

Hawaiian duck

GETTING THERE

From the Kahului Airport, drive south on HI 380 toward Maalaea. Turn southeast onto HI 350, then south on the Mokulele Hwy. (HI 311). Entrance to the refuge is on a dirt road to the right, exactly at Milepost 6.

■ **SEASON:** Refuge open year-round; some areas closed during nesting from about March through Aug.
■ **HOURS:** The ponds at headquarters are open the same hours as headquarters, Mon.–Fri., 8 a.m.–4:30 p.m.
■ **ADDRESS:** Kealia Pond NWR, P.O. Box 1042, Kihei, HI 96753
■ **TELEPHONE:** 808/875-1582

TOURING KEALIA

■ **BY AUTOMOBILE:** North Kihei Rd. (HI 310) follows the isthmus separating Kealia Pond from the Ma'alaea Bay. Several pullouts overlooking the beach and bay are available along the road, and a boardwalk and information kiosk were scheduled for completion in 2000. To drive the road, continue south past the refuge entrance and turn west on Pillani Hwy. (HI 31), which becomes North Kihei Road.
■ **BY FOOT:** Kealia (pronounced keh-AH-lee-ah) has about 1 mile of trails on pond dikes.

WHAT TO SEE

■ **LANDSCAPE AND CLIMATE** Joined by an isthmus that cuts north to south through the middle of Maui, two great mountain ranges form the weather patterns on the island, funneling the trade winds blowing from the northeast through the isthmus and bathing the island lowlands with wind. Kealia Pond lies next to the Pacific at the southern edge of the isthmus and shares the lively breezes

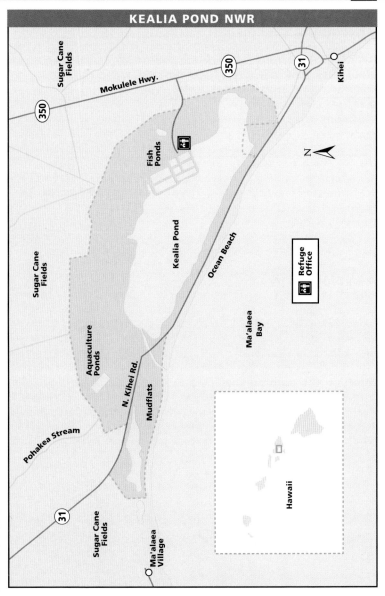

KEALIA POND NWR

Sugar Cane Fields

Mokulele Hwy.

350

31

Kihei

350

Fish Ponds

N

Kealia Pond

Ocean Beach

Refuge Office

Sugar Cane Fields

Ma'alaea Bay

Aquaculture Ponds

N. Kihei Rd.

Mudflats

Pohakea Stream

Hawaii

31

Sugar Cane Fields

Ma'alaea Village

that flow through it. The mountains also catch the rain. Puu Kukui (elevation 5,788 feet) in the West Maui Mountains is soaked each year with more than 400 inches of rain, while Kealia Pond, lying in the mountains' rain shadow, receives only 10 to 12 inches. The Haleakala Mountains, reaching an elevation of 10,032 feet, are drenched with 250 inches of rain annually. (Be sure to see Haleakala National Park, a day trip from Kihei.)

At the end of the west Maui watershed, Kealia Pond serves as a silt basin for runoff—an estuary that captures silt and runoff from agricultural fields before entering the ocean. Silt has lowered the pond's depth to its present 3 feet (approximately). Its waters are brackish, ranging from a seventh as salty as the ocean to half as salty. Sand usually plugs the pond's outlet to the Pacific, although on rare occasions it washes out during heavy rains, allowing more salty water to enter.

Temperatures on the isthmus are balmy but humid and change little throughout the year—in January, the average is around 70 to 80 degrees F.; in July, the thermometer doesn't register much difference—75 to 85 degrees F.

■ PLANT LIFE

Wetlands As much as 90 percent of the vegetation in the refuge is exotic— such aggressive introduced species as mangrove, Indian fleabane, and pickleweed. (Considered an undesirable exotic on Maui, pickleweed in California's San Francisco Bay refuge is protected as a necessary habitat for the endangered salt-marsh harvest mouse.) The kiawe, a type of mesquite, was imported for use as fence posts and firewood. Its smoky flavor is considered tops for barbecuing, but its habit of choking out natives has made it a target for eradication by volunteers who work on the refuge.

Native plants that have regenerated where exotics were removed include the akulikuli, a low-growing ground cover, and a native grass, aki aki.

■ ANIMAL LIFE

Birds Resident birds include the Hawaiian stilt, Hawaiian coot and Hawaiian duck—all endangered species—while the fall migration (October to December) brings many waterfowl to Kealia. Look for wandering tattlers, sanderlings, shovelers, pintails, wigeons, green-winged teal, and ruddy turnstones. The turnstones got their name because they browse on beaches or any flat land covered with small, pebbly stones, which they turn over, searching for bugs.

Reptiles and amphibians Beautiful antique fans and combs displayed in museums testify to the former popularity of objects carved from tortoiseshell. They also testify to the near disappearance of the hawksbill sea turtle. Between 1970 and 1989, more than 1.2 million hawksbills were slaughtered to provide the translucent and elegantly patterned shells used for tortoiseshell crafts.

Hawksbill turtle

Hawksbills live in warm tropical seas, eating jellyfish, sea urchins, sea sponges, and algae growing on the coral reefs they frequent. The turtles take in ocean water while feeding but rid themselves of excess salt by shedding big, salty tears.

Reaching 3 feet in length and weighing as much as 165 pounds, the hawksbill is one of the smaller of the seven species of sea turtle. Its shell, a rich chocolate brown smudged with an irregular pattern of light tan markings, is thicker than that of other sea turtles. Rather than having the smooth, rounded edge found on other sea turtles, the hawksbill's shell is distinguished by a serrated edge around its rear third.

The female comes ashore every two or three years to lay around 160 eggs in a hole she digs in the sand. The hawksbills usually choose isolated beaches for nesting, and even at that only one or two of the 160 can expect to reach adulthood.

Nesting on Kealia Beach across from the refuge (but not a part of it) has proved even more hazardous for the turtles. When they are ready to hatch, the hatchlings break their shells at the same time because they are all needed to climb out of the sand pit where they are buried. Digging up through the sand and shoving it onto the egg shells, they create a platform on which they can crawl out. They race to the sea, attracted by the its shine; but headlights from the nearby highway and artificial light from condominiums and hotels along the shore can confuse them. Until the refuge built a fence to prevent them from reaching the road, an occasional hawksbill crawled toward the highway instead of the ocean.

Residents wanting to protect the fragile safety of these ancient creatures have formed the Dawn Patrol, walking the beach each morning June through October monitoring turtle tracks. For information on this environmental activity, call the refuge.

ACTIVITIES

■ **CAMPING:** No campgrounds are nearby.

■ **WILDLIFE OBSERVATION:** Morning, from around 8 a.m. to 11 a.m., offers best viewing on the refuge. The winds usually rise later, and the sun is angled correctly for seeing the birds.

> **HUNTING AND FISHING**
> There is no hunting or fishing allowed on this refuge.

■ **PHOTOGRAPHY:** Because there is little cover on the refuge, getting close enough to the birds for photographs is difficult. Use a telephoto lens. Stilts can often be seen wading in the wetlands next to the road to headquarters, offering a chance to use your car as a photo blind. The stilts panic easily, so do not try to hop out for a close-up.

■ **HIKES AND WALKS:** A stroll along the beach offers an excellent chance to see humpback whales during their winter stay in Hawaiian waters. The whales arrive from Alaska in late December and depart around mid-March. (See sidebar, Kilauea Point NWR.)

SATELLITE REFUGE

■ **Kakahaia NWR** Kiawe woodlands surround a coastal freshwater pond (formerly a fish pond) on the 45-acre refuge, situated along the south coast of Molokai 5 miles east of Kaunakakai. To observe or photograph the endangered Hawaiian coot, call the refuge manager.

■ **ADDRESS:** Kakahaia NWR, Kaunakakai, Molokai; c/o Kealia Pond NWR, P.O. Box 1042, Kihei, HI 96753

■ **TELEPHONE:** 808/541-1201

Kilauea Point lighthouse

Kilauea Point NWR
Kilauea, Kauai, Hawaii

On a windswept point at the northernmost tip of Kauai, basaltic cliffs—all that is left of an ancient volcanic vent—fall 568 feet straight down to the Pacific Ocean. From the edge of the cliffs, you can see the curve of the earth. Below, waves crash into the basalt while on the point birds drift by at eye level, floating on unseen updrafts. Kilauea Point is a place of mystical, romantic beauty—and among the most visited of all national refuges in states washed by the Pacific.

HISTORY

It was 1927, and a pilot and a navigator flying the *Bird of Paradise*, in the first attempt to fly a land-based plane across the Pacific from the mainland to Hawaii, had missed the islands. As they flew on over the vast, empty ocean, their plane low on gas, they saw the double flash of the Kilauea lighthouse lamp and turned back to a safe landing at Wheeler Field on Oahu.

The lighthouse, now a National Historic Place, and its surrounding lands became Kilauea Point NWR in 1985 when the U.S. Coast Guard transferred the site to the U.S. Fish & Wildlife Service. Both Mokolea Point, east of Kilauea Point, and Crater Hill, between the two points, were added to the refuge in 1988. The tiny 0.3-square mile (204-acre) refuge welcomes around 300,000 visitors annually.

GETTING THERE

From Lihue, drive north on HI 56 (Kuhio Hwy.) about 23 miles to Kilauea. At the entrance to town, follow signs to Kilauea Lighthouse, turning right on Kolo Rd., then left on Kilauea Rd. The refuge is at the end of Kilauea Rd.

■ **SEASON:** Refuge open year-round.

■ **HOURS:** Refuge and visitors' center open daily, 10 a.m.–4 p.m. Closed Thanksgiving, Christmas, and New Year's Day.

■ **FEES:** Entrance fee: $2 per person 16 and older.

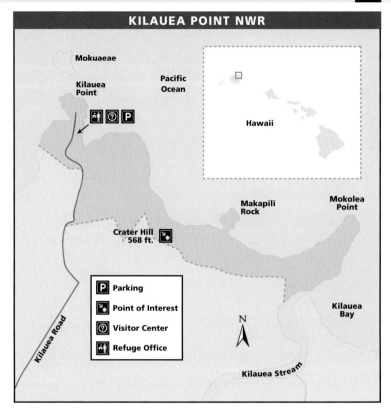

■ **ADDRESS:** Kilauea Point NWR, P.O. Box 1128, Kilauea, Kauai, HI 96754-1128
■ **TELEPHONE:** 808/828-1413

TOURING KILAUEA POINT

■ **BY FOOT:** A 0.1-mile paved path leads from the parking lot to the Visitor Center and lighthouse.

WHAT TO SEE

■ **LANDSCAPE AND CLIMATE** The cliffs of Kilauea Point tell the story of the enormous eroding power of the ocean. The Pacific has worn away half of a massive volcanic vent that last erupted some 15,000 years ago, leaving only a rocky U-shaped section along the northern Kauai coast, defined by Kilauea Point to the west and Mokolea Point at the eastern tip of the U. A small island off Kilauea Point is another segment of the vent. The cliffs, pocked with caves and rock formations carved by the ocean, are a haven for seabirds, making Kilauea Point the best place in Hawaii to view these magnificent birds, which spend much of their lives at sea.

The refuge's climate is typical of the Hawaiian Islands—around 69 to 85 degrees F. and humid enough to curl your hair but consistently cooled by the trade winds. (When the trades occasionally stop, the weather turns hot, humid, and unpleasant.) Rainfall at the point averages around 40 inches annually, but the top ridge of Kauai's mountains, only 8 miles away, is doused with more than 400 inches a year.

Rainfall on the windward side of the island increases by 100 inches for every 1,000 feet of gain in elevation.

■ **PLANT LIFE** Kauai, like the other Hawaiian islands, is overgrown with robust exotic vegetation that has crowded out most of the native flora. At Kilauea Point, the exotics are gradually being removed and replaced with indigenous and endemic Hawaiian plants.

Long before the dinosaurs reigned on earth, hala trees thrived—and have survived as a plant native to the Pacific countries and parts of Asia. The hala came to Hawaii eons ago by way of its floating seeds and may also have been imported by Polynesian voyagers for its many uses. The tree, also know as a screw pine because of its spiraling leaf formation, can grow to 50 feet or 60 feet and inhabits a range of plant zones, from sea level to 2,000 feet. Hala leaves (lauhala)—long, straplike, and with sharp spines—grow in a tuft at the top of bare branches and are used to make table and floor mats. Hawaiians also used them to weave fans, line their roofs, and make sails for voyaging canoes. The female hala branches have a hard exterior but a soft inside that can be hollowed out, allowing the branches to be used for water pipes.

Another endemic being planted is the alula. Look for a plant 2 feet to 3 feet tall (6 feet to 8 feet at maturity) with very large leaves distinguished by their scalloped edges.

■ **ANIMAL LIFE**
Birds Birds that evolved over thousands of years on remote islands inaccessible to land mammals safely nested on the ground. Against the alien species—rats, mongooses, cats, dogs, and pigs—introduced to the islands by people, these land nest-

The nene, Hawaii's state bird

ing birds had no defenses. Their numbers plummeted. Hawaii's state bird, the nene, or Hawaiian goose, disappeared from Kauai even before the arrival of Captain James Cook in 1778, decimated by the arrival of Polynesians from Tahiti and the Marquesas between A.D. 500 and 900. A predator-proof fence built around all of Kilauea Point refuge and a predator-trapping program have restored a safe nesting area for the nene and thousands of seabirds that traditionally nest at the point.

The aerial acrobatics of the red-tailed tropic bird and the fact it can rarely be seen elsewhere in Hawaii (look for it also at Makapuu on Oahu) make it one of the more interesting refuge inhabitants. During breeding sea-

Kilauea Point NWR refuge headquarters

son, the tropic bird puts on an intricate courtship display, flying backwards, remaining motionless on the wind, or diving in a series of spectacular somersaults with its long, narrow red-tail streamer extended into the wind. On land, however, the red-tails are unable to walk without falling over. They nest on Kilauea's cliffs and under bushes and are distinguished from the more common white-tailed tropic birds, also nesting on Kilauea's cliffs, by their larger size, red tail, and red bill. (From a distance it is difficult to distinguish the color of the tail. Look instead for black bands on the top of the white-tail's wings.) Watch for both tropic birds from March through October.

Reintroduced to Kauai several decades ago, the nene prefers land to water and can be found in flocks in grassy areas, on golf courses, and in pastures, where it eats introduced and native plants. The geese, seen year-round, have beautiful patterns of rows of white tips on their back feathers, and the deep furrows in their neck feathers appear as black bands.

Laysan albatross returned to Kilauea Point in the 1970s (see Midway Island NWR for a detailed description) and can be seen from December through July.

Kilauea's most visible seabird is the red-footed booby, a year-round resident at the refuge. In spring and summer Crater Hill—seen from Kilauea Point—looks like it is covered with fluffy white basketball-sized balls—the red-footed boobies in their nests. The boobies were named by sailors, who thought they were dumb because they were so easy to grab when they landed on the ship's rigging. The birds catch their food by diving to depths up to 100 feet. Returning to shore to feed their babies, they must contend with the great frigate birds, who eat by skimming the surface and scooping up fish and squid—or by harassing the boobies until they regurgitate their fish, which the frigate birds catch before it falls into the ocean.

HUMPBACK WHALES Given some savvy with a map and a compass (and a boat), you might be able to find your way from Alaska to Hawaii. Humpback whales summer in the food-rich Alaskan waters but unerringly find their way 2,600 miles to Hawaii each winter without the aid of either. It is believed that these huge mammals—the size of a Greyhound bus—have a built-in compass in the form of a metalloid substance called magnetite near their frontal lobe. The magnetite somehow hones in on the magnetic field that encircles the earth and uses it to pinpoint direction. Sunspots or storms on the sun disrupt the earth's magnetic field (sometimes causing radio blackouts) and may account for one reason apparently healthy whales beach themselves; their compass has nothing to lock on to.

The humpbacks are members of the baleen family of whales. Rather than teeth, long strands of baleen— a fingernail-like substance, but much thicker—grow around the upper jaw, hanging down to form a brush-like layer several feet in length. To eat, the whale takes in a huge gulp of water, then shuts its mouth and squirts out the water. As the water pours out, the baleen catches the tiny krill floating in the water. Krill are shrimplike creatures that are the humpback's preferred food. The whale uses its one-ton tongue to lick the krill off the baleen and work it back into the throat where it is swallowed.

The humpbacks are the only known mammals besides humans that compose music. Only the male humpbacks sing, hanging head down about 59 to 75 feet below the water's surface, singing a series of themes and phrases, always in the same order. But during the season, the whale drops some of the phrases and changes others so that by the time for the return to Alaska, the song has changed—and other whales in the area have changed their songs in the same way. Even more fascinating, the humpbacks off the coasts of both Hawaii and Mexico sing the same tunes—suggesting that humpbacks, just like people, prefer to vary their vacation destinations.

Mammals Humpback whales (October to April), spinner dolphins, and Hawaiian monk seals inhabit the waters off Kilauea Point. Rarely seen in the main Hawaiian Islands, monk seals have begun hauling out on Kilauea's north shore. An endangered species, the monk seals spend most of their time in water, diving about 50 times a day in search of food. To eat the lobsters they catch while at sea, they bring them to the surface and smack them against the water. The lobster's shell breaks open and the monk seal dines on the meat from the tail. The seals give birth to one jet-black pup, weighing around 30 pounds. After six weeks of nursing, the pup will gain 120 pounds!

ACTIVITIES

■ **CAMPING:** No campground is nearby.

■ **WILDLIFE OBSERVATION:** A series of panels on the Visitor Center veranda gives visitors an excellent introduction to the birds and geology of the area. By visiting Kilauea Point in spring (March to May), it is possible to see nesting red-footed boobies and Laysan albatross and their chicks. Walking on the refuge at dusk in spring, you may hear terrible moans and cries that sound like a baby in deep distress. Wedge-tailed shearwaters, living in burrows on the refuge, are busy courting.

Humpback whale

The shearwaters spend the winter on the Gulf of Panama, at sea, and return to Hawaii in spring to breed.

An ongoing project fits Laysan albatross with transmitters that send a signal to a satellite and relay back to earth the location of the birds. By signing up with The Albatross Project, you can receive a daily e-mail message saying where the albatross are. The relay has shown them traveling thousands of miles in just several days. Call Ann Bell Hudgins 808/541-2749 for information or sign on at http://www.wfu.edu/albatross.

■ **PHOTOGRAPHY:** Striking views of the cliffs, ocean, and lighthouse can be photographed without a telephoto lens or other special equipment. With patience and a telephoto lens, it is possible, by waiting near the cliff's edge, to photograph a great frigate bird, Laysan albatross, tropic bird, or booby in flight.

■ **HIKES AND WALKS:** Wildlife naturalists offer a daily two-hour hike up a closed hillside of the refuge that includes a look at the remains of World War II bunkers used as a lookout by day and a radar station by night. Hikers walk near the booby colony and view seabirds from the cliff above the crater. Make reservations by calling 808/828-1068—the popular walk is limited to 15 hikers and fills a day or two in advance—and meet at the Visitor Center at 10 a.m.

HUNTING AND FISHING
There is no hunting or fishing allowed on this refuge.

■ **PUBLICATIONS:** *The Birds of Kauai* by Jim Denny, University of Hawaii Press, 1999. *Hawaii's Humpback Whales* by Gregory Dean Kaufman, Island Heritage Publishing, 1986. *Enjoying Birds in Hawaii* by H. Douglas Pratt, Mutual Publishing. *Kauai's Geologic History* by Chuck Blay, TEOK Investigations. *Plants and Flowers of Hawaii* by S. H. Sohmer and R. Gustafson, University of Hawaii Press.

Hanalei Valley

Hanalei NWR
Hanalei, Kauai, Hawaii

The Hawaiian ducks, moorhens, coots, and stilts that live in Hanalei NWR have picked one of the world's most exquisite settings for their home. In the distance, the misty, green-covered mountains known locally as Bali Hai (after the mystical, magical island in the musical *South Pacific*, which was filmed on Kauai) create an ethereal backdrop for the Hanalei Valley, all green and lush with the Hanalei River flowing through it.

HISTORY

The valley has been used for 1,200 years for taro farming. The broad leaves of this plant, a historic mainstay in the Hawaiian diet, have provided a sheltering home for waterbirds, protecting nesting and feeding habitat for the four endangered birds. Established in 1972 (the first national refuge on Kauai), Hanalei includes 1.5-square miles (1,000 acres) and welcomes around 18,230 visitors each year.

GETTING THERE

From Lihue, drive north on HI 56 about 29 mi. Just after crossing the Hanalei River bridge, turn left onto Ohiki Rd. and continue past the Haraguchi Rice Mill to the last buildings on the right, location of the refuge office.

■ **SEASON:** Refuge open year-round.

■ **HOURS:** Open sunrise to sunset. Office open Mon.–Fri., 8 a.m.–5 p.m. although wildlife personnel are not always there.

■ **ADDRESS:** Hanalei NWR, c/o Kilauea Point NWR, P. O. Box 1128, Kilauea, Kauai, HI 96754-1128

■ **TELEPHONE:** 808/828-1413

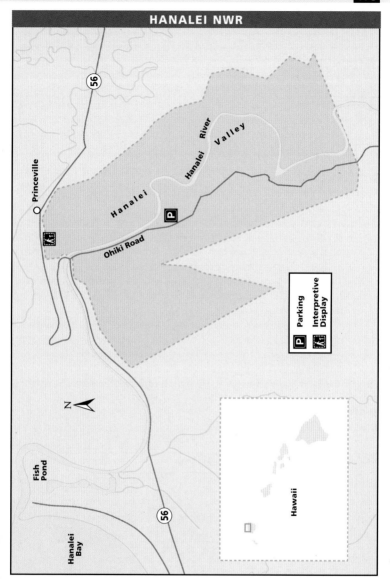

TOURING HANALEI

■ **BY FOOT:** Drive past headquarters to a parking area on the left. The 0.25-mile Kaokaopua (Where the Clouds Settle) Trail begins across the road from the parking area.

WHAT TO SEE

■ **LANDSCAPE AND CLIMATE** The volcano responsible for forming Kauai also laid down a layer of lava (now buried) that makes taro farming possible. Water does not penetrate the dense lava, allowing farmers to create the shallow ponds needed for cultivating the taro. The refuge valley floor, much of it planted in taro, is relatively flat, ranging from about 20 feet to 40 feet above sea level. Steep, wooded hillsides surrounding the valley reach about 1,000 feet. Dense, impermeable lava also forms the base of Hawaii's largest bog, the Alakai Swamp on the summit plateau of Kauai, one of the best places on the island to see native forest birds. The swamp is the highest alpine bog in the world. Mt. Waialeale (5,243 feet), in the mountains above the refuge, is one of the wettest places on earth, drawing enough moisture from the air in the form of more than 400 inches of rain annually that only 75 inches remain to fall on the refuge, most between October and April. Annual temperatures follow the moderate pattern of the islands: 64 to 78 degrees F. average in January and 73 to 84 degrees F. in July.

■ PLANT LIFE

Wetlands A portion of the refuge wetlands is given to growing the historic taro plant. It grows in shallow 1-inch to 4-inch deep wetlands to a height of around 2 feet and is ready to harvest in about 12 to 16 months. Its corm, about twice the size of a large potato, is an important staple throughout the Pacific and in Hawaii is mashed with water into a bland paste called poi. Warning: If you're given a corm, be sure to cook it thoroughly before eating. Taro contains painful calcium oxalate crystals that must be cooked to be destroyed. The large, heart-shaped taro leaves are used as a wrap in the manner of a burrito. The crop is replanted from root stock each year and is harvested by hand.

Growing along the river in periodically inundated freshwater swamps are dense thickets of the hau, or hibiscus, a small tree (to about 20 feet tall) introduced by the Polynesians. The tree's fibrous bark is made into the "grass" skirts worn in various Pacific islands, and the wood was formerly used for outriggers on Hawaiian canoes and fishing floats. Despite its pretty yellow flowers, the hau is considered undesirable because it chokes out wildlife habitat.

■ ANIMAL LIFE

Birds Hanalei's taro patches shelter Hawaii's four endangered shorebirds, which

Taro fields, Hanalei NWR

nest, loaf, and feed under the 2-foot leaves; the nesters use the taro stems as nest supports. These birds look just different enough from their close mainland ancestors to catch the eye of birders. The Hawaiian stilt resembles North America's black-necked stilt but has evolved with more black on its neck and face. It is estimated that only 1,800 Hawaiian stilts remain.

Descended from the American coot, the Hawaiian coot is distinguished by its white frontal shield. Millions of coots were said to live on Kauai in the 1800s; now only a few thousand remain. Both the male and female Hawaiian duck look like a female mallard and have interbred with the mainland species on all the Hawaiian islands but Kauai. Look for the duck in the Hanalei taro patches—it is one of the few places in the islands where the genetically pure Hawaiian duck can be seen. Descended from the common moorhen of North America, the Hawaiian gallinule (also known as the common moorhen or mudhen) sports a red frontal shield. Its solitary habits make it difficult to spot, and the Kauai population is believed to number only a few hundred.

Hawaiian coot

Mammals The absence of a mammal, the mongoose, from Kauai is one reason the native birds haven't been completely wiped out. The story goes that a crate of mongooses was shipped to Kauai to kill rats in the sugarcane fields, but a disgruntled mongoose bit the worker unloading the crate so he tossed the crate overboard.

ACTIVITIES

■ **CAMPING:** No campgrounds are nearby.

■ **WILDLIFE OBSERVATION:** An overlook with interpretive signs on the highway above the refuge, across from the Princeville shopping center, is always open and offers sweeping views of the valley. The taro fields themselves are closed to visitors, but binoculars will help you see birds loafing and eating among the taro.

■ **PHOTOGRAPHY:** It is best to look for stunning shots of scenery and plants in the area. Refuge birds are often hidden under the taro leaves and, because the fields are closed to entry, it is difficult to get close enough for a good photo.

■ **HIKES AND WALKS:** Kaokaopua Trail, though short, is one of the nicest in the western refuges. Bordered by logs salvaged from exotic and dead trees, the trail itself is laid with cobbles collected from the area. Classy enough to have been designed by a landscape architect commissioned to create a *Sunset* demonstration garden, the trail follows an intermittent stream that creates a miniwetland (when it runs), then continues uphill to an ancient shrine where wide-open space gives an expansive view of the refuge, valley, and encircling mountains.

HUNTING AND FISHING
There is no hunting or fishing allowed on this refuge.

The parking area for the trail, next to the Ducks Unlimited pond, is a great place to view all waterbirds.

SATELITTE REFUGE

■ **Huleia NWR** Closed to the public, the refuge, protecting the Hawaiian duck, coot, moorhen, and stilt, encompasses 0.4 square mile (241 acres) along the Huleia River, including the narrow river valley at 5-feet elevation and steep hillsides rising to 200 feet. Taro farming has been reintroduced on the refuge, which can be viewed from the adjoining Menehune Fish Pond or by kayaking the river (kayak rentals and commercial kayaking trips are available in Hanalei and elsewhere). The kayak trip is an interesting reversal of the usual downstream paddle. Because the prevailing wind blows upstream, it is easier to paddle up than down.

■ **ADDRESS:** Huleia NWR, Lihue, Kauai; c/o Kilauea Point NWR, P.O. Box 1128, Kilauea, Kauai, HI 96754-1128

■ **TELEPHONE:** 808/828-1413

■ **GETTING THERE:** From Lihue, drive south for about .5 mi. on Rice St. (which turns into Waapa Rd.) toward Nawiliwili Harbor near Kalapaki Beach. Turn right on Hulemalu Rd. at the Menehune Fish Pond sign and drive 0.6 mi. to the pond overlook, which also affords views of the refuge below.

Laysan albatross

Midway Atoll NWR
Midway Island, U.S.A.

The noise made by 780,000 Laysan albatross overwhelms Midway. As the birds practice their mating dance, they bow to each other; they clack bills together, sounding like woodpeckers on speed; they stretch their long necks to the sky and moan like a foghorn mated to a lovesick cow; they utter shrill, staccato cries like a police whistle stuck on automatic repeat—and they keep it up 24 hours a day. The gooney birds, as the albatross are affectionately known, are so unafraid of people that visitors can walk within one foot of them without causing a distur-

VISITING MIDWAY Visiting Midway is a world-class adventure. Visitors are housed in the remodeled military bachelor-officers' quarters and eat in a cafeteria. An outstanding French restaurant, the Clipper House, is open for breakfast and dinner. Facilities include a bowling alley, movie theater, library, weight room, and gymnasium, but most visitors are too busy looking at the birds, snorkeling, diving, and fishing to use them.

Visitors are urged to contact the refuge for the current list of guides. At time of publication, the following information was accurate: Independent travelers may book a four- or eight-day trip to Midway through MidwayPhoenix Corp., 888/643-9291. The Oceanic Society offers a variety of five- to eight-day nature and research tours to Midway, 800/326-749. Fishing and diving trips should be booked before arriving on the island. Call Midway Sport Fishing, 888/244-8582, or Midway Diving, 888/574-9000.

bance. Midway Atoll, one of the world's most remote places, is a nesting or resting site for 2 million birds—and a star in the country's refuge system.

HISTORY

Midway is the site of one of the greatest naval battles in world history, a battle that marked the turning point in World War II. On June 4, 1942, the Japanese, in control of the Pacific except for Hawaii and Midway, attacked the island. Outnumbered four to one in fighting forces by Japan's Imperial Navy, the Americans, who had broken the Japanese secret code, ambushed the Japanese fleet north of Midway, destroying four Japanese aircraft carriers during the three-day battle and forcing a Japanese retreat. The victory put the Japanese on the defensive, and they never recovered.

Before the war, Midway had been a fuel stop for the Pan Am China clippers—the first planes to make a trans-Pacific flight—and after World War II, for the next 50 years, the atoll served as a naval airbase. Midway Atoll NWR was established in 1988 as an overlay refuge; the Navy closed its base on the island in 1996, turning the entire atoll over to the refuge, and the island was opened to civilian visitors in August 1996.

The refuge, which welcomes around 3,500 visitors annually, includes 466 square miles (298,369 acres). Three islands cover 2.4 square miles (1,549 acres). The remaining 463,8 square miles (296,820 acres) are water.

GETTING THERE

A plane flies from Honolulu, HI, to Midway and back twice a week, with visitors limited to 100 at a time. For information and reservations, call Midway Phoenix Corp., 888-643-9291.
■ **SEASON:** Refuge open year-round.
■ **HOURS:** Open 24 hours. Office open Mon.–Fri., 7:30 a.m.–4 p.m.
■ **ADDRESS:** Midway Atoll NWR, c/o Midway Island Station #4, P.O. Box 29460, Honolulu, HI, 96820-1860
■ **TELEPHONE:** 808/599-3914

TOURING MIDWAY

■ **BY FOOT:** Sand Island, which offers complete visitor facilities, is laced with

MIDWAY ATOLL NWR

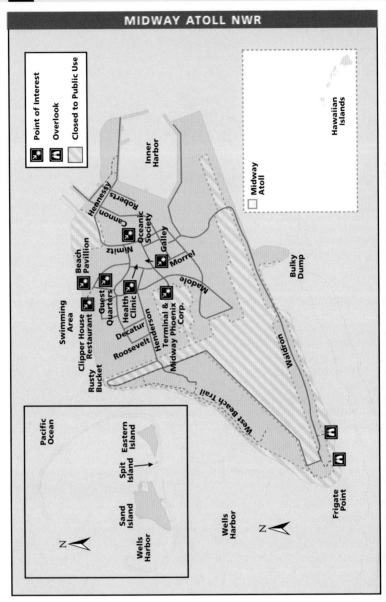

12 miles of narrow paved and gravel roads left over from World War II and the postwar naval air base; all are open for walking. The West Beach Trail is 2 miles one-way.

■ **BY BICYCLE:** All roads are open to bicycles, which can be rented.

■ **BY CANOE, KAYAK, OR BOAT:** Snorkeling, diving, and fishing expeditions from Sand Island are offered daily.

■ **BY GOLF CART:** Several golf carts are available for rent ($25 per day) for persons unable to walk.

WHAT TO SEE

■ **LANDSCAPE AND CLIMATE** Midway—a coral atoll about 5 miles in diameter—lies 2,800 miles west of San Francisco and 2,200 miles east of Japan at a latitude of 28 degrees N. Created some 25 to 30 million years ago by an upwelling of lava from a hot spot in the Pacific Plate near what is now the Big Island of Hawaii, Midway, and the chain of islands in the Hawaiian Archipelago formed by the hot spot, are moving steadily northwest at a rate of 4 inches a year. Midway is now 1,200 miles from Hawaii's Big Island, the southernmost island of the chain and the latest to be formed over the hot spot.

Highest elevation on the atoll, which consists of three small islands surrounded by the emergent reef, is 45 feet. Like all islands in the chain, Midway is gradually sinking into the ocean as the Pacific Plate continues to move northwest—and wind, waves, and rain erode it.

Midway's moderate temperatures and humidity are cooled by nearly constant winds. In January the thermometer averages a low of 63 to a high of 73 degrees F. July heats up, with an average low of 75 degrees F. to a high of 88 degrees F. The 40 inches of annual rain can fall at any time, but heaviest precipitation occurs November through February.

■ **PLANT LIFE** Before humans first arrived at Midway in 1859, Sand Island had little native vegetation. What was there consisted mostly of grasses and a low-lying shrub called naupaka, a plant colonizing sandy areas and helping hold down the sand. Its survival rate is high, because nothing eats it, and it does well in the salt air.

In 1903, however, the Commercial Pacific Cable Co., while laying the first trans-Pacific telegraph cable, brought in ironwood trees, which were planted along the north side of Sand Island for shade and windbreaks. The ironwoods took over, spreading across the entire island and onto Eastern Island. The tree's fallen needles prevent other plants from growing; and the dense accumulation of dead wood and fallen branches forces the albatross to expend great amounts of energy getting through the maze and makes flying out impossible for the birds, which need a running start to get off the ground. Island biologists are gradually removing ironwoods and controlling other weeds throughout the three islands, replacing them with naupaka, beach morning glory, and bunchgrasses—all native plants.

Pacific golden plover

■ **ANIMAL LIFE**
Birds Two million birds use Midway's three islands, including about 70 percent of the world's breeding population of Laysan albatross. With a wingspan of 6 feet, the albatross is

graceful and elegant in flight, comical on the ground with its bouncing waddle—and totally endearing. The birds spend from three to seven years at sea, never touching ground, then return to the grassy open spaces of Midway to mate. The gooney bird mating ritual is one of the great sights of nature. Facing each other, the birds bounce up and down, bow to each other, clack bills together, then stretch their long necks up and moan. The juveniles, looking for a lifelong mate, repeat the dance endlessly, wandering off when they tire of it or turning to dance with a third bird that bounces up to investigate.

The albatross begin arriving on Midway in October. By December the mature females lay an egg, which is incubated by both parents for 65 days. The adults fly off to sea to find food, often leaving the chick for 5 to 10 days. When they return, the chick rattles its beak against its parent's beak until the adult regurgitates a meal for the chick. By July the adults have abandoned land, leaving the chicks on their own to learn to fly—or die. Best viewing of the albatross is December through June. Midway also is home to 22,000 pairs of black-footed albatross, the second largest nesting population in the world.

The male great frigate bird, called "Iwa," or "thief," by the Hawaiians, puffs out its bright red throat pouch and displays vigorously, waiting for a female to notice. A spectacular flyer—but unable to walk or swim—the great frigate bird attacks other birds in the sky, forcing them to drop their food, which it catches midair. Look for it on Eastern Island from February to November.

The sooty tern arrives in March after spending the first two to three years of its life in flight, skimming the water, taking food on the wing and rarely floating on the ocean. The white tern, visible on Midway all year, is beautiful in flight but a careless nester. It lays a single egg directly on a tree branch, and chicks must cling to their precarious perch.

Twenty species of birds can easily be seen on Midway, including the black and brown noddies, bonin petrel red-tailed tropic bird, and red-footed booby. The

Great frigate birds

Green sea turtles on the beach

Pacific golden plover flies nonstop almost 2,800 miles from Alaska to Midway, as does the bristle-thighed curlew.

Mammals Only 1,300 to 1,400 monk seals—the second most endangered seal in the world—remain in the Pacific, and about 65 of those live at Midway. The seals eat octopi, lobsters, reef fishes, and eels, and they are able to dive to a depth of 1,640 feet when searching for food. They haul out on remote beaches, retreating to the water if approached.

A herd of around 250 Hawaiian spinner dolphins play, breed, and rest in Midway's lagoon. These agile dolphins perform spectacular aerial displays, leaping high out of the water and spinning on their axis and slapping their tails. Look for them near Welles Harbor to the west and the mooring basin just north of Sand Island an hour after sunrise until early evening. Lucky visitors may see the Midway spinners approach boats.

Rats, brought to Midway aboard ships, were decimating seabirds that nested on the ground. At its height, a rat eradication program trapped 400 rats a day. The rats having been eliminated, seabird numbers are increasing. Tiny house mice that do not appear to damage wildlife still abound and scurry about the trails at night.

Reptiles and amphibians The green turtle gulps a tiny man-o-war jellyfish floating at the surface, then dives gracefully, its three-foot shell a dark shadow in the clear turquoise water. The endangered turtles feed in Midway's lagoon and swim some 600 miles to nest at French Frigate Shoals within the Hawaiian Islands NWR, an atoll about halfway between Midway and Kauai. The females, which nest every two to three years, crawl onto a beach above high tide line and deposit around 90 eggs in an egg chamber that they have dug. They can lay up to nine

MIDWAY ATOLL FISHING SEASONS

Fishing	Jan	Feb	Mar	Apr	May	Jun	Jul	Aug	Sep	Oct	Nov	Dec
ahi (tuna)	■	■	■	■	■	■	■	■	■	■	■	□
mahimahi (dolphin)	■	■	■	■	■	■	■	■	■	■	■	□
blue marlin	■	■	■	■	■	■	■	■	■	■	■	□
giant trevally	■	■	■	■	■	■	■	■	■	■	■	□
bluefin trevally	■	■	■	■	■	■	■	■	■	■	■	□
sailfish	■	■	■	■	■	■	■	■	■	■	■	□
amberjack	■	■	■	■	■	■	■	■	■	■	■	□
African/Pacific pompano		■	■	■	■	■	■	■	■	■	■	□
spiny lobster	■	■	■	■	■	■	■	■	■	■	■	□
slipper lobster	■	■	■	■	■	■	■	■	■	■	■	□

Because commercial fishing vessels have been excluded from waters around the atoll for nearly 50 years, the area is rich in fish. Catch-and-release fishing is expected to preserve the heavy fish population and assure good sport fishing. All fish caught within the lagoon must be released alive. No one may eat fish from within the atoll's fringing reef because of the threat of ciguatera poisoning. Those fishing outside the lagoon but within refuge boundaries may keep one fish per person per day for consumption on Midway only. There is an abundance of species of pelagic fish on the refuge. Spiny and slipper lobsters may be caught Jan. to Nov. during daylight hours and only by skindivers. Limit one lobster per day per skindiver to be consumed on-island only.

Hunting is not permitted on the refuge.

clutches at two-week intervals, totaling about 90 eggs per season. Researchers estimate only one of every 20,000 hatchlings survives to breed.

Invertebrates Several of the older buildings have been undermined by termites. Both ground termites and air termites are found on Midway, as are giant cockroaches.

ACTIVITIES

■ **SWIMMING:** Lagoon waters inside the reef vary from 4 feet to 40 feet in depth. More than 250 species of fish inhabit the coral reef, and snorkelers may see butterflies, parrots, damsels, angelfish, and wrasses. Water temperatures in the lagoon reach 80 degrees F. during the summer, but winter waters are cold enough to require a wetsuit for comfortable snorkeling and diving. Outside the reef, divers can explore waters ranging in depth from 40 feet to 60 feet and inhabited by manta rays, snappers, groupers, and reef sharks, as well as shipwrecks dating from the 1800s.

■ **WILDLIFE OBSERVATION:** Sand Island, where all visitor facilities are situated, is small—about 1.8 miles long and 1.2 miles wide—allowing visitors to explore all corners. Twice weekly boat trips to Eastern Island that include a short walk and tour on the uninhabited island may allow glimpses of monk seals, green turtles, and a number of seabirds nesting on Eastern.

■ **PHOTOGRAPHY:** A telephoto lens isn't needed for close-up photos of the gooney birds, which may waddle up to inspect you and your camera. On Eastern Island, you will need a telephoto lens for shots of great frigate birds perched in low-growing naupaka trees—and fast film to catch the white terns in flight. A shot of sunset over the north swimming beach with white sand, turquoise water, and pale gray clouds shaded to pinks and apricots will convince everyone that they are in paradise.

■ **HIKES AND WALKS:** A leisurely day-long hike (or bike ride) around the perimeter of the island takes visitors past a large colony of black-footed albatross. A short stroll from living quarters leads to the north swimming beach, where Laysan albatross wheel over the heads of vacationers. The West Beach trail through a thick stand of ironwood shows how an introduced species can change the environment. Wildlife rangers offer several hikes covering the flora and fauna and history of Midway.

Laysan albatross with young

Pacific/Remote Islands NWRs

Honolulu, Hawaii

■ **ADDRESS:** Pacific/Remote Islands Complex, P.O. Box 50167, Honolulu, HI 96850-5167

■ **TELEPHONE:** 808/541-1201

WHAT TO SEE

All islands except Johnston are closed to the public and must be viewed from a boat, although several allow entry by special-use permit, chiefly for scientists and educators.

■ **Baker Island NWR** Halfway between Hawaii and Australia, this tiny island lies just north of the equator about 1,600 miles southwest of Honolulu and is 0.5 square mile (340 acres), or about 2.5 times the size of The Mall in Washington, D.C. The refuge also includes 49 square miles (31,397 acres) of submerged lands. With a high point of 26 feet above sea level, the island has scant rainfall, no natural freshwater, constant winds, and is scorched by burning sun. Vines, grasses, and low-growing

Red-footed booby

shrubs are roosting and foraging habitat for four species of migratory seabirds. Baker, Jarvis, and Howland islands were designated as wildlife refuges in 1974.

■ **Hawaiian Islands NWR** This chain of eight islands, reefs, and atolls, designated as a refuge in 1909 by President Theodore Roosevelt, stretches around 800 miles between the main Hawaiian islands and Midway Atoll. The isolated islands protect the Laysan duck and finch and the Nihoa finch and millerbird as well as 14 million seabirds of 18 species. Several thousand species of tropical fish, algae, coral, and other marine invertebrates live in the 391 square miles (250,000 acres) of marine habitat.

■ **Howland Island NWR** Situated in the central Pacific within 200 miles of Baker Island, Howland had a moment of fame in the 1930s when an airstrip was built there for Amelia Earhart's failed flight. Its 0.9 square mile (400 acres) of emergent land and 50 square miles (32,150 acres) of submerged land support eight species of migratory seabirds.

■ **Jarvis Island NWR** Just below the equator 1,300 miles south of Honolulu, the island, like Howland and Baker, was a source for guano in the 18th and 19th centuries. Eight species of migratory seabirds nest on Jarvis, the largest of the three islands at 1.7 square miles (1,100 acres). The refuge includes another 79 square miles (36,419 acres) of submerged lands.

■ **Johnston Atoll NWR** A former nuclear-weapons test site and now a storage and destruction site for chemical weapons being destroyed under international treaty, Johnston Atoll was established as a refuge in 1926. Near the center of the North Pacific between the Hawaiian Islands and the Marshall Islands, the atoll is one of the most isolated in the world. The four islands within the atoll are home to 12 species of seabird and a nesting site for the green turtle. Around 300 species of fish have been recorded in waters around the reefs.

■ **Rose Atoll NWR** The southernmost refuge in the national wildlife system— established in 1974—and the easternmost emergent land in the Samoan Archipelago, Rose is one of the smallest atolls in the world. Lying at 14.5 degrees south latitude, a square reef dominated by coralline algae surrounds two small islets, together less than 0.03-square mile (20 acres). A dense forest of pisonia and tournefortia trees on the larger islet provides cover and nesting sites for 12 species of migratory seabirds, including red-footed boobies and great and lesser frigate birds. Reef herons nest within the trees' root systems. A permit issued by the refuge manager and American Samoa government is required for landing.

Appendix

NONVISITABLE NATIONAL WILDLIFE REFUGES

Below is a list of other national wildlife refuges in California and Hawaii. Although these refuges are not open to the public, many can be viewed from a nearby road or from a boat.

Antioch Dunes NWR
c/o San Pablo Bay NWR
P.O. Box 2012
Mare Island, CA 94592-0012
707/562-3000

Bear Valley NWR
c/o Klamath Basin Complex
Rt. 1, Box 74
Tulelake, CA 96134-9715
530/667-2231

Bitter Creek NWR
c/o Hopper Mountain Complex
P.O. Box 5839
Ventura, CA 93005-0839
805/644-5185

Blue Ridge NWR
c/o Kern Complex
P.O. Box 670
Delano, CA 93216-0670
805/725-2767

Butte Sink WMA
c/o Sacramento NWR
752 County Rd. 99W
Willows, CA 95988-9639
530/934-2801

Castle Rock NWR
c/o Humboldt Bay NWR
1020 Ranch Rd.
Loleta, CA 95551-9633
707/733-5406

Ellicott Slough NWR
c/o San Francisco Bay Complex
P.O. Box 524
Newark, CA 94560-0524
510/792-0222

Farallon NWR
c/o San Francisco Bay Complex
P.O. Box 524
Newark, CA 94560-0524
510/792-0222

Hopper Mountain NWR
c/o Hopper Mountain Complex
P.O. Box 5839
Ventura, CA 93005-0839
805/644-5185

Marin Islands NWR
c/o San Pablo Bay NWR
P.O. Box 2012
Mare Island, CA 94592-0012
707/562-3000

Pixley NWR
c/o Kern Complex
P.O. Box 670
Delano, CA 93216-0670
805/725-2767

San Joaquin River NWR
c/o San Luis NWR
P.O. Box 2176
Los Banos, CA 93635-2176
209/826-3508

Stone Lakes NWR
2233 Watt Ave., Ste. 230
Sacramento, CA 95825-0509
916/979-2085

Baker Island NWR
c/o Pacific/Remote Islands Complex
P.O. Box 50167
Honolulu, HI 96850-5167
808/541-1201

Hawaiian Islands NWR
c/o Pacific/Remote Islands Complex
P.O. Box 50167
Honolulu, HI 96850-5167
808/541-1201

Howland Island NWR
c/o Pacific/Remote Islands Complex
P.O. Box 50167
Honolulu, HI 96850-5167
808/541-1201

Huleia NWR
c/o Kilauea Point NWR
P.O. Box 1128
Kilauea, Kauai, HI 96754-1128
808/828-1413

James Campbell NWR
66-590 Kamehameha Hwy., Rm. 2C
Haleiwa, HI 96712-1484
808/637-6330

Jarvis Island NWR
c/o Pacific/Remote Islands Complex
P.O. Box 50167
Honolulu, HI 96850-5167
808/541-1201

Kakahaia NWR
c/o Kealia Pond NWR
P.O. Box 1042
Kihei, HI 96753-1042
808/875-1582

Pearl Harbor NWR
c/o James Campbell NWR
66-590 Kamehameha Hwy., Rm. 2C
Haleiwa, HI 96712-1484
808/637-6330

Rose Atoll NWR
c/o Pacific/Remote Islands Complex
P.O. Box 50167
Honolulu, HI 96850-5167
808/541-1201

FEDERAL RECREATION FEES

Some—but not all—NWRs and other federal outdoor recreation areas require payment of entrance or use fees (the latter for facilities such as boat ramps). There are several congressionally authorized entrance fee passes:

■ ANNUAL PASSES

Golden Eagle Passport Valid for most national parks, monuments, historic sites, recreation areas and national wildlife refuges. Admits the passport signee and any accompanying passengers in a private vehicle. Good for 12 months. Purchase at any federal area where an entrance fee is charged. The 1999 fee for this pass was $50.00

Federal Duck Stamp Authorized in 1934 as a federal permit to hunt waterfowl and as a source of revenue to purchase wetlands, the Duck Stamp now also serves as an annual entrance pass to NWRs. Admits holder and accompanying passengers in a private vehicle. Good from July 1 for one year. Valid for *entrance* fees only. Purchase at post offices and many NWRs or from Federal Duck Stamp Office, 800/782-6724, or at Wal-Mart, Kmart, or other sporting good stores.

■ LIFETIME PASSES

Golden Access Passport Lifetime entrance pass—for persons who are blind or permanently disabled—to most national parks and NWRs. Admits signee and any accompany passengers in a private vehicle. Provides 50 percent discount on federal use fees charged for facilities and services such as camping, or boating. Must be obtained in person at a federal recreation area charging a fee. Obtain by showing proof of medically determined permanent disability or eligibility for receiving benefits under federal law.

Golden Age Passport Lifetime entrance pass—for persons 62 years of age or older—to national parks and NWRs. Admits signee and any accompanying passengers in a private vehicle. Provides 50 percent discount on federal use fees charged for facilities and services such as camping, or boating. Must be obtained in person at a federal recreation area charging a fee. One-time $10.00 processing charge. Available only to U.S. citizens or permanent residents.

For more information, contact your local federal recreation area for a copy of the *Federal Recreation Passport Program* brochure.

VOLUNTEER ACTIVITIES

Each year, 30,000 Americans volunteer their time and talents to help the U.S. Fish & Wildlife Service conserve the nation's precious wildlife and their habitats. Volunteers conduct F & W Service population surveys, lead public tours and other recreational programs, protect endangered species, restore habitat, and run environmental education programs.

The NWR volunteer program is as diverse as are the refuges themselves. There is no "typical" Fish & Wildlife Service volunteer. The different ages, backgrounds, and experiences volunteers bring with them is one of the greatest strengths of the program. Refuge managers also work with their neighbors, conservation groups, colleges and universities, and business organizations.

A growing number of people are taking pride in the stewardship of local national wildlife refuges by organizing nonprofit organizations to support individual refuges. These refuge community partner groups, which numbered about 200 in 2000, have been so helpful that the F & W Service, National Audubon Society, National Wildlife Refuge Association, and National Fish & Wildlife Foundation now carry out a national program called the "Refuge System Friends Initiative" to coordinate and strengthen existing partnerships, to jump-start new ones, and to organize other efforts promoting community involvement in activities associated with the National Wildlife Refuge System.

For more information on how to get involved, visit the F & W Service Homepage at http://refuges.fws.gov; or contact one of the Volunteer Coordinator offices listed on the U.S. Fish & Wildlife General Information list of addresses below or the U. S. Fish & Wildlife Service, Division of Refuges, Attn: Volunteer Coordinator, 4401 North Fairfax Drive, Arlington, VA 22203; 703/358-2303.

U.S. FISH & WILDLIFE GENERAL INFORMATION

Below is a list of addresses to contact for more information concerning the National Wildlife Refuge System.

U.S. Fish & Wildlife Service Division of Refuges

4401 North Fairfax Dr., Room 670
Arlington, Virginia 22203
703/358-1744
Web site: fws.refuges.gov

F & W Service Publications:
800/344-WILD

U.S. Fish & Wildlife Service Pacific Region

911 NE 11th Ave.
Eastside Federal Complex
Portland, OR 97232-4181
External Affairs Office: 503/231-6120
Volunteer Coordinator: 503/231-2077
The Pacific Region office oversees the refuges in California, Hawaii, Idaho, Nevada, Oregon, and Washington.

U.S. Fish & Wildlife Service Southwest Region

500 Gold Ave., SW
P.O. Box 1306
Albuquerque, NM 87103
External Affairs Office: 505/248-6285
Volunteer Coordinator: 505/248-6635
The Southwest Region office oversees the refuges in Arizona, New Mexico, Oklahoma, and Texas.

U.S. Fish & Wildlife Service Great Lakes–Big Rivers Region

1 Federal Dr.
Federal Building
Fort Snelling, MN 55111-4056
External Affairs Office: 612/713-5310
Volunteer Coordinator: 612/713-5444
The Great Lakes-Big Rivers Region office oversees the refuges in Iowa, Illinois, Indiana, Michigan, Minnesota, Missouri, Ohio, and Wisconsin.

U.S. Fish & Wildlife Service Southeast Region

1875 Century Center Blvd.
Atlanta, GA 30345
External Affairs Office: 404/679-7288
Volunteer Coordinator: 404/679-7178
The Southeast Region office oversees the refuges in Alabama, Arkansas, Florida, Georgia, Kentucky, Louisiana, Mississippi, North Carolina, South Carolina, Tennessee, and Puerto Rico.

U.S. Fish & Wildlife Service Northeast Region

300 Westgate Center Dr.
Hadley, MA 01035-9589
External Affairs Office: 413/253-8325
Volunteer Coordinator: 413/253-8303
The Northeast Region office oversees the refuges in Connecticut, Delaware, Massachusetts, Maine, New Hampshire, New Jersey, New York, Pennsylvania, Rhode Island, Vermont, Virginia, West Virginia.

U.S. Fish & Wildlife Service Mountain-Prairie Region

P.O. Box 25486
Denver Federal Center
P. O. Box 25486
Denver, CO 80225
External Affairs Office: 303/236-7905
Volunteer Coordinator: 303/236-8145, x 614
The Mountain-Prairie Region office oversees the refuges in Colorado, Kansas, Montana, Nebraska, North Dakota, South Dakota, Utah, and Wyoming.

U.S. Fish & Wildlife Service Alaska Region

1011 East Tudor Rd.
Anchorage, AK 99503
External Affairs Office: 907/786-3309
Volunteer Coordinator: 907/786-3391

NATIONAL AUDUBON SOCIETY
WILDLIFE SANCTUARIES

National Audubon Society's 100 sanctuaries comprise 150,000 acres and include a wide range of habitats. Audubon managers and scientists use the sanctuaries for rigorous field research and for testing wildlife-management strategies. The following is a list of 24 sanctuaries open to the public. Sanctuaries open by appointment only are marked with an asterisk.

EDWARD M. BRIGHAM III ALKALI LAKE SANCTUARY*
c/o North Dakota State Office
118 Broadway, Suite 502
Fargo, ND 58102
701/298-3373

FRANCIS BEIDLER FOREST SANCTUARY
336 Sanctuary Rd.
Harleyville, SC 29448
843/462-2160

BORESTONE MOUNTAIN SANCTUARY
P.O. Box 524
118 Union Square
Dover-Foxcroft, ME 04426
207/564-7946

CLYDE E. BUCKLEY SANCTUARY
1305 Germany Rd.
Frankfort, KY 40601
606/873-5711

BUTTERCUP WILDLIFE SANCTUARY*
c/o New York State Office
200 Trillium Lane
Albany, NY 12203
518/869-9731

CONSTITUTION MARSH SANCTUARY
P.O. Box 174
Cold Spring, NY, 10516
914/265-2601

CORKSCREW SWAMP SANCTUARY
375 Sanctuary Rd. West
Naples, FL 34120
941/348-9151

FLORIDA COASTAL ISLANDS SANCTUARY*
410 Ware Blvd., Suite 702
Tampa, FL 33619
813/623-6826

EDWARD L. & CHARLES E. GILLMOR SANCTUARY*
3868 Marsha Dr.
West Valley City, UT 84120
801/966-0464

KISSIMMEE PRAIRIE SANCTUARY*
100 Riverwoods Circle
Lorida, FL 33857
941/467-8497

MAINE COASTAL ISLANDS SANCTUARIES*
Summer (June–Aug.):
12 Audubon Rd.
Bremen, ME 04551
207/529-5828

MILES WILDLIFE SANCTUARY*
99 West Cornwall Rd.
Sharon, CT 06069
860/364-0048

NORTH CAROLINA COASTAL ISLANDS SANCTUARY*
720 Market St.
Wilmington, NC 28401-4647
910/762-9534

NORTHERN CALIFORNIA SANCTUARIES*
c/o California State Office
555 Audubon Place
Sacramento, CA 95825
916/481-5440

PINE ISLAND SANCTUARY*
P.O. Box 174
Poplar Branch, NC 27965
919/453-2838

RAINEY WILDLIFE SANCTUARY*
10149 Richard Rd.
Abbeville, LA 70510-9216
318/898-5969 (Beeper: leave message)

RESEARCH RANCH SANCTUARY*
HC1, Box 44
Elgin, AZ 85611
520/455-5522

RHEINSTROM HILL WILDLIFE SANCTUARY*
P.O. Box 1
Craryville, NY 12521
518/325-5203

THEODORE ROOSEVELT SANCTUARY
134 Cove Rd.
Oyster Bay, NY 11771
516/922-3200

LILLIAN ANNETTE ROWE SANCTUARY
44450 Elm Island Rd.
Gibbon, NE 68840
308/468-5282

SABAL PALM GROVE SANCTUARY
P.O. Box 5052
Brownsville, TX 78523
956/541-8034

SILVER BLUFF SANCTUARY*
4542 Silver Bluff Rd.
Jackson, SC 29831
803/827-0781

STARR RANCH SANCTUARY*
100 Bell Canyon Rd.
Trabuco Canyon, CA 92678
949/858-0309

TEXAS COASTAL ISLANDS SANCTUARIES
c/o Texas State Office
2525 Wallingwood, Suite 301
Austin, TX 78746
512/306-0225

BIBLIOGRAPHY AND RESOURCES

Aquatic and Marine Biology

Kaufman, Gregory D. *Hawaii's Humpback Whales*, Aiea, Hawaii: Island Heritage Publishing, 1986.

Norris, Kenneth S. *The Hawaiian Spinner Dolphin*, Berkeley, Calif.: University of California Press, 1994.

Birds

Denny, Jim. *The Birds of Kaua'i*, Honolulu: University of Hawaii Press, 1999.

Kemper, John. *Birding Northern California* (Birding Guides Series), Helena, Mont.: Falcon Publishing Co., 1999.

Kerlinger, Paul. *How Birds Migrate*, Mechanicsburg, Pa.: Stackpole Books, 1995.

MacGowan, Craig. *California Coastal Birds*, Seattle: The Mountaineers Books, 1990.

Soehren, Rick. *The Birdwatcher's Guide to Hawaii*, Honolulu: University of Hawaii Press, 1996.

Botany

Faber, Phyllis M. and Robert F. Holland, *Common Riparian Plants of California*, Mill Valley, Calif.: Pickleweed Press, 1988.

Fuller, Thomas C. and Elizabeth McClintock. *Poisonous Plants of California*, Berkeley, Calif.: University of California Press, 1986.

Johnston, Verna R. *California Forests and Woodlands*, Berkeley, Calif.: University of California Press, 1994.

Kepler, Angela Kay. *Hawaiian Heritage Plants*, Honolulu: University of Hawaii Press, 1998.

Munz, Phillip A. *California Mountain Wildflowers*, Berkeley, Calif.: University of California Press, 1972.

Valier, Kathy. *Ferns of Hawaii*, Honolulu: University of Hawaii Press, 1995.

Cultural and Environmental History

de Montalvo, Garcia Ordones. *The Exploits of Esplandian,* as quoted in *Broken Shore,* by Arthur Quinn, Inverness, Calif.: Redwood Press, 1987.

Dougherty, Michael. *To Steal a Kingdom*, Waimanalo, Hawaii: Island Style Press, 1992.

Gifford, Terry, ed. *John Muir His Life and Letters and Other Writings,* Seattle: The Mountaineers Books, 1996.

Up and Down California in 1860-1864 The Journal of William H. Brewer, Berkeley, Calif.: University of California Press, 1975.

Geology

Alt, David D. and Donald W. Hyndman. *Roadside Geology of Northern California*, Missoula, Mont.: Mountain Press Publishing Co., 1975.

Hawaii's Volcano Watch: A Pictorial History, 1779-1992, Honolulu: University of Hawaii Press, 1998.

Hazlett, Richard W. and Donald W. Hyndman. *Roadside Geology of Hawaii*, (Roadside Geology Series), Missoula, Mont.: Mountain Press, 1996.

McPhee, John. *Assembling California*, New York: Noonday Press, 1994.

Hill, Mary. *Geology of the Sierra Nevada*, Berkeley, Calif.: University of California Press, 1989.

Sharp, Robert P. and Allen F. Glazner. *Geology Underfoot in Southern California*, Missoula, Mont.: Mountain Press Publishing Co.,1993.

Mammals

Jameson, E.W., Jr. and Hans J. Peeters. *California Mammals*, Berkeley, Calif.: University of California Press, 1998.

Outdoor/Natural History Writings

Bakker, Elna. *An Island Called California*, Berkeley, Calif.: University of California Press, 1984.

Daws, Gavan. *Shoal of Time a History of the Hawaiian Islands*, Honolulu: University of Hawaii Press, 1989.

Farquhar, Francis P. *History of the Sierra Nevada*, Berkeley, Calif.: University of California Press, 1989.

Jaeger, Edmund C. *The California Deserts*, Stanford, Calif.: Stanford University Press, 1983.

King, Clarence. *Mountaineering in the Sierra Nevada*, Lincoln, Nebr.: University of Nebraska Press, 1997.

Muir, John. *The Mountains of California*, New York: Penguin U.S.A., 1997.

Schoenherr, Allan A. *A Natural History of California*, Berkeley, Calif.: University of California Press, 1995.

Regional/State Guides

Clark, Jeanne L. *California Wildlife Viewing Guide*, Helena, Mont.: Falcon Press, 1996.

Foster, Lynne. *Adventuring in the California Desert* (Sierra Club Adventure Travel Guide), San Francisco: Sierra Club Books, 1997.

Perry, John. *The Sierra Club Guide to the Natural Areas of California*, San Francisco: Sierra Club Books, 1997.

Wall, Dennis. *Wildlife Refuges*, Santa Fe: Museum of New Mexico Press, 1996.

Reptiles and Amphibians

Brown, Philip. *A Field Guide to Snakes of California*, Houston: Gulf Publishing Co., 1997.

Stebbins, Robert C. *A Field Guide to Western Reptiles and Amphibians* (The Peterson Field Guide Series), Boston: Houghton Mifflin Co., 1998.

GLOSSARY

'A'a Rough, sharp lava (Hawaiian, noun).

Accidental A bird species seen only rarely in a certain region and whose normal territory is elsewhere. *See also* occasional.

Acre-foot The amount of water required to cover one acre one foot deep.

Alkali sink An alkaline habitat at the bottom of a basin where there is moisture under the surface.

Alluvial Clay, sand, silt, pebbles, and rocks deposited by running water. River floodplains have alluvial deposits, sometimes called alluvial fans, where a stream exits from mountains onto flatland.

Aquifer Underground layer of porous water-bearing sand, rock, or gravel.

Arthropod Invertebrates, including insects, crustaceans, arachnids, and myriapods, with a semitransparent exoskeleton (hard outer structure) and a segmented body, with jointed appendages in articulated pairs.

Atoll A coral reef surrounding a lagoon and an island.

ATV All-terrain vehicle. *See also* 4WD and ORV.

Baleen The flexible, bonelike straps in a whale's mouth used to strain food from the seawater.

Barrier island Coastal island produced by wave action and made of sand. Over time the island shifts and changes shape. Barrier islands protect the mainland from storms, tides, and winds.

Basking The habit of certain creatures such as turtles, snakes, or alligators to expose themselves to the pleasant warmth of the sun by resting on logs, rocks, or other relatively dry areas.

Biome A major ecological community such as a marsh or a forest.

Blowout A hollow formed by wind erosion in a preexisting sand dune, often due to vegetation loss.

Bog Wet, spongy ground filled with sphagnum moss and having highly acidic water.

Bottomland Low-elevation alluvial area, close by a river. Sometimes also called "bottoms."

Brackish Water that is less salty than seawater; often found in salt marshes, mangrove swamps, estuaries, and lagoons.

Breachway A gap in a barrier beach or island, forming a connection between sea and lagoon.

Bushwhack To hike through territory without established trails.

Cambium In woody plants, a sheath of cells between external bark and internal wood that generates parallel rows of cells to make new tissue, either as secondary growth or cork.

Canopy The highest layer of the forest, consisting of the crowns of the trees.

Carnivore An animal that is primarily flesh-eating. *See also* herbivore *and* omnivore.

Climax In a stable ecological community, the plants and animals that will successfully continue to live there.

Colonial birds Birds that live in relatively stable colonies, used annually for breeding and nesting.

Competition A social behavior that organizes the sharing of resources such as space, food, and breeding partners when resources are in short supply.

Coniferous Trees that are needle-leaved or scale-leaved; mostly evergreen and cone-bearing, such as pines, spruces, and firs. *See also* deciduous.

Cordgrass Grasses found in marshy areas, capable of growing in brackish waters. Varieties include salt-marsh cordgrass, hay, spike grass, and glasswort.

Crust The outer layer of the earth, between 15 to 40 miles thick.

Crustacean A hard-shelled, usually aquatic, arthropod such as a lobster or crab. *See also* arthropod.

DDT An insecticide ($C14H9Cl5$), toxic to animals and human beings whether ingested or absorbed through skin; particularly devastating to certain bird populations, DDT was generally banned in the U.S. in 1972.

Deciduous Plants that shed or lose their foliage at the conclusion of the growing season, as in "deciduous trees," such as hardwoods (maple, beech, oak, etc.). *See also* coniferous.

Delta A triangular alluvial deposit at a river's mouth or at the mouth of a tidal inlet. *See also* alluvial.

Dominant The species most characteristic of a plant or animal community, usually influencing the types and numbers of other species in the same community.

Ecological niche An organism's function, status, or occupied area in its ecological community.

Ecosystem A mostly self-contained community consisting of an environment and the animals and plants that live there.

Emergent plants Plants adapted to living in shallow water or in saturated soils such as marshes or wetlands.

Endangered species A species determined by the federal government to be in danger of extinction throughout all or a significant portion of its range (Endangered Species Act, 1973). *See also* threatened species.

Endemic species Species that evolved in a certain place and live naturally nowhere else. *See also* indigenous species.

Epiphyte A type of plant (often found in swamps) that lives on a tree instead of on the soil. Epiphytes are not parasitic; they collect their own water and minerals and perform photosynthesis.

Esker An extended gravel ridge left by a river or stream that runs beneath a decaying glacier.

Estuary The lower part of a river where freshwater meets tidal saltwater. Usually characterized by abundant animal and plant life.

Evergreen A tree, shrub, or other plant whose leaves remain green through all seasons.

Exotic A plant or animal not native to the territory. Many exotic plants and animals displace native species.

Extirpation The elimination of a species by unnatural causes, such as overhunting or overfishing.

Fall line A line between the piedmont and the coastal plain below which rivers flow through relatively flat terrain. Large rivers are navigable from the ocean to the fall line.

Fauna Animals, especially those of a certain region or era, generally considered as a group. *See also* flora.

Fledge To raise birds until they have their feathers and are able to fly.

Floodplain A low-lying, flat area along a river where flooding is common.

Flora Plants, especially those of a certain region or era, generally considered as a group. *See also* fauna.

Flyway A migratory route, providing food and shelter, followed by large numbers of birds.

Forb Any herb that is not in the grass family; forbs are commonly found in fields, prairies, or meadows.

Frond A fern leaf, a compound palm leaf, or a leaflike thallus (where leaf and stem are continuous), as with seaweed and lichen.

4WD Four-wheel-drive vehicle. *See also* ATV.

Glacial outwash Sediment dropped by rivers or streams as they flow away from melting glaciers.

Glacial till An unsorted mix of clay, sand, and rock transported and left by glacial action.

Gneiss A common and rather erosion-resistant metamorphic rock originating from shale, characterized by alternating dark and light bands.

Grassy bald A summit area devoid of trees due to shallow or absent soil overlying bedrock (ledge).

Greentree reservoir An area seasonally flooded by opening dikes. Oaks, hickories, and other water-tolerant trees drop nuts (mast) into the water. Migratory birds and other wildlife feed on the mast during winter.

Habitat The area or environment where a plant or animal, or communities of plants or animals, normally live, such as an alpine habitat.

Hammock A fertile spot of high ground in a wetland that supports the growth of hardwood trees.

Hardwoods Flowering trees such as oaks, hickories, maples, and others, as opposed to softwoods and coniferous trees such as pines and hemlocks.

Herbivore An animal that feeds on plant life. *See also* carnivore *and* omnivore.

Heronry Nesting and breeding site for herons.

Herptiles The class of animals including reptiles and amphibians.

Holdfast The attachment, in lieu of roots, that enables seaweed to grip a substrate such as a rock.

Hot spot An opening in the earth's interior from which molten rock erupts, eventually forming a volcano.

Humus Decomposed leaves and other organic material found, for instance, on the forest floor.

Impoundment A man-made body of water controlled by dikes or levees.

Indigenous species Species that arrived unaided by humans but that may also live in other locations.

Inholding Private land surrounded by federal or state lands such as a wildlife refuge.

Intertidal zone The beach or shoreline area located between low and high tide lines.

Introduced species Species brought to a location by humans, intentionally or accidentally; also called nonnative or alien species. *See also* exotic.

Lava Underground molten rock that has erupted through the surface of the earth.

Lichen A ground-hugging plant, usually found on rocks, produced by an association between an alga, which manufactures food, and a fungus, which provides support.

Loess Deep, fertile, and loamy soil deposited by wind, the deepest deposits reaching 200 feet.

Magma Underground molten rock.

Management area A section of land within a federal wildlife preserve or forest where specific wildlife-management practices are implemented and studied.

Marsh A low-elevation transitional area between water (the sea) and land, dominated by grasses in soft, wet soils.

Mast   A general word for nuts, acorns, and other food for wildlife produced by trees in the fall.

Meander   A winding stream, river, or path.

Mesa   Flat-topped landforms with steeply sloping sides, larger than buttes but smaller than plateaus. From "table" in Spanish.

Mesozoic   A geologic era, 230-65 million years ago, during which dinosaurs appeared and became extinct, and birds and flowering plants first appeared.

Midden   An accumulation of organic material near a village or dwelling; also called a shell mound.

Migrant   An animal that moves from one habitat to another, as opposed to resident species that live permanently in the same habitat.

Mitigation   The act of creating or enlarging refuges or awarding them water rights to replace wildlife habitat lost because of the damming or channelization of rivers or the building of roads.

Moist-soil unit   A wet area that sprouts annual plants, which attract waterfowl. Naturally produced by river flooding, moist-soil units are artificially created through controlled watering.

Moraine   A formation of rock and soil debris transported and dropped by a glacier.

Neotropical   New world tropics, generally referring to central and northern South America, as in *neotropical* birds.

Nesting species   Birds that take up permanent residence in a habitat.

Occasional   A bird species seen only occasionally in a certain region and whose normal territory is elsewhere.

Oceanic trench   The place where a sinking tectonic plate bends down, creating a declivity in the ocean floor.

Old field   A field that was once cultivated for crops but has been left to grow back into forest.

Old-growth forest   A forest characterized by large trees and a stable ecosystem. Old-growth forests are similar to precolonial forests.

Omnivore   An animal that feeds on both plant and animal material. *See also* carnivore *and* herbivore.

ORVs   Off-road vehicles. *See also* 4WD *and* ATV.

Oxbow   A curved section of water (once a bend in a river) that was severed from the river when the river changed course. An oxbow lake is formed by the changing course of a river as it meanders through its floodplain.

Pahoehoe   Smooth lava (Hawaiian noun).

Pacific Plate   A huge segment of matter that floats over the earth's molten core, carrying with it islands, continents, and the matter that welds to continents when two plates collide.

Passerine   A bird in the *Passeriformes* order, primarily composed of perching birds and songbirds.

Peat   An accumulation of sphagnum moss and other organic material in wetland areas, known as peat bogs.

Petroglyph   Carving or inscription on a rock.

Photosynthesis   The process by which green plants use the energy in sunlight to create carbohydrates from carbon dioxide and water, generally releasing oxygen as a by-product.

Pictograph   Pictures painted on rock by indigenous people.

Pit-and-mound topography   Terrain characteristic of damp hemlock woods where shallow-rooted fallen trees create pits (former locations of trees) and mounds (upended root balls).

Plant community   Plants and animals that interact in a similar environment within a region.

Pleistocene   A geologic era, 1.8 million to 10,000 years ago, known as the great age of glaciers.

Prairie   An expansive, undulating, or flat grassland, usually without trees, generally on the plains of mid-continent North America. In the southeast, "prairie" refers to wet grasslands with standing water much of the year.

Prescribed burn   A fire that is intentionally set to reduce the buildup of dry organic matter in a forest or grassland, to prevent catastrophic fires later on or to assist plant species whose seeds need intense heat to open.

Proclamation area   An area of open water beside or around a coastal refuge where waterfowl are protected from hunting.

Rain shadow   An area sheltered from heavy rainfall by mountains that, at their higher altitudes, have drawn much of the rain from the atmosphere.

Raptor   A bird of prey with a sharp curved beak and hooked talons. Raptors include hawks, eagles, owls, falcons, and ospreys.

Rhizome   A horizontal plant stem, often thick with reserved food material, from which grow shoots above and roots below.

Riparian   The bank and associated plant life zone of any water body, including tidewaters.

Riverine   Living or located on the banks of a river.

Rookery   A nesting place for a colony of birds or other animals (seals, penguins, others).

Salt marsh   An expanse of tall grass, usually cordgrass and sedges, located in sheltered places such as the land side of coastal barrier islands or along river mouths and deltas at the sea.

Salt pan   A shallow pool of saline water formed by tidal action that usually provides abundant food for plovers, sandpipers, and other wading birds.

Scat   Animal fecal droppings.

Scrub   A dry area of sandy or otherwise poor soil that supports species adapted to such conditions, such as sand myrtle and prickly pear cactus, or dwarf forms of other species, such as oaks and palmettos.

Sea stack   A small, steep-sided rock island lying off the coast.

Second growth   Trees in a forest that grow naturally after the original stand is cut or burned. *See also* old-growth forest.

Seeps   Small springs that may dry up periodically.

Shield volcano   A volcano erupting with fluid lava flowing for miles in sheaths rarely more than 30 feet thick, creating characteristic gently sloping sides.

Shorebird   A bird, such as a plover or sandpiper, frequently found on or near the seashore.

Shrub-steppe   Desertlike lands dominated by sagebrush, tumbleweed, and other dry-weather-adapted plants.

Slough   A backwater or creek in a marshy area; sloughs sometimes dry into deep mud.

Spit   A narrow point of land, often of sand or gravel, extending into the water.

Staging area   A place where birds rest, gather strength, and prepare for the next stage of a journey.

Successional   Referring to a series of different plants that establish themselves by territories, from water's edge to drier ground. Also, the series of differing plants that reestablish themselves over time after a fire or the retreat of a glacier.

Sump   A pit or reservoir used as a drain or receptacle for liquids.

Swale   A low-lying, wet area of land.

Swamp   A spongy wetland supporting trees and shrubs (as opposed to a marsh, which is characterized by grasses). Swamps provide habitat for birds, turtles, alligators, and bears and serve as refuges for species extirpated elsewhere. *See also* extirpated.

Test   The hard, round exoskeleton of a sea urchin.

Threatened species   A species of plant or animal in which population numbers are declining, but not in immediate danger of extinction. Threatened species are protected under the Endangered Species Act of 1973. *See also* endangered species.

Tradewinds   Winds blowing from east to west on latitudes just north and south of the equator.

Tuber   A short, underground stem with buds from which new shoots grow.

Understory   Plants growing under the canopy of a forest. *See also* canopy.

Vascular plant   A fern or other seed-bearing plant with a series of channels for conveying nutrients.

Vernal pool   Shallow ponds that fill with spring ("vernal") rains or snowmelt and dry up as summer approaches; temporary homes to certain amphibians.

Wader   A long-legged bird, such as a crane or stork, usually found feeding in shallow water.

Wetland   A low, moist area, often marsh or swamp, especially when regarded as the natural habitat of wildlife.

Wilderness Area   An area of land (within a national forest, national park or a national wildlife refuge) protected under the 1964 Federal Wilderness Act. Logging, construction, and use of mechanized vehicles or tools are prohibited here, and habitats are left in their pristine states. "Designated Wilderness" is the highest form of federal land protection.

Wrack line   Plant, animal, and unnatural debris left on the upper beach by a receding tide.

INDEX

abalone, 25
acacia, catclaw, 49
aeakepa, 157
aeakiapola'au, 157
aeohi'a trees, 155, 156
ae'o, 160
akulikuli, 164
'alae ke'oke'o, 160
'alae'ula, 160
'alala, 155, 157
albatross, Laysan, 169, 171, **176**,
    176–177, 179–180, 183, 183
alder, 74
Aleut, 25
alfalfa, 29, 30, 74, 86, 149
algae, 165
alligator, **7**
alluvial fans, 34
alula, 168
Alviso Slough Trail (CA), 41–42
Anahuac NWR (TX), **7**
animal life, 24
Antioch Dunes NWR (CA), 139–140
aquatic plants, 29–30
arid lands, 29
arrowweed, 29, 64
aspen, 88
aster, Mojave, 48
Audubon, John James, 1
Audubon Refuge Keepers (ARK), x
auklets
    Cassin's, 44
    rhinocerous, 44
avocets, 31, 65, 94, 103
    American, 106, 107, 111, 149, **152**, 153

baccharis, 39
badgers, 70, 93, 125, 150
Baker Island NWR (HI), 183–184
barley, 65
barred sandbass, 115
bass, 67
    largemouth, 32, 93, 100, 135, 150, 153
    smallmouth, 32
    striped, 32, 41, 141
bats, 41, 59, 93, 99, **150**, 150
    brown, 24
    hoary, 150
    Mexican long-tongued, 150
    pepistrel, 150

    silver-haired, 76
    spotted, 150
bat rays, 115
bears, 75
    black, 24, 55, 76
    grizzly, 25
Bear Valley NWR (CA), 77–78
beavers, 76, 81, 87, **87**, 99, 153
bees, 114
berry
    Christmas, 114–115
    lemonade, 124
bighorn, 45
bird's beak, salt-marsh, 39, 114, **118**
Bitter Creek NWR (CA), 55–56
bitterns
    American, 135
    least, 31
blackberry, 98
blackberry vines, 152
blackbirds
    Brewer's, 86, 131
    red-winged, 31, 50, 106, 108, 131, 135
    tricolored, **128**, 131, 137
    yellow-headed, 31, 82, 106, 131
blackfish, Sacramento, 153
blennies, combtooth, 115
blue dicks, 39, 128–129
Blue Ridge NWR (CA), 56–57
bluebirds
    mountain, 79, 91
    western, 91
bluegill, 153
boa, rubber, 76
bobcats, 31, 24, 50, 55, 57, 70, 93, 125
bogweed, 69
bonytail chub, 66
boobies
    blue-footed, **146**, 149
    red-footed, 169, 180, **184**, 185
Bosque del Apache NWR, 29
brant, 120
    Pacific black, **58**, 59
Brazoria NWR, 29
brittlebush, 49, 64
brodiaea, 98, 153
buckwheats, 110
bufflehead, 103
bullfrogs, 26
bullhead
    brown, 100
    yellow, 100

bulls, Roosevelt, 131
bulrush, 29, 40, 87, 97
  alkali, 148
  American great, 48–49
  California, 128
  hardstem, 90
  river, 64
  salt-marsh, 97
  three-square, 64
  tuberous, 97
bunchgrasses, 70, 75, 128, 179
buntings, lazuli, 131
burros, feral, 66
bushes, 152
bushtits, 115
Butte Sink NWR (CA), 108
butterflies
  Lange's metalmark, **140**
  Smith's blue, 110
buttonbush, 134

Cabeza Prieta NWR (AZ), 5
cactus, 21, 29, 64
  barrel, 49, 124
  beavertail, 49, 64
  saguaro, 5
California Condor Recovery Plan, 52, 56
California fan plans, 21
canvasbacks, 88
caribou, barren-ground, **xii**
carp, 135, 150
Carson, Rachel *(Silent Spring)*, 7
Cascade Mountains, 20
Castle Rock NWR (CA), 60
caterpillars, 157
catfish, 32, 67, 135
  channel, 93, 150
  white, 153
cats, 26, 168
  feral, 160
cattail, 29, 48–49, 50, 64, 66, 74, 82, 87, 90, **90**, 97, 99, 148, 160
ceanothus, 55
cedar, 57
  incense, 57
  salt, 49, 64, 148
Center Trail (CA), 120
chamise, 55
chaparral, 55
chaparral broom, 39
Chapman, Frank, x

Charlie Bell 4WD trail (AZ), 5
chipmunk, 76
cholla, 124
chuckwalla, 28, 66
chuparosa, 65
Cibola NWR (AZ), **28**, 28–32
clams, 60
  jackknife, 116
  littleneck, 116
  purple, 116
Clear Lake NWR (CA), 78–80
climate, 19–21
Coachella Valley NWR (CA), 19, 21, **33**, 33–35
coachwhip, 125
coatis, 150
codfish, 41
Colorado Desert, 19, 33
Colusa NWR (CA), 106–108
condors, **25**, **54**, 57
  California, **52**, 52–55, 56
conifers, 74
Cook, Captain James, 23
coontail, 74
coots, 24, 106, 135, 172, 176
  American, 65, **98**
  Hawaiian, 160, 164, 175, **175**
coral, 179
corbina, 116
cordgrass, 114, 115, 119, 143
cormorants, 44, 60
  Brandt's, 44
  double-crested, 44, 75, 79, 94, 153
  pelagic, 44
corn, 29
corvina, orangemouth, 150
cottonwoods, 27, 29, 51, 88, 94, 100, 104, 124, 134, 148, 152, 153
  Fremont, 49, 64, 98, 130
cowbirds, brown-headed, 31
coyotes, **8**, 31, 50, 66, 67, 70, 76, 86, 91, 92, 93, 99, 115, 125, **125**, 131, 150, 153
coyote brush, 39, 134, 143
Coyote Trail (CA), 120
crabs, 41, 60
  hermit, 116
  yellow shore, 116
cranes, sandhill, 28, 30, 32, 65, 66, 70, 75, 82, 92, 94
  lesser sandhill, **136**
  sandhill, 89, **93**, 106, 130, 136

crappie, 32, 67
  white, 100
creosote, 29, 34, 64, 70
cropland, 26, 27, 74, 83, 107, 137, 149
crows, 143, 157
curlews, 103
  bristle-thighed, 160

Darling, Jay Norwood "Ding," 5
deer, 75, 103–104
  black-tailed, 59, 99, 108
  black-tailed mule, 57
  mule, 31, 32, 67, 76, **76**, 93
deerweed, 124
Delevan NWR (CA), 108
dogs, 26, 168
dolphins, spinner, 170, 181
Don Edwards San Francisco Bay NWR
    (CA), 36–42
doves, 32, 67
  Inca, 50
  mourning, 50, 51
  spotted, 160
  white-winged, 31
  zebra, 160
dowitchers, 65, 111
  long-billed, 31, 50, 160
downingia
  blue, 133
  folded, 98
  harlequin, 98
  Hoover's, 98
ducks, 26, 28, 31, 32, 40, 41, 49, 75, 84,
    90, 94, 95, 98, 100, 111, 123, 130, 135,
    140, 151, 160
  blue-winged, 41
  bufflehead, 31, 139
  canvasback, 40, 41, 139, **139**
  diving, 40
  gadwall, 31, 106, 107, 111
  green-winged, 31
  Hawaiian, 24, 160, **162**, 164, 172, 176
  Laysan, 184
  lesser scaup, 139
  mallards, 31, 88, 94, **104**, 106, 107,
    111, 130, 135, 139
  mergansers, 31
  northern pintail, 31, 41, **75**, 111, 130
  northern shoveler, 31, 41, 130, 139,
    153
  pintail, 106, 107, 149, 153, 164

ring-necked, 103
ruddy, 41, 65, 82, 83, **83**, 86, 103, 111,
    130, 149
shovelers, 106, 107, 164
  northern, **32**, 65, 103
teal, 45, 94, 103
  blue-winged, 49
  cinnamon, 31, 41, 49, 50, 65, 82, 111,
    139
  green-winged, 65, 106, 107, 111,
    130, 135, 149, 153, 164
  turnstones, 164
  wigeons, 94, 153, 164
  wood, **101**, 104
Ducks Unlimited, 8
dunes, 110
dunlin, 111

eagles, bald, 31, 32, 50, 65, 72, 75, 76, **77**,
    77–78, 88, 92, 94, 99
earthquakes, 18
eelgrass, 59, 112
eels, cusk, 115
egrets, 65, 94, 103, 108, 150
  cattle, 26, 160
  great, **40**, 40, 140, 153
  snowy, 31, **31**, 40, 140
elder, box, 98
elderberry
  blue, 98
  Mexican, 124
elk, 75, 76
  North American, 131
  Rocky Mountain, 80
  tule, 24, 130, 131, **131**, 135
Ellicott Slough NWR (CA), 42
encelia, 143
  California, 124
endangered species, 25–26
  animals, 114
  birds, 50, 66, 115, 119, 139, 143, 157–158,
    159, 160, 164, 174–175
  butterflies, 140
  fish, 76
  mammals, 164, 170
  plants, 23, 39, 110
  reptiles and amphibians, 181–182
Endangered Species Act (1973), 7, 10
eucalyptus, Red River, 100
evergreen shrub, 39, 56, 69, 124

falcons
  peregrine, 31, 51, 65, 106, 111
  prairie, 79–80, 86
Farallon NWR (CA), 43–44
farmlands, 29–30, 49, 65
fat hen, 40, 139
ferns, 155
finch, Nihoa, 184
fleabane, Indian, 164
Flicker, John, xi
flounder, 41
  starry, 41
flycatchers, 32, 65, 88, 125
  Pacific-slope, 31
  southwestern willow, 31, 50, 66
foxes, 24, 67
  desert kit, 150
  gray, 41, 99, 125, 153
  kit, 45, 50
  red, 41, 99
  San Joaquin kit, **68**, 70, 131
freshwater marsh, 55
frigate birds, 149, 169, 180, 182–183, 185
  great, **180**
frogs, 31, 59
  Pacific, 76
  spotted, 76
  western, 76

gadwalls, 88, **88**, 94
gallinule, 160
geese, 28, 32, 49, 82, 90, 94, 98,100, 106, 123, 135
  Aleutian Canada, 60
  Canada, **25**, 30, 65, 88, 94, 99, 137, 149, 151
  Hawaiian, 169
  lesser snow, **107**
  Pacific white-fronted, 99
  Ross', 99, 103, 107, 130, **135**, 137, 149, 151
  snow, 75, 95, 99, 103, 107, 130, 137, 149, 151
  tule, 99
  white-fronted, 75, 94, 99, 106, **126**, 130, 137
geology, 15, 18
gilia, 110
glasswort, 114
goldfields, 133
  yellow, 98

gophers, 76, 93
  pocket, 150
grain, 74, 86
grape, California wild, 98
grapevines, wild, 104, 152
grasses, 29, 98
  aki aki, 164
  alkali, 128
  Bermuda, 49
  Ithuriel's spear, 98
  knot, 128
  Lemmon's canary, 98
  squirreltail, 128
grass nut, 98
grasshoppers, 70
Grassy, John, 9
grebes, 75, 92, 103
  Clark's, 49, 51, 92, 150
  eared, 49, 86, 92, 145, 149, 151
  pied-billed, 82
  western, 92, 150
Grinnell, George Bird, 1, 4
grosbeaks
  black-headed, 131
  blue, 66, **67**
  blue-headed, 131
grouse
  blue, 57
  sage, 91
guano, 44
gulf croaker, 150
gulls, 44, 75, 94, 117, 119, 149
  California, 79, 86, **86**
  Heermann's, **120**
  ring-billed, 79
  yellow-footed, **148**, 149

Hakalau Forest NWR (HI), 23, 24, 26, **155**, 155–157
hala trees, 168
halibut, 41, 60, 116
  California, 115
Hanalei NWR (HI), **22–23**, 172–176, **172**, **174**
hardpan, 129
harriers, northern, 50, 59, 65, 111
hau, 174
Havasu NWR (CA), 45–51
Hawaiian and Pacific Islands NWR Complex, 154–185
Hawaiian Islands NWR (HI), 184

hawks, 77, 99
  Cooper's, 119
  ferruginous, 119
  Harris's, 65
  marsh, 59
  northern harrier, 119
  red-shouldered, 119
  red-tailed, 50, 65, 111, 119, 125
  sharp-shinned, 119
  sparrow, 86
heath, alkali, 40, 48–49, 114, 143
heather, mock, 110
hemlock, 129
herons, 37, 75, 94, 103, 108, 150
  black-crowned, 49, 82, 140
  black-crowned night-, **80**, 160
  great blue, 31, **49**, 50, 59, 65, 86, 140, 153
  green, 31
  night-, 31
  reef, 185
herring, 41
hibiscus, 174
history, 15
hog wallows, 133
holly, California, 114–115
honeybees, 104
honeycreepers, 24, 157
honohono, Hawaiian, 160
Hookton Slough Trail (CA), 59–60
Hopper Mountain NWR Complex (CA), 52–57
Howland Island NWR (HI), 184
Huleia NWR (HI), 176
Humboldt Bay NWR (CA), 19, 58–60, **60**
hummingbirds
  Allen's, 99
  Anna's, 65, 99
  black-chinned, 65
  Costa's, 65
  rufous, 99
hyssop, English water, 160

ibis, white-faced, 49, 65, 75, 107
iguana, desert, 66
Imperial NWR (AZ), 29, **61**, 61–67
iodine bush, 70, 148
ironwood trees, 64, 179

jackrabbits, black-tailed, 66, 108, 115, 116, 131, 143

James Campbell NWR (HI), 23, 24, 157–161
Jarvis Island NWR (HI), 184–185
jaumea, 143
jays, 91
  scrub, 131
  Steller's, 82
jellyfish, 44, 165
  man-o-war, 181
jimsonweed, 129
Johnny-tucks, yellow, 129
Johnston Atoll NWR (HI), 185
junipers, 56, 79
  California, **56**
  western, 91

Kakahaia NWR (HI), 165
Kaokaopua Trail (HI), 173, 175
Kealia Pond NWR (HI), 21, 161–165
Kealie Pond marsh refuge, 24
kelp, 119
  giant, **119**
Kern NWR (CA), 19, 20, 68–70
Kesterson NWR (CA), 129
kestrel, American, 32, 41, 86, **110**, 111, 125
kiawe, 164
Kilauea Point lighthouse, **166**
Kilauea Point NWR (HI), **154**, 166–171, **169**
killdeer, 41, 49–50, 94
kites, black-shouldered, 41, 111
Klamath Basin NWR Complex (CA), **20, 71, 74**, 71–88
Klamath Marsh NWR (OR), 80–82
Klamath Reclamation Project, 71
koa trees, 23, 155, 157
koloa maili, 160
koloas, 160

Lake Havasu (CA), **45**
lamprey, Pit-Klamath brook, 76, 93
lava, 174, 179
lavender, sea, 143
Lea Act (1945), 107
lesser yellowlegs, 119
lily
  mariposa, 98
  pond, 80
  wocus water, 81
  yellow pond, 81, **81**

yellow water, 74
lions, mountain, 24, 55, 57, **57**, 93
lizards, 31, 59, 67, 121
    coast horned, 125
    desert whiptail, 66
    fringe-toed, 24, 34–35, **35**
    horned, 63
    legless, 120
    leopard, 70
    sagebrush, 93
    side-blotched, 93
    western collared, 93
    western whiptail, **66**
    zebra-tailed, 66
lobster, 170
lodgepole, 75
loons, 120
Lower Klamath NWR (CA), 27, 82–84
lupine
    blue, 153
    blue beach, 110

magpies, yellow-billed, 131
makai, 160
Mallard Slough Trail (CA), 42
mangroves, 164
Marin Islands NWR (CA), 140–141
marmots, yellow-bellied, 24, **24**, 86
marsh birds, 90
marshes, 23, 24, 103, 113–114, 136
meadowfoam, white, 133
meadowlarks, 31, 32
    western, 31
Merced NWR (CA), 22, 135–137
mergansers, 120
merlins, 111
mesquite, 164
    honey, 29, 64, 148–149
    screwbean, 29
mice, 50, 59, 93
    deer, 91
    house, 181
    salt-marsh harvest, 40, 164
Midway Atoll NWR (Midway Island),
    176–183
Migratory Bird Conservation Act
    (1945), 107
millerbird, 184
millet, 29, 65, 97
milo, 29
minks, 93

mockingbirds, northern, 31, 50
Modoc NWR (CA), 25, **25**, 89–94
Mojave desert, 19
mongoose, 24, 26, **160**, 160, 168, 175
moorhens, 24, 172, 176
    common, 131, 35
    Hawaiian, **159**, 160
morning glory, 153
    beach, 110, 179
    English swamp, 160
mosquitoes, 76
Mount Whitney (CA), 19
mudsuckers, longjaw, 115
mullet, 115, 162
murres, **19**, 60
muskrats, 90, 103–104, 153
mussels, 41

Native Americans, 25, 129
    Aztec, 84
    Klamath, 81
    La Jolla, 118
    Ohlone, 42
The Nature Conservancy, 8
naupaka trees, 179, 182–183
nene, **168**, 169
Newark Slough Trail (CA), 42
noddies, 180

oaks, 104, 134, 153
    coast live, 39
    live, 123
    scrub, 56
    seedlings, 27
    valley, 98, 130, 152
Ocean Beach Trail (CA), 109–110
ocotillo, 64
'ohi'a trees, 23
onions, 74
opossums, 115, 121, 125, 153
orcuttgrass, hairy, 98
orioles, 103
osprey, 65, 88
otters, 103–104
    river, 76, 153
    sea, 25
owls, 32, 104
    barn, 26, 79–80, 86, 99
    burrowing, **123**, 125, **149**, 149–150
    great grey, 80
    great horned, 51, 99

horned, 86
long-eared, 99
northern pygmy, 99
northern saw-whet, 99
short-eared, 99, 111
western screech, 99
oystercatchers, 44
black, **43**

Pacific/Remote Islands NWRs (HI),
    183–185
paintbrush, 153
    red-orange Monterey, 110
palms, fan, 35
palo verde trees, 49, 149
Partners in Flight, 8
pear, coastal prickly, 124
Pearl Harbor marsh refuge, 24
pelicans, 31, 32, 60
    American white, 65, **78**, 153
    brown, 122–123, 143
    California brown, 115
    white, **46**, 49, 50, 79, 88, 94, 149, 150
penstemon, 143
perch, surf, 116
Petit Manan NWR (ME), 4
petrels
    ashy storm-, 44
    bonin, 180
phainopepla, 31, 65
phalaropes, 31, 111
pheasants, 135
    ring-necked, 106, 108
phlox, 110
    black, 65, 115
    Say's, 65
phragmites, 39, 40, 70, 64, 114, 119, 139,
    143, 148, 160, 164
pigeon guillemots, 44
pigeons, band-tailed, 57
pigs, 168
    feral, 24, 26, **156**, 157
pine, 80
    bristlecone, 21
    Jeffrey, 57
    piñon, 56
    ponderosa, 57, 75
    screw, 168
    yellow, 57
pintails, 88, 94
pisonia, 185

Pixley NWR (CA), 70
plaintain
    arrowhead, 128
    water, 128
plant communities, 21–23
plovers, 31
    golden, 25
    Pacific golden, **179**, 180–181
    snowy, 111
poison oak, **105**, 105, 124, 140–141, 152
popcorn flowers, white, 133
poppies
    blue lupine, 129
    California, **14**, 39, **127**, 129
    golden-orange, 153
porcupines, 93
potatoes, 74
primroses, 65, 97, 110
    evening, 140
pronghorns, 24, 75, 76, 79, 89, 91, 93
puffins
    Atlantic, 4
    tufted, **44**, 44
purslane, English sea, 160

quail, 32, 51, 67
    Gambel's, **65**, 65
    mountain, 57
quailbush, 29

rabbits, 31, 32, 67, 93
    black-tailed jack, 50
    cottontail, 50, 51, 66, 115, 121, 131, 143
rabbit brush, 48, 90–91
raccoons, 41, 70, 93, 108, 125, 150, 153
rails
    California black, 66
    California clapper, 139
    clapper, 41, **114**, 115, 119, 143
    least clapper, 123
    secretive yellow, 88
    sora, 31, 55, 90
    Virginia, 55, 90
    Yuma clapper, 31, 50, 66
rain forest, 23
rain forest wildlife refuge, 155. *See also*
    Hakalau Forest NWR (HI)
"Range of Light," 19–20
raptors, 65, 94, 111, 122
rats, 26, 27, 93, 160, 168, 181
    pack, 50

Tipton kangaroo, 70
rattlesnakes, 55, 80, 99–100. *See also* snakes
  desert diamondback, 150
  Mojave, 31–32
  red diamond, 125
  sidewinder, 31, 35
  western, 76, 93
  western diamondback, 31, 50, **50**
razorback sucker, 66
redwoods, 21
reed, giant bur, 128
ringtail, 150
River Mouth Trail (CA), 123
roadrunners, 28, 50, 149
  greater, 31, 65
robins, 91
rock quarry, 60
Rock Hill Trail (CA), 151
Roosevelt, President Theodore, viii, 1, 4, 83
Roosevelt, Theodore IV, ix
rose, California, 143
Rose Atoll NWR (HI), 185
rubber brush, 90–91
rushes, 49, 65, 97
  Baltic, 97
  common toad, 97
  congested toad, 97
  Pacific, 97
  spike, 128

Sachuest Point NWR (RI), **6**
Sacramento NWR (CA), 100–104
Sacramento NWR Complex (CA), **95**, 95–108
Sacramento River NWR (CA), 104–106
sage, 55
  purple, **124**
sagebrush, 70, 75, 90, 91–92
  black, 124
  purple, 124
  white, 124
sago pondweed, 74
sailfin molly, 150
Salinas River NWR (CA), 109–111
salmon, 60
  chinook, 59, 100
  coho, **59**, 59
  king, 41

Kokanee, 76
salt grass, 40, 139
saltbush, 69–70
  arrowscale, 69–70
  crown, 69–70
saltwort, 114, 143
Salyer, J. Clark, 5
San Diego NWR (CA), 123–125
San Diego NWR Complex (CA), 112–125
San Luis NWR Complex (CA), 126–137
San Luis NWR (CA), 22, 24, 27, 132–135
San Pablo Bay NWR (CA), **138**, 138–141
sand dabs, 60
sand dollar, 115–116
sand dunes, 34
sand verbena, 34
sanderlings, 111, 164
sandpipers, 31, 65, 103, 153
  least, 31
  pectoral, 160
  spotted, 31
  western, 50
scarlet pimpernels, 39
scorpion weed, 65
screwbean trees, 64, 149
sculpin
  Klamath Lake, 76
  prickly, 153
sea blite, 114
sea lions
  California, 44
  Steller, 44
sea purslane, 23
sea sponges, 165
seabirds, 43, 60, 167, 169, 181, 182, 184
Seal Beach NWR (CA), 142–143
seals
  fur, 25
  elephant, 41, 44
  harbor, 37, 40–41, **41**, 44, 59, 60
  Hawaiian monk, 170
  monk, 24, 26, 181, 182
  northern fur, 44
sedges, 29, 49, 65, 160
selenium, 129
sharks, 141
  blue, 44
  leopard, 116
  soupfin, 59
  white, 41, 44
shearwaters, wedge-tailed, 170–171

sheep
  bighorn, 50
  desert bighorn, 51, 66–67
shiner perch, 41
Shorebird Loop Trail (CA), 59
shorebirds, 32, 49, 58, 65, 75, 90, 94, 103,
    112, 119, 122, 139, 151, 157, 174–175
  migratory, 60
shrew, Pacific water, 76
shrikes, 32
  loggerhead, 50, 65
shrimp
  bay, 41
  brine, 147
  fairy, 133
  ghost, 116
  tadpole, 133
shrubs, native, 27
Sierra Nevada mountain range, 19–20
skimmers, black, 149
skunks, 115, 121
  spotted, 70, 99
  striped, 70, **99**, 99, 150, 153
  western spotted, 125
smartweed, 84, **96**
  swamp, 97
smoke trees, 21, 34
snails, California horned, 116
snakes, 31, 67, 93. *See also* rattlesnakes
  coach whip, 50
  garter, 76, 108
  giant garter, **108**, 108
  gopher, 86, 99–100
  red racer, 50
snipe, 106
  common, 135
sole, 41, 60
songbirds, 31, 65–66, 82, 103, 105, 122,
    151
Sonny Bono Salton Sea NWR (CA), 21,
    25, **144**, 144–151
Sonoran Desert (AZ), 29
Sousa Trail (CA), 135
sparrows, 32
  Belding's savannah, 114, 115, 119, 143
  lark, 31
  white-crowned, 106, 107
spiders, 121
spineflower, Monterey, 110
squawfish, Sacramento, 93
squirrels, 93

California, 143
California ground, 115, 131–132
ground, **132**
staghorn sculpin, 41
steelhead, 60
  native, 100
sticklebacks, threespine, 59
stilts, 24, 31, 165, 172, 176
  black-necked, **36**, 65, 94, 103, 111,
    109, 149, 153
  Hawaiian, **157**, 160, 161, 164, 175
stingrays, 115
Stone Lakes NWR (CA), 152–153
sturgeon, 141
suckers
  lost river, 76
  Sacramento, 153
  shortnose, 76
sugar beets, 74
sunfish, 32, 67
sunflowers, 48
  bush, 115, 143
  San Diego, 124
Sutter NWR (CA), 108
swallows
  barn, 50
  cliff, 79–80, 86
  northern rough-winged, 65
swamp timothy, 128
swans, 49
  tundra, 49, **82**, 94, 99
Sweetwater Marsh NWR (CA), 19, **116**,
    116–120
sycamores, 104, 152, 153
  western, 98, 124

tamarisks, 29, 49, 50, 148
tanagers, 103
taro, 173–174, 175, 176
tattlers, 164
termites, 182
terns, 94, 123
  California least, 115, 119, **142**, 143
  Caspian, 149
  Forster's, 41
  gull-billed, 149
  least, 111
  sooty, 180
  white, 180, 183
thickets, 49
thorns, desert, 149

thrasher, crissal, 65
Tidelands Trail (CA), 41
tidytips, 153
Tijuana Slough NWR (CA), 19, 120–123, **112**
tilapia, 32, 147, 150
toads, 31
    Great Basin spadefoot, 93
    green, 50
Topock Marsh (CA), 47
topography, 19–21
tortoise
    desert, 66
    upland desert, 31
tortoiseshell, 164
tournefortia, 185
toyon, 39, 114–115
tropic bird, red-tailed, 169
trout
    brook, 76
    brown, 76, 93
    Goose Lake redband, 93
    rainbow, 76, 93
Tubbs Island Trail (CA), 139
Tule Lake NWR (CA), **84**, 84–86
tules, 28, 74, 82, 83–84, 85, 87, 90, 97, 153
tumbleweed, 70
turnstones, migrating ruddy, **161**
turtles, 31, 182
    green, 181, 185
    green sea, **181**
    hawksbill sea, 161, **164**, 164–165
    leatherback sea, 44
    pond, 99, 108
    spiny softshell, 31

Upper Klamath NWR (CA), 87–88
urchins, sea, 165

verbena
    sand, 110
    sea-rocket, 110
    yellow-flowered, 110
verdin, 65
vernal pools, 133
vetch, milk, 34
vireo, least Bell's, 115, **115**
volcanoes, 18, 79, 108, 167, 173
vole, 86

wallflowers, Contra Costa, 140
walnuts, 55
warblers, 88, 94, 103
    Lucy's, 31
    Townsend's, 91
    yellow-rumped, 107, 131
    yellowthroat, 31
water hyssop, 23
waterbirds, 40, 94
    migratory, 59
waterfowl, 28, 30, 32, 40, 49, 51, 61, 65, 66, 67, 74, 75, 82, 89, 94, 95, 98, 103, 105, 106, 107, 112, 126, 135, 136, 137, 139, 149, 151, 159–160, 164
watergrass, 97
weasels, long-tailed, 70, 76, 115
wetlands, 27, 29, **39**, 31, 38, **61, 89, 100**, 97, 103, 126–127, 128, 136, 148, 159, 164, 175
whales
    blue, 44
    grey, 122
    humpback, 25, 44, 140, 165, 170, **171**
wheat, 29, 65, 149
wildflowers, 21, 64–65, **68**, 75, 80, 98, 110, 128, 135, 153
wildrose, 98
willets, 94
willows, 27, 29, 51, 88, 94, 100, 124, 130, 134, 148
    Goodding, 49, 64
    Goodding's black, 98
wocus, 74
wood-pewee, western, 31
woodpeckers, 104
    Gila, 50
    white-headed, 82
worms, 60
wrens
    Bewick's, 115
    marsh, 50, 65, 135

yarrow, golden, 143
yellowlegs, 65
    greater, 153
    lesser, 160

ACKNOWLEDGMENTS

The writing of a book like this doesn't get done without a lot of help. I can't list the hundred or so U.S. Fish & Wildlife personnel from California, Hawaii, and Midway—and Alaska, Washington, Oregon (I've written two books in that series)—who answered my endless questions and showed me their refuges, expressing a pride in them that was contagious; but I can offer a big thank-you, because without them these books wouldn't have been written.

I do want to mention three behind-the-scenes people who toil away without getting the recognition they deserve:

Will Balliett, editor extraordinaire, who can take the worst piece of banal writing and turn it into prose that sparkles.

David Embledge, the editor who envisioned these books in the first place and whose eagle-eyed overview carried the entire series of nine books through to completion.

Don Young, who edited this book and prevented any number of gaffes from getting into print.

I'd also like to thank two good friends, Jan and Bob Burns, who pitched in when this project seemed overwhelming. Bob's extensive knowledge of plants and birds added immensely to the book, and Jan's logistical help assured that visits to the California and Hawaii refuges went smoothly.

To the readers, I want to say this: Go see these refuges. They're special.

—Loren Mac Arthur

ABOUT THE AUTHOR

Loren Mac Arthur has been a U.S. Forest Service naturalist interpreter in Alaska, a features writer and editor on a California newspaper, and a nationally published freelance writer, working in adventure travel and natural history.

PHOTOGRAPHY CREDITS

We would like to thank the U. S. Fish & Wildlife Service for letting us publish photos from their collection, as well as the other contributing photographers for their wonderful imagery. The pages on which the photos appear are listed after each contributor.

Dan Gibson: 5

John & Karen Hollingsworth: 4, 6, 20, 25, 28, 33, 36, 39, 45, 61, 69, 71, 74, 79, 84, 89, 93, 112, 114, 116, 126, 140, 159, 166, 169, 174, 179, 183

Gary Kramer: ii–iii, xii, 7, 8, 22–23. 24, 26, 31, 41, 43, 49, 50, 52, 57, 58, 60, 65, 67, 75, 77, 78, 80, 82, 88, 95, 98, 101, 104, 107, 108, 109, 110, 120, 123, 128, 131, 135, 144, 148, 152, 154, 156, 157, 168, 172

Omni-Photo Communications: 14, 87, 146, 161, 180, 184

U.S. Fish & Wildlife Service: 19, 35, 54, 68, 100, 115, 118, 125, 132, 138, 142, 149, 155, 171, 176, 181

NATIONAL AUDUBON SOCIETY
Mission Statement

The mission of National Audubon Society, founded in 1905, is to conserve and restore natural ecosystems, focusing on birds, other wildlife, and their habitats for the benefit of humanity and the earth's biological diversity.

One of the largest, most effective environmental organizations, Audubon has more than 560,000 members, numerous state offices and nature centers, and 500+ chapters in the United States and Latin America, plus a professional staff of scientists, lobbyists, lawyers, policy analysts, and educators. Through our nationwide sanctuary system we manage 150,000 acres of critical wildlife habitat and unique natural areas for birds, wild animals, and rare plant life.

Our award-winning *Audubon* magazine, published six times a year and sent to all members, carries outstanding articles and color photography on wildlife and nature, and presents in-depth reports on critical environmental issues, as well as conservation news and commentary. We also publish *Field Notes*, a journal reporting on seasonal bird sightings continent-wide, and "Audubon Adventures," a bimonthly children's newsletter reaching 500,000 students. Through our ecology camps and workshops in Maine, Connecticut, and Wyoming, we offer professional development for educators and activists; through Audubon Expedition Institute in Belfast, Maine, we offer unique, traveling undergraduate and graduate degree programs in Environmental Education.

Our acclaimed *World of Audubon* television documentaries on TBS deal with a variety of environmental themes, and our children's series for the Disney Channel, *Audubon's Animal Adventures*, introduces family audiences to endangered wildlife species. Other Audubon film and television projects include conservation-oriented movies, electronic field trips, and educational videos. National Audubon Society also sponsors books and interactive programs on nature, plus travel programs to exotic places like Antarctica, Africa, Australia, Baja California, Galapagos Islands, Indonesia, and Patagonia.

For information about how you can become an Audubon member, subscribe to *Audubon Adventures*, or learn more about our camps and workshops, please write or call:

National Audubon Society
Membership Dept.
700 Broadway
New York, New York 10003
212/979-3000
http://www.audubon.org/audubon

JOIN THE NATIONAL AUDUBON SOCIETY—RISK FREE!

Please send me my first issue of AUDUBON magazine and enroll me as a temporary member of the National Audubon Society at the $20 introductory rate—$15 off the regular rate. If I wish to continue as a member, I'll pay your bill when it arrives. If not, I'll return it marked "cancel," owe nothing, and keep the first issue free.

____ Payment Enclosed   ____ Bill Me

Name _____

Street _____

City _____

State/zip _____

Please make checks payable to the National Audubon Society. Allow 4–6 weeks for delivery of magazine. $10 of dues is for AUDUBON magazine. Basic membership, dues are $35.

Mail to:

NATIONAL AUDUBON SOCIETY
Membership Data Center
PO Box 52529
Boulder, CO 80322-2529